# RENAISSANCE HUMANISM

TWAYNE'S STUDIES IN
INTELLECTUAL AND CULTURAL HISTORY

Michael Roth, General Editor
*Scripps College and the Claremont Graduate School*

# RENAISSANCE HUMANISM

❧

Donald R. Kelley

*Twayne Publishers • Boston*
A DIVISION OF G. K. HALL & CO.

Renaissance Humanism

Twayne's Studies in Intellectual and Cultural History Series, No. 2

Copyright 1991 by Donald R. Kelley.
All rights reserved.
Published by Twayne Publishers
A division of G. K. Hall & Co.
70 Lincoln Street
Boston, Massachusetts 02111

Copyediting supervised by Barbara Sutton.
Book design and production by Janet Z. Reynolds.
Typeset by Huron Valley Graphics, Inc., Ann Arbor, Michigan.

10 9 8 7 6 5 4 3 2 1 (hc)
10 9 8 7 6 5 4 3 2 1 (pb)

The paper used in this publication meets the minimum requirements
of American National Standard for Information Sciences—Permanence
of Paper for Printed Library Materials, ANSI Z39.48-1984. ♾™

Printed and bound in the United States of America.

**Library of Congress Cataloging-in-Publication Data**

Kelley, Donald R.
    Renaissance humanism / Donald R. Kelley.
       p.  cm. — (Twayne's studies in intellectual and cultural
history ; no. 2)
    Includes bibliographical references and index.
    ISBN 0-8057-8606-6 (alk. paper). — ISBN 0-8057-8631-7 (pbk. :
alk. paper)
    1. Humanism.  2. Renaissance.  I. Title.  II. Series.
B778.K44  1991
144'.09'024—dc20                          91-4776

# Contents

| | | |
|---|---|---|
| *Foreword* | | vii |
| *Preface* | | ix |
| 1. | The Origins of Humanism | 1 |
| 2. | The Context of Humanism | 14 |
| 3. | Humanism and Philosophy | 34 |
| 4. | Humanism and the World of Nations | 55 |
| 5. | The Structure of Humanism | 74 |
| 6. | Beyond Humanism | 111 |
| *Document and Commentary: Valla's* Elegances of the Latin Language | | 137 |
| *Chronology* | | 142 |
| *Notes and References* | | 148 |
| *Bibliographic Essay* | | 161 |
| *Index* | | 169 |

# *Foreword*

Twayne's Studies in Intellectual and Cultural History consists of brief original studies of major movements in European intellectual and cultural history, emphasizing historical approaches to continuity and change in religion, philosophy, political theory, aesthetics, literature, and science. The series reflects the recent resurgence of innovative contextual as well as theoretical work in these areas, and the more general interest in the historical study of ideas and cultures. It will advance some of the most exciting work in the human sciences as it stimulates further interest in cultural and intellectual history. The books are intended for the educated reader and the serious student; each combines the virtues of accessibility with original interpretations of important topics.

Donald R. Kelley's book provides a broad overview of Renaissance humanism, paying particular attention to the fourteenth to sixteenth centuries. The study has an Italian focus, but it also covers relevant developments in Germany, France, and England. Kelley offers a synthetic account of humanism's various guises. Rather than choose between those who see humanism as a form of rhetoric and those who see it as a way of life, he examines the varieties of humanism in politics, the arts, philosophy, and the world of learning generally. He traces the movement's history in the context of the Renaissance and shows its structure and connections to various cultural changes and continuities. Kelley explicates the links between Renaissance humanism and subsequent developments in philosophy and critically questions what it might mean to move beyond humanism. The result is a multifaceted picture of the Renaissance with contemporary relevance.

Donald Kelley explores one of the intellectual movements central to the European understanding of modernity and its history. This study makes sense of complex phenomena by conveying what was, and still may be, at stake in the humanist project. *Renaissance Humanism* gives to this project a past, a political and social context, and a legacy for our own times.

MICHAEL S. ROTH
*Scripps College and the*
*Claremont Graduate School*

# *Preface*

Renaissance humanism was—virtually by definition—present at the birth of the modern world. It is true that humanists looked back to antiquity for their cultural and political ideals, yet their larger aim was the cultivation of "humanity" for practical purposes and indeed for the benefit not only of immediately contemporary disciples but also for a more remote "posterity." Of course, the humanism of the fourteenth and fifteenth centuries preceded and in some ways was at odds with the modern scientific and industrial revolutions of the seventeenth and eighteenth centuries; but almost from its fourteenth-century beginnings the intellectual program of humanism was open to expansionist, ostensibly progressive, and—as later observers would say—"modernizing" developments. The Enlightenment concern for *l'Humanité*, its progress and its "perfectibility," looked back to the classical ideal of *humanitas* and its potential—as indeed have darker visions of the career and the fate of humankind. In any case, it seems to me that a full understanding of Renaissance humanism in a long historical perspective requires an appreciation of all of these more remote and retrospective linkings.

This approach is all a matter of interpretation, of course, but it is quite in keeping with the perceptions and expressions of the humanists themselves, who likewise wanted to pass their cultural message on to later generations. One enthusiastic sixteenth-century humanist (Louis Le Roy), celebrating not only "good letters" but also "the many fine things restored or recently invented," declared that it was the mission of modern scholars "to transmit them to those who come after us, just as we have received them from our ancestors." For Le Roy, this featured especially that magical trinity of modernism also publicized by Bacon—namely, printing, the marine compass, and gunpowder—although, again, the cultural euphoria so characteristic of humanism did not preclude the possibility of decline and a return to confusion, ignorance, destruction, and "barbarism."

Thus, humanism had larger implications beyond its original temporal and geographical horizons. Though parochial in origin, the humanist agenda was universal in its aspirations; though a product of its late medieval environment, it transcended those limitations, too, looking ahead to the future as well as back to the past. If humanism originated in Italy and reached back for ancient Roman inspiration, it soon acquired an international and later universal scope, whose implications are still with us. If it started out in the fourteenth century as an elitist literary movement based on an interest in classical Latin and Greek, it soon came to inform educational, social, and even (in the form of "civic humanism") political efforts. If it centered originally on the "humanities," especially grammar and rhetoric, it soon made its aims and methods felt in other fields of study, including the study of law, theology, and all branches of philosophy. If it rested on ancient conventions of the "dignity of man" (as well as the obverse "misery of man"), it came also to recognize and occasionally to celebrate the "other half" of mankind. If humanism, finally, was obsessed with "words" (according to a famous humanist formula), it had a more fundamental concern for "things"—and especially for human things.

The humanist tradition has been interpreted by a scholarly canon that has continued down to the present; and among its most distinguished members I am happy to count several of my own mentors—especially Paul Kristeller, Hans Baron, Felix Gilbert, and Myron Gilmore. If I have gone beyond the limits of that scholarly canon, this may in itself reflect the expansionist character of humanism as a historical phenomenon and the controversies left in its wake. In any case I have tried to address some of the significant features of this phenomenon, going beyond the narrow confines of the classicist tradition properly speaking. This is quite in keeping, I believe, with the attitudes and values of the humanists and the hopes they had for their "posterity"—which, if we like, means us.

Over the years I have accumulated many debts to colleagues and students. I should like to pay special tribute to Charles Schmitt and John D'Amico, both important contributors to the humanist tradition despite their much-too-early deaths, and to Michael Roth, Anthony Grafton, and Albert Rabil for corrections and useful suggestions. I am also, and more specifically, grateful to Robin Ladrach, John Ehman, and Morris Pierce for their help with the manuscript, and, as always, to Bonnie Smith—my Beatrice and my Laura and much more besides.

# 1

# The Origins of Humanism

Francesco Petrarch was the first with a talent sufficient to recognize and call back to light the ancient elegance of the lost and extinguished style.

—Leonardo Bruni

"Renaissance humanism" joins two debatable abstractions, one that suggests a cultural revival and the other a secular philosophy, perhaps divested of higher religious concerns. Taken together, the terms designate a more specific historical theme—that is, a European cultural movement based on a fascination with classical and patristic antiquity, its sources, and its ideals. But even in this specific historical context, various issues of interpretation and debate have arisen. Was there really such a thing as a "Renaissance"? Does "humanism" have any intellectual, philosophical, or moral force beyond the literary conventions of the classical tradition? Can "Renaissance humanism" be defined apart from its late medieval political, economic, social, and cultural context? Can it be attributed to an identifiable group of persons with common values and aims? How is it related to modern thought and action? These are a few of the questions underlying this historical and interpretive survey.

## Italian Humanism

"To each eye, perhaps, the outlines of a given civilization present a different picture," Jacob Burckhardt has written about the Renaissance in Italy;[1] and this diversity is compounded with a double abstraction such as "Renaissance humanism." To simplify, the humanist movement, beginning in the later thirteenth century and representing the intellectual and cultural aspect of the Renaissance in Europe, may be approached from at least two angles of vision. From the first, it may be seen as an expression of urban culture that turned with renewed interest to the moral and political values of human society—especially to those reflected in the ancient Greek *polis* and developed by the Roman Republic and Empire. Perhaps the best example of this is Dante's (and before him Cicero's) ideal of *humanitas,* which is mankind united for the achievement of its human potential under a single world monarch. By some such political fulfillment, whether in a universal empire or in a free city-state such as Dante's own Florence, man comes to control his own fate; he comes to realize his "potential intellect," as Dante put it, and to occupy a place in God's creation "a little lower than the angels."[2] The emergence of this sort of human philosophy, in a number of forms, is one of the central themes of fourteenth-century cultural history.

But from a second angle of vision, the agenda of humanism existed apart from the particular context of Italian politics, as the humanists themselves insisted it did; and it is essential to understand these intellectual foundations as well. As usual, the explanation the humanists offered was of classical origin—in this case, the second-century scholar Aulus Gellius. "Those who have spoken Latin and have used the language correctly," Gellius wrote,

> do not give to the word *humanitas* the meaning it is commonly thought to have, namely, what the Greeks call *philanthropia,* signifying a kind of friendly spirit and good feeling toward all men without distinction. Rather they gave to *humanitas* about the force of the Greek *paideia,* that is, what we call "learning and instruction in good or liberal arts." Those who earnestly desire and seek after these are most highly humanized. For the pursuit of that knowledge and the training given by it have been given to man alone of

all animals, and for that reason it is termed *humanitas,* or humanity.[3]

What distinguished the "humanist," in other words, was a mastery of the arts and sciences of the classical "encyclopedia," which in effect transformed the medieval ladder of technical learning into a "circle" of human arts—the "encyclo-paideia," whose fortunes and encounters will be traced in this essay.

In the Italian Renaissance, Aulus Gellius' prescription seems confirmed by the origin of the term "humanist" itself. The word comes from *umanista,* which was school jargon for students in the liberal arts (on the analogy of *jurista,* for one studying civil law, and of *canonista,* for canon law), and this in turn was derived from the term defining their course of study, the *studia humanitatis.* Originally, these "humanities" included two of the three members of the medieval *trivium*—grammar and rhetoric (the arts of reading and speaking or writing, on the lowest level), excluding dialectic, the third member, and separated from the mathematical aspect of the several *artes liberales,* called the *quadrivium;* but to these we should add the three supplementary fields of poetry, history, and moral philosophy. Such was the circle of disciplines locating the headquarters of the original humanists and providing the general method of study of all the subjects that caught their fancy. What humanism did not imply was a particular ideological program. Rather, as Paul O. Kristeller has argued: "Renaissance humanism as such was not Christian or pagan, Catholic or Protestant, scientific or antiscientific, Platonist or Aristotelian, Stoic or Epicurean, optimistic or pessimistic, active or contemplative, although it is easy to find for these attitudes, and for many others, a certain number of humanists who favored them. What they all have in common is something else: a scholarly, literary, and educational ideal based on the study of classical antiquity."[4]

In general, Renaissance humanism was a European and indeed an ecumenical phenomenon, although it originally had an Italian focus. To begin with, it was an expression of the urban culture of the northern Italian city-states; its adherents were characteristically lawyers, city officials, teachers, ambassadors ("orators"), and occasionally churchmen and independent scholars. Fourteenth-century humanism must be understood against a background of the development of practical, epistolary rhetoric (the *ars dictaminis*), centered in the communes of northern and central Italy. It was enhanced by a general revival of interest in the Latin classics, which had been located primarily not in the universities but rather in the cathedral schools of northern Europe, especially that of Chartres, and in secular courts such as those of Emperor Frederick II and Robert of Anjou. Medieval biblical commentaries, for example, reflect interest in classical literature and the grammatical and "historical" approach to textual interpretation characteristic of the humanists, as did the imperialist ideology of Frederick II, who boasted of his descent from the ancient Roman Caesars, and the ideology of Dante's own "lord," Henry VII. However, it was the needs and aspirations of a secular, commercial, expanding urban society that most directly promoted the arts of communication and, in this connection, literacy, literature, and their attendant cultural attitudes. In a very general sense Renaissance humanism was a form of civic ideology, and it never entirely lost these birthmarks.

## Dante and the *Studium*

Except in the strictest sense, "humanism" is not an exclusively modern phenomenon, for similar interests and attitudes had been apparent in the work of various medieval authors, from John of Salisbury in the twelfth century down to Dante in the early fourteenth. In his *Divine Comedy* Dante speaks of passing through seven gates (the seven "liberal arts") to meet the great spirits of pagan antiquity, especially "the master of those that know," Aristotle, who sat among a "philosophic family" that included Plato, Socrates, and the pre-Socratics.[5] In general Dante's *Comedy* represents on one level an ascending pilgrimage—a progressive education leading to the higher realms of speculation, culminating in philosophy and theology and ending in religious epiphany, yet grounded in the pagan classics and liberal arts. In his *De monarchia* Dante celebrated humanity (*humanitas*) as a companion of divinity and the world empire of Rome (and his own imperialist—"Ghibelline"—party) as the earthly vehicle of the intellectual values associated with the classical tradition. Only marginally, however, can Dante be regarded as a "humanist," for despite his appreciation of the mentality of ancient Rome, he lacked both a self-conscious, historical perspective on antiquity and a commitment to the methods and priorities of the humanities.[6] According to his own view of his life, Dante turned from poetry and the liberal arts specifically to Scholastic philosophy.

For Dante, the classical ideal as described by Kristeller represented not a new, or renewed, cultural ideal but only something preliminary and ancillary to the higher goal of philosophical synthesis and theological revelation—and to the conceptualizations of Aristotle and his Christian sponsor, Thomas Aquinas, who ranked at the very top of Dante's own grade sheet.

The first generation of humanists, more or less contemporary with Dante, departed from his philosophical orthodoxy. More than that, they offered a direct challenge to the sort of intellectual totalitarianism reflected in the last books of Dante's *Comedy*—which was indeed, in its purpose if not in all of its substance, "divine" and not "human." Humanism began, then, as an insurrection of the liberal and lowly "arts"—in which children learned their "letters"—against the intellectual hegemony of the "sciences" (theology, law, medicine, and the theoretical parts of philosophy), installed at the top of the *Studium*, which was the term employed both for the medieval hierarchy of learning and for its principal institutional embodiment, the medieval university. Humanism defined itself in separation from, and largely in reaction to, the "clerical" and professional monopoly of learning reflected in the university from its twelfth-century inception through the Renaissance and well into the seventeenth century.

The medieval *Studium* formed one element in the trinity of European culture in the age of Dante, and it was associated with the idea (or rather the myth) of the transmission of both power and learning—both a "translation of empire" (*translatio imperii*) and a "translation of studies" (*translatio studii*)—from the succession of world empires of the past (from the Medes, Persians, Greeks, and Romans) to the modern "Holy Roman Empire" to which Dante was devoted. In his conventional *Translation of Empire* (1282) Alexander of Roes explains that the threefold division of European culture occurred after the division of the Carolingian Empire, by which the Germans were given in trust the Empire, the Italians the Church, and the French "the studium of philosophy and the liberal arts, which [Charlemagne] transferred from the city of Rome to the city of Paris," where the studium found institutional incarnation in the University in the twelfth (legend said ninth) century. Thus, Alexander concluded, as the Germans protect the Catholic faith and the Italians upheld it spiritually, so the French "prove[d] and demonstrate[d] with the firmest reasoning that it should be held by all."[7]

The *Studium* was largely a creation of the Church, especially in the North, where the ecclesiastical hierarchy, analogous to the ladder of university learning, dominated university administration. Masters and disciples alike were subject to its "discipline," and theology remained, at least in theory and in Dante's *Comedy*, the "queen of sciences." The medieval university, especially the Parisian model, was fundamentally authoritarian not only in the sense that it acted as an apologist for ecclesiastical and political authority but also in the sense that it privileged certain "authorities," certain traditional authors, and indeed defined disciplines in terms of these *auctores* and their *auctoritas*. It is true that the standard method of teaching was logical or dialectical, but for the most part this "Scholastic" method (the *scholasticus* being the teacher of dialectic) was designed to justify, to order, to inculcate, and to criticize—rather than to investigate—the received doctrine in particular fields of study. So the *Studium*, the doctrinal aspect of Christendom, was in a way quite practical, designed to train and to indoctrinate persons to occupy certain professions, especially doctors, lawyers, theologians, and of course more teachers to carry the tradition over into future generations. In short, the *Studium* established the framework of Christian knowledge, its expansion, and its teaching, within which debates over human science, art, values, and goals would be carried on for many generations.

Against both of these reactionary trends—against both the authoritarianism and the utilitarianism of the medieval university—humanists revolted, following the old pattern of generational conflict between "ancients" and "moderns." The classicist program referred to by Kristeller was the creation of scholars, poets, and dropouts who wanted in effect to declare the liberal arts independent of the—illiberal—professions. As Erasmus complained, orthodox scholars were always ready with the rebuff that the humanist "is a Grammarian, not a Philosopher," or "a Rhetorician, not a Lawyer," or "an Orator, not a Theologian"—"but before long," Erasmus added, "things will take another turn." In effect, humanists wanted to establish the humanities as free and equal forms of human inquiry and creation. Although humanists were not committed to particular doctrines, as Kristeller argues, they were committed to the forms and content of the liberal arts; and deliberately or inadvertently, many of them conceived an antipathy toward the professional methods acquired in the higher faculties. The ensuing rivalry between humanism and scholasticism, explicit as well as implicit, revived and gave new meaning to the ancient quarrel between rhetoric and dialectic—or between philology and philosophy.

## Petrarch and His Legend

All this is prologue to the work of Francesco Petrarca, the founder and the prototype of Renaissance humanism. Actually, Petrarch's significance stems at least as much from the legend he created (and which his disciples perpetuated) as from his actual accomplishments. Through self-promotion and single-minded careerism, as well as literary talent and a sense of destiny, Petrarch established an image of himself as a lonely but lauded, and laureated, pioneer who became a sort of cultural hero, whose followers preserved and tried to publicize his ideals and his campaign against "barbarism." In any number of ways, Petrarch is a paradigm of Renaissance humanism—not only through his public career but also through his private ordeals and posthumous legend. For this reason—and also because autobiography was for Petrarch, as it had been for Dante, the primary mode of discourse and discovery—it is enlightening to listen to Petrarch reflect on his life and its meaning not only for him but also for us, his intended posterity.

In 1351, when he was forty-seven, Petrarch provided a portrait—indeed, a sort of time capsule—of himself that touches on the most significant aspects of his character and of the humanist program. "It is possible that some word of me may have come to you," he begins his famous *Letter to Posterity* (modeled after Ovid's *Tristia*), "though even this is doubtful, since an insignificant and obscure name will scarcely penetrate far in either time or space."[8] The qualifying remark displays not only the kind of false or ironic modesty, or at least employment of the "humility topos" dear to self-conscious authors like Petrarch, but also his characteristic concern for his own place in history. In the following pages Petrarch describes his character and family background, his mainly idealized relationship with "Laura" (the poetic counterpart to Dante's philosophical and theological Beatrice); his extraordinary circle of acquaintances among the great figures, authors, emperors, and popes, of his day; his education and travels; his manuscript discoveries; his political enthusiasms; his retreat at Vaucluse (a hideaway that today has been transformed into a still-beautiful tourist trap); and his (despite his disclaimers, not-so-reluctant) acceptance of the laurel crown, which symbolized his position as national poet in succession to Virgil, or at least to Dante.

As for his studies, Petrarch was, he tells us, "especially inclined to moral philosophy and the art of poetry." He attended the universities first of Montpellier and then of Bologna, but after his father's death he gave up the study of law to devote himself entirely to the *studia humanitatis* and to communion with his classical models in Latin and Greek antiquity. "Among the many subjects which interested me," Petrarch continued, "I dwelt especially upon antiquity, for our own age has always repelled me, so that, had it not been for the love of those dear to me, I should have preferred to have been born in any other period than our own. In order to forget my own time, I have constantly striven to place myself in spirit in other ages, and consequently I delighted in history."[9] A similar sentiment is expressed in one of Petrarch's most touching and revealing Latin sonnets:

> Living, I despise what melancholy fate
> has brought us wretches in these evil years.
> Long before my birth time smiled and may again,
> for once there was, and yet may be, more joyful days.
> But in this middle age times dregs sweep
> around us, and we bend beneath a heavy
> load of vice. Genius, virtue, glory now
> have gone, leaving chance and sloth to rule.
> Shameful vision this! We must awake or die.[10]

This combination of discontent and nostalgia represents the other face of Petrarch's fascination with historical perspective—he was looking not only forward to a more enlightened posterity but also back, to an antiquity that had created the language, institutions, and values of the literate and civilized humanity into which Petrarch wanted to gain entry. Yet he recognized this as a dream world. In his own words, he looked backward and forward as if he were on the frontiers of two countries, neither of which was entirely his, since he continued to live in the "middle" or "dark" age before the classical revival. He stood, in the famous words of C. H. Haskins's undergraduate, "with one foot in the middle ages, while with the other he saluted the rising star of the Renaissance"—and this Renaissance was nothing less (though it might be more) than the triumph of the humanist program.

For the "Scholastic" methods of the academic establishment of his own day, Petrarch had nothing but contempt. He revered the "fathers of Roman law" but despised the technical, mercenary, and corrupt civil law as taught in the universities.[11] He objected to the abuses of dialectic associated with Aristotle, or rather his modern interpreters, such as Averroës; and ironically (or sarcastically), he contrasted the pompous pedantry of his critics to his own "ignorance," which was to say his preference for human "eloquence" and the values of the human studies.[12] On various grounds Petrarch preferred the teachings of Plato to those of his wayward disciple. "Plato is praised by the greater men," Petrarch remarked in his elitist way, "Aristotle by the bigger crowd"[13]—and indeed, Plato was to be the philosopher most favored by scholars devoted to the humanist program, especially Petrarch's Florentine successors, Pico della Mirandola and Marsilio Ficino.

For Petrarch, the revival of antiquity began with "letters"—language and literature—and this involved classical forms as well as classical Latin style, especially the genre of the letter. Six years before his *Letter to Posterity*, Petrarch, in a visit to Verona, made the discovery of a lifetime: a manuscript of Cicero's letters to Atticus. This discovery turned Petrarch into a correspondent not only of his Italian and other European contemporaries and of posterity, but also of the ancients, beginning with Cicero himself. In his fanciful letter to Cicero, Petrarch criticized him for wasting his time and his intellect on politics when he should have devoted himself entirely to philosophy. In a second letter, answering an imagined response from Cicero (which a later scholar actually tried to reproduce), Petrarch apologized for his criticism but insisted on the superiority of the contemplative over the active life. "It was your life that I criticized, not your mind, nor your tongue," Petrarch wrote, "for the one fills me with admiration, the other with amazement."[14] It was in large part this encounter that inspired Petrarch to think that his own work—his *fama*, meaning earthly immortality as well as honor—might survive for a more (as Cicero's had for a less) deserving posterity.

Was Petrarch, then, a Ciceronian? In his ironic discussion of "his own ignorance and that of many others," Petrarch answered that he was indeed a *Ciceronianus* in the sense that he admired the man and his work. "However," he added (thinking no doubt of the answer to the same question given centuries before by Jerome in his famous dream), "when we come to think or speak of religion, then I am certainly not a Ciceronian but a Christian."[15] As classical civilization provided the letter, so Christianity provided the spirit of Renaissance culture. As Petrarch's disciple Coluccio Salutati later put it, "Whence did the primitive church learn to express itself if not from the heritage of the heathen?"

Petrarch was the author of a wide range of works that, like his letters, continued or revived classical models—Italian as well as Latin poetry, his neo-Virgilian, republican epic *Africa*, the lives of famous ancients (*De viris illustribus*), dialogues, contributions to moral philosophy, and many other topics, though usually in an autobiographical context. Petrarch celebrated Christian as well as classical antiquity, and his admiration of Cicero was matched by his admiration of Augustine. As Cicero represented the highest standard of moral philosophy, so Augustine represented the most profound sort of Christian self-examination; and both reflected the most exalted goal of humankind, which was wisdom (*sapientia*). In a dialogue with Augustine called *The Secret*, Petrarch again seems to stand on the borders of two countries, displaying in this no-man's-land his anxieties about the tensions between Christianity and classical culture and the attendant problem of virtue: was it based on reason or faith? His famous letter on his ascent of Mount Ventoux (which has also become a tourist trap these days) represents a sort of allegory of his own intellectual development—ascending, like Dante's, from the liberal arts to higher forms of wisdom. Here Petrarch again invoked Augustine, in this case to exalt humanist and Christian self-knowledge above curiosity about the natural world and its distracting secrets. Opening his copy of Augustine's *Confessions*, Petrarch was led, he remarked, "from the contemplation of space to that of time . . . [and] turned my inner eye toward myself."[16] And on that dramatic object, indeed, Petrarch's "inner eye" remained for most of his life. In this sense he was not only a "Ciceronian" but also, at least as deeply, an "Augustinian," though often an ironic one.

Petrarch was a poet, an introvert, and a careerist, and above all he prized the fruits of a literary and contemplative life; yet he was not without political ideals and even public hopes beyond his carefully cultivated private sphere. His national piety shone through various works, including his famous sonnet "Italia mia," which Machiavelli would quote at the very end of *The Prince*. Like Dante, Petrarch looked in particular to Roman tradition—"What is all history but the praise of Rome?" he once asked—and it was this enthusiasm, or nostalgia, that entangled him in one of the most fascinating and, from the standpoint of humanism, if not Italian history, significant political episodes of the fourteenth century. For like Dante, Petrarch too had a national hero; and this hero was one of the most curious figures—romantic to some, pathetic to others—of the Renaissance.

This was Cola di Rienzo—"Rienzi, the last of the tribunes," as he is called in the most famous of the novels written about his career.[17]

## The First of the Humanists and the Last of the Tribunes

Rienzi's life is worthy of the opera and the popular literature that have been devoted to him. Cola di Rienzo, son of a Neapolitan tavernkeeper, was born in 1314 (and so it was at least plausible that, as he later claimed, he was a bastard son of Emperor Henry VII, who had passed that way just before his death in 1313); he certainly drew on the national legacy represented by Dante and Petrarch in his later career. Beyond this, Rienzi was self-educated, visionary, supremely ambitious, and undoubtedly neurotic in more ways than one. His active career began in 1343, when he was sent as an envoy of the Roman people to the papal court at Avignon. Inspired by the fashionable classicism that had been publicized by Petrarch's laureation a couple of years before, Rienzi took it upon himself to send back an inflated, rhetorical report, declaring that the Pope was the savior of Italy (and was on the verge of returning to his Roman home); and in antiquarian fashion he styled himself "consul." This was the beginning of a propaganda campaign aimed at restoring ancient Roman virtue and government; and to Petrarch this suggested the possibility of restoring Italian unity and so of providing a political framework for his humanist program.

The peak of Rienzi's republican ideology was reached in a famous speech he delivered on the legendary *Lex Regia*—that ancient Roman law that had bestowed the "majesty" (that is, the sovereignty) of the people on the prince. Rienzi's aspiration was to proclaim the *majestas* of the Roman people, whom he claimed to represent. It is worth noting that he also performed a pioneering act of deciphering an ancient inscription—since the *Lex Regia* (now on display in the Capitoline Museum) had supposedly been undecipherable for centuries before Rienzi's explication. For such reasons Rienzi has often been regarded by historians as an early representative, if not a founder, of Renaissance humanism in its political and utopian incarnation.

But there was another side to Rienzi's mad scheme; for he was also under the spell of the revivalist ideas of the spiritualist wing of the Franciscan order—thus combining mysticism with classicism, religious fanaticism with political humanism. His program was a sort of synthesis of Franciscan reform, which envisaged a return to primitive Christianity, and a political ideal, which hoped to return to ancient republicanism and thereby to achieve a federal Italy under the leadership of Rome. He claimed direct inspiration both from the Holy Spirit and from the majesty of Rome. His arms incorporated both the keys of Saint Peter and the "SPQR" of the Roman republic. Yet concealed beneath this wild ideological façade, Rienzi had the mind of a practical and indeed unscrupulous politician. He became a notary in the Roman commune and, through a combination of demagoguery and intrigues among the Roman merchants, took advantage of the political chaos in a popeless Rome to carry off a revolution. This coup d'etat occurred in 1347, when Rienzi proclaimed himself "Candidate of the Holy Spirit, Knight Nicholas, Severe and Clement Deliverer of the City, Zealot for Italy, Friend of the World, TRIBUNE AUGUSTUS."[18] He sent letters out to all the Italian cities, proclaimed the restored "majesty of Rome," and summoned a pan-Italian congress to establish himself throughout the peninsula.

It was in the course of these sensational exploits—and rhetorical excesses—that Petrarch became Rienzi's admirer and supporter. In his first letter to Rienzi, Petrarch placed him "on a high pinnacle, exposed to the gaze, the judgment, and the comments not only of the Italians but of the whole human race," including, of course, that final earthly judge which was posterity. Yet within five years those "firmest of foundations" laid by Rienzi had crumbled, and Petrarch withdrew his support from the one who "preferred to live a coward rather than die with dignity." In fact, Rienzi's reality had not matched his rhetoric. Whatever his mental condition, he was not equal to the majesty of the Roman people; and shortly after his coup, he showed himself to be a petty tyrant, turning everyone against him, alienating first Pope Clement VI, who called him to Avignon for an accounting, and then Emperor Charles IV, who threw him into prison.

Rienzi was liberated and returned to Rome as "senator," representing the papacy, but the second act of his tragicomedy was even briefer. Rome was still in chaos, and the antipapal nobles turned on Rienzi. The traditional cry, *"Popolo! Popolo!"* went up, and in 1354 Rienzi was assassinated on the steps of the Capitol. This was the end of Rienzi's mad scheme—and likewise of Petrarch's sad dream. Yet like Emperors Frederick II and Henry VII, Rienzi left a potent legend and a lingering memory among humanists. Afterward, Petrarch turned to Charles IV for national leadership, but he too proved a political disappointment and gave up the imperial crown, as Petrarch lamented, for his miserable Bohemian kingdom.

These failures could only reinforce Petrarch's disillusionment with his own times, his fondness for the contemplative life, and his nostalgia for the good old days of Italian virtue, power, and civilization. They also sharpened his historical sense—the disparity between ancient ideals and modern reality—and inspired the methods of historical criticism characteristic of humanist scholarship that Petrarch was again one of the first to exemplify. A year after Rienzi's death, Petrarch responded to an appeal from Charles IV to evaluate a claim made by the Habsburgs for exemption from imperial jurisdiction on the basis of an original grant of territory by Julius Caesar. The basis of this so-called "Habsburg donation" was quickly demolished by Petrarch on various linguistic and historical grounds: the obviously forged document employed the first rather than the Caesarean third person singular; Austria was falsely and un-Romanly termed "eastern"; and the language in which it was written was in many ways "both barbarous and modern."[19] Here are some of the essentials of those techniques of philological and historical criticism that represent one of the major bequests of Renaissance humanism to modern scholarship.

Petrarch obviously had neither the head nor the heart for politics; his major accomplishment was to set an example as a poet and a scholar, to act as publicity agent for the best of classical and Christian antiquity. In this connection he proposed a new (or renewed) ideal of humanity and a new vision of history. For these literary and symbolic achievements he was canonized by his disciples, beginning especially with Giovanni Boccaccio (who, as Leonardo Bruni put it, received the Florentine muses "as if by hereditary succession"). Boccaccio, who died in 1375, a year after Petrarch, was himself succeeded by a distinguished line of Florentine disciples, most notably Coluccio Salutati (d. 1406), Leonardo Bruni (d. 1444), Poggio Bracciolini (d. 1459), and in certain respects Ficino (d. 1499), Pico (d. 1494), and even Machiavelli (d. 1527). In a long perspective, then, the legacy and legend of Petrarch are virtually to be identified with the dual and debatable abstraction called Renaissance humanism.

# 2

# The Context of Humanism

Florence has the greatest minds; whatever they undertake they easily surpass other men, whether they apply themselves to military or political affairs, to study philosophy, or to merchandize.

—Leonardo Bruni

The humanist movement did not arise in a social vacuum, of course. If it derived its style from classical antiquity and its emotional impetus from resentment of the intellectual establishment of the fourteenth century, it drew its strength and substance from the urban, educational, and familial culture of Renaissance Italy. In fact, the convergence between humanism and the political, social, and economic life of the Italian communes was one of the central themes of the fourteenth and fifteenth centuries.[1] "Civic humanism" (Hans Baron's coinage from *Bürgerhumanismus*, which could also be translated as "bourgeois humanism") is the name that has been given to this general phenomenon, and in order to understand its significance, it is necessary to look briefly at the social and political environment of the striking cultural changes that gave the Renaissance its name.

## The Civic Environment

In many ways Italian history is an exception to the general political trends of late medieval Europe. Late medieval Italian society was local, not national; largely urban rather than agrarian; and in social terms postfeudal and postmanorial. Politically, it was a patchwork, shattered by invasions and kept divided by the old Guelf-Ghibelline rivalry and by the political behavior of the Church, both of which divisions were still being deplored by Machiavelli in the sixteenth century. Although it was impoverished and depopulated after the disappearance of the Roman Empire in the West, Italy remained to some extent a land of cities. Some of these cities had survived through the agency of the Church, which had taken them over as administrative centers; other had been rebuilt after the tenth and eleventh centuries, that is, on the threshold of the demographic and economic revival that made Italy a commercial force; and even the barbarian Lombard invaders adopted urban habits, organization, and a tendency to factionalism. The distinctive institution of Italian society, in other words, was the *civitas,* the collateral descendant of the Greek *polis;* and though the city went through profound transformations, it did retain some of its original identity.

Civic consciousness predated the Renaissance in various ways, and the early communes had at least a dim awareness of their links with antiquity. This rudimentary sort of historical sense was expressed by a late eleventh-century poet, who declared his patriotic intentions in this way:

> I am going to write the history of the famous Pisans,
> And revive the memory of the ancient Romans:
> For Pisa only carries on the admirable glory
> Which Rome achieved by vanquishing Carthage.[2]

In some ways the first humanists were only carrying on, in more "elegant," self-conscious, and critical ways, this medieval version of "civic humanism," and reviving and imitating the culture of the Roman and Greek prototypes.

One factor often overlooked in the emergence of civic culture (because it is also associated with "medieval" developments) is the significance of Roman law ("civil law") in Italy after its revival in the twelfth century and its founding role in the law faculty of Bologna and other universities. Roberto Weiss has pointed out the role of the lawyers in "starting the Renaissance";[3] they did much to preserve it as well. It should not be forgotten that "civil science" (*civilis scientia*), a term used by humanists like Salutati and Vergerio as well as professional jurists, reached its highest level in the work of Bartolus, a younger Florentine contemporary of Petrarch, and especially his disciple Baldus, who died at the height of the "crisis of the early Italian Renaissance."[4] Under the leadership of such *legisti*, jurisprudence "Italian style" (*mos italicus*) applied the resources of Roman law to the commercial, social, and political affairs of the Italian city-states and thereby gave them a sort of borrowed legitimacy notwithstanding the theoretical sovereignty of the Holy Roman Emperor. In general the "civil science" of these modern jurists was founded on notions of citizenship and civilization (*civilitas; civiltà*) and other social qualities associated with "civil humanism"—which might with equal justice and propriety be called "civil" humanism.[5]

Besides the legitimizing force of civil law, what transformed and modernized the remnants of the ancient *civitas* (and the "new towns" of the Middle Ages) was the complex of economic and social processes called the "commercial revolution." Much of this process is not directly visible to historians, and we can see mainly the results of it, the tip of the iceberg. But we can make indirect inferences about what must have underlain the revolution. Two long-range phenomena in particular preceded the commercial successes of the thirteenth and fourteenth centuries, including the improvement of agricultural techniques and the major efforts of land reclamation and colonization. Related to this was a substantial rise in population, which not only permitted the "agrarian revolution" but consumed its fruits. The outlines of these interrelated phenomena are not entirely clear, but their principal consequences—the rapid growth of towns, or "communes," in the twelfth and thirteenth centuries—is unmistakable.

The first "commercial revolution" reached its climax during Petrarch's early manhood in the 1330s. It had been made possible by the accumulation of capital—"primitive accumulation," Marxists used to call it—and by the investment in local industry, especially cloth production, silk as well as wool, and the establishment of markets. Most conspicuous was Mediterranean trade, especially the luxury trade, the so-called long voyage, and the formation of an axis between London and the Levant. But local trading has recently come to be recognized as equally significant in many areas—that is, trading with the countryside, the *contado* around urban centers. On the basis of such local trade, individual fortunes were accumulated and that other essential institution, the civic family of the Renaissance— the true source of both "fortune" and "virtue"—was established. This early period of prosperity was followed by the creation of investment banking and exchange—corresponding to the financial phase of early capitalism—and by the great families who preserved the factional state of Italian politics and were celebrated in extravagant civic and perhaps nostalgic terms in Alberti's treatise *Della famiglia*.[6]

But above all, humanism was a phenomenon of city culture. The first great center of commercial expansion—and in Italy, the last great center as well—was Venice, whose great success story dates back to the time of the crusades. By the era of Petrarch, Venice was a well-established maritime empire, whose influence (though slight on European *terra firma*) extended from the Atlantic and the fairs of northern Europe to the merchant colonies in the eastern Mediterranean. Venice's "myth" of liberty, social balance, and political order, moreover, was already in ascendence. Up to the eighteenth century, Venice preserved a republican form of government, but from the fourteenth century it already had a restricted aristocratic monopoly and a "closed" governing council. Maritime distractions, diplomatic ingenuity, urban patriotism, and love of civic "liberty" were conspicuous features of Venetian tradition, and Venetian humanism shared the conservative and narrowly "patrician" values of its ruling elite. In the later fifteenth century, Venice also became a primary center of printing, which operated powerfully to shape and to fix as well as to disseminate humanist learning and values.[7]

The model of Renaissance despotism was the Lombard city of Milan, by contrast, which had passed through the communal stage and fallen under a tyranny before emerging, under the Visconti family, as the dominant power and leader of the imperialist (Ghibelline) party in Italy. The greatest political figure was Duke Giangaleazzo Visconti, who by the end of the fourteenth century had assembled what amounted in all but title to a "kingdom" of northern Italy. The Milanese court, schools, and especially the chancery featured a number of significant scholars (Pier Candido Decembrio and Francesco Filelfo being the most important), but they remained largely under the spell of Florentine humanism and the influence of Petrarch. Politically, on the other hand, Milan was the chief opponent of Florence and the Guelf party in Italy; and indeed the so-called "crisis of the early Italian Renaissance" centered on the threat Giangaleazzo, who assumed the title of "Duke of Milan," posed to the republic of Florence in the course of his drive to transform his duchy into a "Kingdom of Italy." Giangaleazzo's death in 1402 eased the immediate challenge, but the ideological rivalry between Guelf "liberty" and Milanese "despotism" has resounded throughout the modern tradition of republican political thought.[8]

If Milan was the classic Renaissance despotism, Florence was even more clearly—at least according to its "myth"—the classic Renaissance republic, as well as the dominant center of humanist culture. By the mid-thirteenth century Florence had established its "first democracy" (*primo popolo*) on the basis of Guelf commitments and had secured its economic base by moving from manufacture (especially of cloth) to banking. Economically, Florence was dominated by a guild arrangement, of which its social structure and its government were in effect extensions. Social groups—the old aristocracy and the "little people" (*popolo minuto*)—struggled for survival, if not control, while the commercial elite (*popolo grasso*) struggled for profit and political domination, to the ruination of the old nobility (as Machiavelli lamented) and hence of military "virtue" and the independence that it had made possible. The remaining great families of Florence hardly distinguished the political program of civic liberty from their own interests and investments in the public debt, which reinforced the intense feelings of patriotism that underlay the art and architecture as well as the political propaganda of the city's governing elite.

But in the fourteenth century internal as well as external pressures grew, as economic depression and plague exacerbated political instability. From the time of Dante to that of Machiavelli, Florentine history was marked by a succession of economic shocks; natural threats (most notably, the plague); class divisions; corporate rivalries; party struggles (the papalist Guelfs versus the imperialist Ghibellines); conflicts with the Church, both in Rome and in its "Babylonian captivity" in Avignon (1305–78); and especially political "crisis," arising from the threats of external invasion as well as internal "tyranny" and the discontents of the lower classes (*sottoposti*). Such was the historical environment—and the material base—of Florentine humanism in its heyday between the time of Dante and Petrarch and that of Machiavelli and Erasmus, and such the first context of "civic humanism."

The humanist movement served, expressed, and reacted to the commercial milieu of the Italian city-states. One can see a certain convergence between the program of the *studia humanitatis* and the civic (or bourgeois) pursuit of wealth in violation of ecclesiastical restrictions of "usury" and (especially Franciscan) celebrations of poverty. Such Christian prejudices were bad for learning and worse for business. At first merchants carried out their business "in the name of God and of profit," but by the fifteenth century they were offering secular and social arguments in defense of their value to the commonwealth. Like humanists, merchants praised the faculty of memory; and they depended on literacy, written records, and secular virtues, as well as a concept of merit based not on birth or self-deprivation but on human achievement. "The pen is an instrument so noble and excellent that it is absolutely necessary not only to merchants," wrote the author of *The Perfect Merchant* in the fifteenth century, "but also in any art, whether liberal, mechanical, or mercantile."[9] Accompanying the "civic humanism" celebrated by historians and political theorists, in short, was a set of underlying economic attitudes that might be called "mercantile humanism."

Other Italian cities besides Florence were subject to similar cultural impulses (as well as direct Tuscan influence), especially the republican states of Siena and Bologna. In Milan, the "despotic humanism" was analogous to, and competed with, the civic humanism of pre-Medici Florence. In Venice, humanist scholarship shared the conservative values of the ruling (and, by the fifteenth century, "closed") aristocracy. Humanism also flourished at the courts of the Kingdom of Naples and the Roman papacy, especially from the pontificate of Nicholas V onward, in which another humanist "academy" was founded. In Rome, the humanities were joined to ecclesiastical orthodoxy and later to a rigid "Ciceronian" view of literary and intellectual tradition; and the conspicuous presence of ancient Roman monuments and their ruins were a constant inspiration for celebrations of and lamentations over classical culture and values.

But Florence remained the haven and headquarters of the humanist movement. Having passed through a variety of social, economic, and epidemic crises in the fourteenth century, Florence entered its period of political trauma, centering above all on the threat of an expanding and imperialistic Milanese state. In this connection its need to marshal civic resources and patriotic spirit became intense. The mercantile drive to accumulate civic wealth converged with the political impulse to promote civic independence, and the result was the consolidation of Florentine political spirit in the form of an articulated Guelf ideology. "The glorious

Guelf company . . . is doubly praiseworthy," declared Bruni: "for its Catholic faith, because, following the true religion, it does not deviate from the church; and for its civil polity, because it is dedicated to Liberty, without which no Republic can survive, and without which wise men do not think life worth living."[10]

Florence was spared a Milanese invasion by Giangaleazzo's death in the autumn of 1402—miraculously, as some thought—but the conflicts among the city-states of Italy continued. The most significant results of this "crisis," certainly from the standpoint of our age, were in the realm of thought: ideas about man, his society, his history, and his earthly aspirations. These themes had been discussed by humanists for a century and more, but never before with the sense of political urgency and historical perspective as in this period. The transformation of thought and values is especially apparent in the work of Bruni, the successor of Petrarch and Salutati, who emerged at this time as the leading spokesman both for humanist aspirations and for Florentine civic ideals. He was in retrospect the founder and archetype of "civic humanism."

## Leonardo Bruni and the Active Life

The humanist program of Leonardo Bruni was shaped in the context of the first Florentine "crisis" (1400–1402), invoked so eloquently by Hans Baron, and an attendant series of fundamental ideological issues associated with Italian Renaissance culture. Of these issues, one had to do with the reputations of Dante and Petrarch (and the more or less invidious comparisons between them), one with the image of Cicero as a model of humanism, and another with the origins and history of Florence. All were associated with the political conflict between the Florentine republic and the Milanese despotism, as well as with Bruni's eagerness to celebrate the government he served as chancellor. Nor did Bruni's enthusiasm for Florentine liberty diminish after the crisis of 1400–1402. "We do not tremble beneath the rule of one man . . . ," he continued to boast a quarter-century later, "nor are we slaves to the rule of a few. Our liberty is equal for all, is limited only by the laws, and is free from the fear of men."[11] A few years later in a virtuoso exercise in Greek prose concerning "the Florentine constitution," Bruni analyzed the social and institutional sources of this *libertas Florentina*, while in his little treatise on the *militia* he celebrated the vital (but declining) military dimension of civic culture. In his commentary on the pseudo-Aristotelian *Economics,* he defended the need to increase civic as well as familial wealth, against older ecclesiastical doctrine.

It was on this foundation that the great edifice of Florentine culture was erected. Bruni moved easily between his politico-economico-military patriotism and the humanist program of learned eloquence. Bruni's chauvinistic opinions were expressed not only in his polemical and panegyrical works but also in connection with his Greek translations. These included especially translations of the works of Aristotle, which represented a sort of idealization of the Greek *polis,* and above all a pioneering history of Florence (1415), which was the prototype of Renaissance humanist historiography (and so of modern national historiography). Unlike Petrarch, who admired Cicero for his writings rather than for his political activities, Bruni praised Cicero for combining the active life and the contemplative life. According to Bruni, Cicero was "the only man to have fulfilled both of these great and difficult accomplishments," that is, writing philosophy and serving the republic.[12] "As in the public sphere he served his country as consul and countless persons as orator," marveled Bruni, "so in learning and letters he truly served not only his fellow citizens but in fact all who use the Latin language. He seemed to be the very light of education and of wisdom." "Accordingly," Bruni added, "he should be called not just Father of his Country, but the father of our speech and letters."

Bruni compared and judged his two great Florentine predecessors in the same terms. Although deficient in Latin elegance, Dante was a matchless poet in the *volgare,* and like Cicero he made enormous efforts and suffered equally great personal sacrifices, including many years in exile, in pursuit of his Ghibelline political ideals. By contrast, Petrarch attained great mastery in Ciceronian and Virgilian Latin and displayed personal "virtue." But he also enjoyed a "wise" and rather selfish solitude in his retreat in Vaucluse, as well as great honors, including the friendship of the ruling figures of his day and the crown of the poet laureate. In his concluding comparison, Bruni acknowledged the superiority of Petrarch over Dante in both prose and poetry (in Latin at any rate) and in his "prudent" avoidance of political disputes and factions. Yet despite adverse fortune, Dante was the more learned in philosophy and mathematics, and above all, "is of greater worth than Petrarch in the active and civic life."[13]

The philosophical expression of this twofold ideal appeared

most clearly in Aristotle's writings on "practical philosophy," (that is, political and moral philosophy), which Bruni himself translated into Ciceronian language. As Dante had pointed out, Aristotle had prized a life both active and contemplative, since human beings were too weak to achieve virtue or the "good life" apart from civil society. In this respect, the *vita contemplativa* and the *vita activa* were both praiseworthy, but in other respects they were inadequate when taken by themselves. "The contemplative life is, to be sure, the more divine and rare," as Bruni summed the matter up, "but the active is more excellent with respect to the common good" (*in communi utilitate*).[14]

As Bruni extended the humanist ideal from the private to the public sphere, and from the moral to the political sphere, so he expanded the historical horizons of humanism by looking critically at the Florentine past and the conditions of the current cultural revival, which he hoped was also a political revival. Ranking the *studia humanitatis*, Bruni gave first place to history, for the sake not only of learning but also of civic pride. Bruni prized history for its literary and moral value but especially for its utility in political decisions. "Knowledge of the past," he remarked, "gives guidance to our counsels and our practical judgment, and the consequences of similar undertakings [in the past] will encourage or deter us according to our circumstances in the present."[15]

These were classical commonplaces, but to them Bruni added a new perspective on the Renaissance past. In general, his view was based on a revisionist argument about Florentine origins. He traced these origins not to conventional Caesarean (imperial, by imputation Ghibelline) foundations but to the republican (Guelf) colonization by Sulla. From Caesar's time, both Roman liberty and the Latin language had entered into decline, then into the oblivion created by "barbarian" invaders, and it was not to be recovered for many centuries. The revival had come most directly from Petrarch, who was, for Bruni, "the first" to have restored the ancient style (and its attendant values) through his discovery and emulation of Cicero, though he did not perfect that style. But Bruni was also aware of the necessary preconditions of this accomplishment.[16] Among these were not only the individual work of Dante and other vulgar poets but also, and more fundamentally, the revival of civic liberties and Latin style in the northern Italian towns after the expulsion of the Lombards. The denouement of the story, of course, came with the fame achieved by Petrarch and his disciples and the Florentine culture of Bruni's own day, which added Greek philosophy to Latin learning to fulfill the ideal of civic humanism and to furnish an even more elegant model for it. Thus, to the old hagiographical convention that derived the classicial revival from the genius of Petrarch, Bruni added an awareness of the political and social dimensions of that revival's cultural achievement.

After Bruni, the civic ideal was preserved in an intellectual tradition, if not in the realities of Medici domination in Florence, which began with the return of Cosimo de' Medici ten years before Bruni's death in 1444. The civic ideal reemerged in another Florentine republic (which survived from 1498 to 1512) and in the work of Machiavelli, who was Bruni's most famous successor as champion of republican Florence, as historiographer of the city, and as a founder of modern ideas of the state and the "science" thereof. The "Machiavellian moment" (as it has been called) was the classic expression of civic humanism and the principal vehicle by which this cluster of political values—liberty, "virtue," and republican government—have passed into the modern political tradition.[17] It is in this sense that Renaissance humanism became a public force in modern history.

## Liberal Education

In one fundamental respect the disciples of Petrarch departed from his example (if not always his teaching), and this was in the matter of public service. From the fifteenth century on, most Italian "humanists" were engaged in putting the *studia humanitatis* to practical use in their various roles as secretaries to civic or papal government, as official historians and/or propagandists, and as ambassadors. Above all, they put it to use as "masters" (*magistri*) in the quintessential humanist calling, teaching the liberal arts, from the most elementary to the most advanced levels. For the "cultivation," the "indoctrination," and especially the "institution" of the young was the most practical and fundamental expression of Renaissance *humanitas*— and the means of guaranteeing its transmission to the "posterity" to which Petrarch had referred.

The term *institution* has a marvelously rich and suggestive semantic heritage. It suggests at once the founding of something, its methodical teaching, the established and approved condition of something, and the social formations on the basis of which it is preserved, developed, and disseminated. From the *Institutes* of Justinian and the *Institution of Oratory* of Quintilian to the *Institution of the Prince* of Guillaume Budé, the *Institutes of a Christian Prince* of Erasmus, and *Institution of Christian Religion* of Calvin, the term designated fundamental instruction in an important topic, and in its social sense it applies to the humanist movement of the Renaissance. For humanism became in its essence a vehicle of education on all levels, the basis for a conception of individual and social life, and an established intellectual tradition with its characteristic "institutions" and centers of instruction, promotion, and graduation.

The honor roll of great humanist educators and their disciples is long and impressive. Vittorino da Feltre and his school at Mantua, Guarino at Ferrara, and Vergerio at Padua are only a few of the most influential figures in Italian communal education, while Rudolf Agricola, Alexander Hegius, Erasmus, and Melanchthon carried on the same pedagogical project beyond the Alps, though in very different cultural contexts.[18] Humanistic educational efforts were pursued in private tutorships and civic schools like Vittorino's, which were devoted to physical as well as mental culture; in academies, such as those of the court of Naples, Medicean Florence, and papal Rome; and by the sixteenth century in some universities, in which professorships of classical scholarship (especially of rhetoric, poetry, and history) were established in the arts faculties. By that time, in any case, the *studia humanitatis* had been spread far and wide, especially in elementary schools, in Italy and beyond, and this had made the schools fit even for such a man of letters as Petrarch.

"Trivial" though this movement might seem (being derived from the *trivium*), it was the mark of what George Holmes has called a "humanist avant garde," a "lunatic fringe . . . ostentatiously observing a set of values outside the normal intellectual framework."[19] What they did in effect was to radicalize Petrarch's position: "To deny that Aristotle was the 'master of those that know' and to prefer Cicero's approach to philosophy, or to regard the niceties of Latin style as all-important while denying value to the intricacies of logic, was an intellectual rebellion more complete and bizarre . . . than the rebellion of [the contemporary heretics] Wycliffe and Hus." And humanist pedagogy was further radicalized by the Greek phase of the humanist movement. The teaching of Greek was begun with the coming of Byzantine scholar Manuel Chrysoloras to Florence in 1397 and was continued by his students, including Bruni, Guarino, and Vergerio; and it led to even more subversive texts and ideas.

The essence of humanistic education was the teaching of that most basic of all human intellectual creations—"letters" (*litterae*, or literature), meaning primarily the liberal arts of grammar and rhetoric, based on the reading of Latin orators, historians, and poets. It was the study of these authors that first gave the *umanisti* their nickname. According to Erasmus, knowledge acquired by these boys (and, marginally, girls) was divided into two categories, viz., words and things (corresponding to the old classical topos, *res et verba*). Nor could an understanding of the human world be separated at all, in either theory or practice, from the medium of language.[20] Indeed, it was the aim of humanism to subject other disciplines to its own literary and "historical" methods.

Humanist education was concerned with action as well as discourse, and here the classical model was Cicero's and Quintilian's prescriptions for the training (*institutio*) of the "orator." One of the characteristic humanist genres was devoted to analogous treatises on the "institution" of the perfect person—the well-rounded, or at least well-grounded, yet professionally, socially, or politically competent, person; the Perfect (or Complete) Courtier, Citizen, Christian, Prince, Artist, Jurist, Historian, or even Baconian Man of Science. The horizons of these social roles were variously defined—ranging from the scholar's study to the family, from the classroom to the artist's studio, from the court to the courtroom, from civic government to the royal council, from the Christian Elect to the community of modern natural philosophers. Alberti's *Della famiglia*, Palmieri's *Della vita civile*, Erasmus' *Education of a Christian Prince*, and Machiavelli's notorious obverse portrait in his *Prince* and more generally Machiavelli's celebration of world-citizenship all suggested the possible human horizons of the "universal man" (*uomo universale*) envisioned by Renaissance educators.

In education, the masculine monopoly of culture was breached by humanism—"virtue" and "nobility" became detached from birthright in terms of gender as well as class. Vittorino accepted the principle of sexual equality in his school, broad-mindedness that itself had good classical precedent. As Bruni wrote to a lady of Montefeltro (who herself was the authoress of a Latin oration dedicated to the Emperor Sigismund), "There is, indeed, no lack of examples of women renowned for their letters and their eloquence"—Scipio's daughter Cornelia, Sappho, and the lady Aspasia, "from whom even so great a philosopher as Socrates did not blush to admit that he had learned certain things."[21] Bruni himself stressed moral philosophy and virtues chiefly practical and domestic, although he did want women to enjoy the larger benefits of the *studia humanitatis;* and so, even more conservatively, did Juan Luis Vives, who adapted the views of Quintilian to the education of Christian women—especially unmarried women and widows. Vives did not encourage the notion that they might also be teachers, at least beyond the stage of infant care, or preachers, or engage in public affairs, or indeed challenge the husband's position as "king" in his household.[22]

Undeniably, numerous women authors and scholars, especially in the noble classes, contributed to Renaissance scholarship. Yet despite the hyperbole of a humanist like Boccaccio, writing about "famous women," or of a Renaissance "feminist" like Bartolommeo Goggio, writing passionately "in praise of women,"[23] or an apologist like Christine de Pisan, Joan Kelly-Gadol's question remains in doubt: "Did women have a Renaissance?"[24] The answer may be a qualified yes, but only for a relatively small number of "women worthies" and even then outside the major institutions of learning, except for salons. Because of the importance of scriptural reading, a greater emphasis may have been placed on the literary education of Protestant women, but again, such benefits were limited largely to noblewomen. Nor did breaking the male monopoly of the priesthood by Protestant confessions signify an upsurge in women's participation in preaching, education, or ecclesiastical offices, except in conventional wifely roles. As one French Huguenot declared, nursing a child was the highest accomplishment a good woman might hope to make.

Despite the emergence of public instruction in the sixteenth century, especially in Protestant schools, liberal education was for the most part designed for the professional, social, and political elite—in general, the movers and shakers of Renaissance society. "Amongst his scholars," wrote Vespasiano about Vittorino, "were cardinals, bishops and archbishops, as well as temporal rulers and cultured gentlemen from Lombardy, Venice, Padua, Vicenza and all the chief places of the province."[25] It is true that the study of grammar and the classical *auctores* taught submission to "authority"—on that level *magister dixit*—but more advanced training in rhetoric departed from elementary deference and demands for imitation (suggested by the extremes of "Ciceronianism") and opened the way to persuasion, social influence, administrative counsel, political representation and leadership, potentially subversion, and other forms of public communication and action, whether commendable or reprehensible. And

needless to say, the growing power of the printing press—the prolif-
eration of textbooks, teaching aids, reference works, and other
means of public instruction—served to magnify all of these tendencies in public communication.

Humanist pedagogy implied ideas of psychology and determined attitudes toward philosophy, especially in the endless search
for "methods" of studying, organizing knowledge, and achieving
some measure of originality. It should be noted here that "originality" implied not absolute novelty but rather an informed as well as
ingenious sort of imitation (*mimesis*) that selected an appropriate
source and treated it with elegant and perhaps virtuoso skill.[26] Nevertheless, in the early stages of education, especially in grammar,
the emphasis was on the faculty of memory, later—in rhetoric and
poetry—moving to more original expression, and finally, perhaps,
rising to higher levels of rationality and communication. This trajectory suggested the form of Bacon's scientific method, which was
likewise based on the combination of memory (experience) and
reason, though normally marginalizing the third faculty, that of
imagination.

In the eighteenth century Giambattista Vico, discussing educational "method" at the very end of the tradition of Renaissance humanism, took the Baconian scheme as the point of departure and
argued that training should begin not with theories but with "topics"
(*ars topica*), the essential category of rhetoric, but including, for Vico,
"the totality of arts and sciences," because "common sense predomi-
nates in youth, while reason is strongest in old age."[27] For Vico,
writing in the wake of the scientific revolution, "the greatest draw-
back of our educational methods is that we pay an excessive amount
of attention to the natural sciences and not enough to ethics"—with
the result that, listening for "the authentic voice of Nature," "the
science of politics lies almost abandoned and untended." Resurrect-
ing the old theme of civic humanism, Vico urged that anyone interested in public affairs "should not waste too much time, in his adoles-
cence, on those subjects that are taught by abstract geometry." His
"new science"—in opposition to that of Galileo and Descartes—
embraced history, humanist erudition, and the Renaissance encyclopedia in which, originally and ideally, "all arts and disciplines were
interconnected and rested in the lap of philosophy."[28]

In this educational, or educationist, context, "philosophy" was
generally conceived in practical terms—whether moral, social, political, or religious (as in Erasmus' *philosophia Christi*). Philosophy

thus implied not the study of nature and her laws but rather the study of the arts of human culture (itself originally an educational term) and civilization (*civilitas* being the root of this concept, which linked the ideals of Renaissance and Enlightenment). In humanist education as in humanist philology, in short, language and the liberal arts devoted to language preserved their primacy over abstract conceptualization and disputation. For such, from the time of Vives to Vico, was the road to self-knowledge, self-mastery, and true "wisdom"—and thereafter, perhaps, service to one's community and mankind in general.

## The Horizons of Humanism

In breaking out of the rigid framework of the medieval *Studium*, the early humanists expanded their horizons in a variety of ways—temporally, spatially, emotionally, and conceptually. To Petrarch and his followers, nothing that was human (and little that was divine) was foreign. Curiosity, nostalgia, and an attitude of tolerance would lead to a deeper understanding of the past and a willingness to extend such understanding beyond the boundaries of Christendom. What resulted was a transformation not only of knowledge but also of values and assumptions about the human condition. Burckhardt's famous formula, "the discovery of the world and of man," remains a good characterization of these cultural phenomena even within the strictly defined terrain of the *studia humanitatis* and the classical tradition.

Coinciding with, or even preceding, the humanist movement associated with Petrarch was the extraordinary pursuit of classical manuscripts, Latin and Greek, carried on by Petrarch and his school. (That this pursuit did not really constitute "discoveries" does not detract from the significance of these scholarly voyages of discovery.) Petrarch's own love of books is illustrated by the story that his father, angry at his son's literary indulgences, threw two volumes into the fire and then, responding to Petrarch's distress, rescued them. Petrarch himself acquired manuscripts of the works not only of Cicero, Livy, Pliny, and Quintilian but also of Homer and Plato; and these relics of the past occasioned in him feelings of both depression and exaltation. To Quintilian he wrote a letter lamenting the tattered condition of a copy of the *Institution of Oratory:* "I recognized therein the hand of time," he wrote, "destroyer of all things."[29] On the other hand, Petrarch's discovery of Cicero's letters to Atticus was the source of a veritable epiphany and inspired Petrarch to his remarkable correspondence with ancient authors. Among these were Homer, whom Petrarch thanked for his explanation of the origin of poetry, and Livy, whose historical work Petrarch edited in part (in a manuscript that later became the basis of Valla's critical notes).[30]

Petrarch's first disciples, Boccaccio and Salutati, carried on the antiquarian enterprise. Boccaccio produced a translation of Homer from Petrarch's manuscript and turned up a manuscript of part of Tacitus's historical writings in the monastery of Monte Cassino. Salutati's most famous discovery was a copy of Cicero's familiar letters, which contributed further to the image and legend of Cicero and the controversies surrounding them. The great age of manuscript-hunting came in the early fifteenth century, especially with the efforts of Poggio. Poggio's finds included the codex of Tacitus known to Boccaccio, six more orations of Cicero (in a heap of waste paper), and above all a copy of Quintilian's *Institution of Oratory*. According to Vespasiano, "as he could not obtain the volume he spent thirty-two days in copying it with his own hand; this I saw in the fairest manuscript."[31] "Oh wondrous treasure!" exclaimed Poggio's friend Bruni when he learned of this discovery in 1416. "Oh unexpected joy! Shall I see you, Marcus Fabius, whole and undamaged, and how much will you mean to me now?"[32] What Quintilian's work provided, among other things, was a systematic discussion of the theory and practice of rhetoric, rivaled only by the work of Cicero on rhetoric—and perhaps even (as Valla suggested) preferable to it. In this way the conversation between ancients and moderns struck up by Petrarch became a central theme of humanism, especially Florentine humanism.

It was in this connection that the essential theme, image, and myth of the "Renaissance" and of the interplay between ancients and moderns was formulated. "What have you not accomplished in restoring to us the Orators, Poets, Historians, Astronomers, and Grammarians who would undoubtedly now be lost forever?" Francesco Barbaro, former student of Guarino, exclaimed in a letter to Poggio in 1417. "Forthwith no debased or worn-out honor ought to be paid to you but something special and new."[33] Anticipating the more famous pretensions of Valla in his *Elegancies of the Latin Language*, Barbaro expressed the superiority of such literary efforts to material achievements. "Will there be anyone so jealous as to think that I do you too much honor?" Barbaro continued. "Whom more-over do I honor? Those truly who have brought more assistance than ever and finer ornaments to this Republic of letters." This is one of the first references to that "Republic of Letters" which, through the forces of printing and journalism, would give coherence to European intellectual life.

For humanists who cared for such things, there were even more tangible residues of the lamented classical past: *Antiquitas* had a material as well as a literary aspect. Recalling perhaps his own motive for writing the *Decline and Fall,* Edward Gibbon quoted the complaints of Poggio, in his essay on "the variety of Fortune," about the ruins of Rome:

> The hill of the Capitol, on which we sit, was formerly the head of the Roman Empire, the citadel of the earth, the terror of kings; illustrated by the triumphs, enriched with the spoils of so many nations. The spectacle of the world, how it is fallen! how changed! how defaced! the path of victory is obliterated by vines, and the benches of the senators are concealed by a dunghill. Cast your eyes on the Palatine hill, and seek among the shapeless and enormous fragments the marble theatre, the obelisks, the colossal statues, the porticoes of Nero's palace: survey the other hills of the city, the vacant space is interrupted only by ruins and gardens. The forum of the Roman people, where they assembled to enact their laws and elect their magistrates, is now enclosed for the cultivation of pot-herbs, or thrown open for the reception of swine and buffaloes. The public and private edifices, that were founded for eternity, lie prostrate, naked, like the limbs of a mighty giant; and the ruin is the more visible, from the stupendous relics that have survived the injuries of time and fortune.[34]

Even before Petrarch, pilgrims, travelers, and tourists had been impressed by such pitiable sights, but they looked on them with different eyes. For Dante, the empire was still a part of living tradition, but for Rienzi it needed resuscitation. Dante's universal *Romanitas* was replaced by a kind of idealization that spurred the study of "antiquities" in a number of areas, as Roberto Weiss has shown; and politics furnished a further motive, as Rienzi's pioneering study of Roman inscriptions demonstrates. Archaeology, topography, epigraphy, numismatics, sphragistics, and other "auxiliary sciences" of history (as well as the "fine" arts of painting and architecture) were among the by-products of sentimental—and increasingly scientific—antiquarianism.[35] The ruins described by Poggio had been visible for centuries, but they had not been regarded primarily as stirring monuments or even relics (except of course for the remains of Christian Rome), or at least they had not inspired the literary emotion and historical emotion and curiosity that they did in the antiquarian writings of Poggio and especially of Flavio Biondo (papal secretaries, both). Biondo's *Roma instaurata* and *Roma triumphans* directed attention to the antiquities of medieval Christian as well as ancient imperial and republican Rome; and his *Historiarum ab inclinatione romanorum imperii decades*, the most distinguished antecedent of Gibbon's *Decline and Fall*, served as a model for the investigations of northern scholars, who delved into their own national traditions, reconstructed genealogies, fabricated myths, and devised the critiques thereof.

In the second half of the fifteenth century this antiquarian assault on the Western past was expanded through a growing expertise in and fascination with Greek literature and philosophy. This shift of attention from Rome to Greece was intensified by contacts between the Eastern and Western churches during the Conciliar period (most notably the Council of Ferrara-Florence) and more particularly after the fall of the Ottoman Empire, which sent Greek scholars into exile into the West or made their residence there permanent. To this was also added the study of Hebrew and other "oriental" languages. The purpose of these ventures included not only Christian tradition and Greek philosophy, especially Neoplatonism, but also occult, Hermetic, and Cabalistic thought that led scholars into suspicious areas of unorthodoxy, forbidden knowledge, and even heresy. *Romanitas* and *Hellenismus* were joined by strange but even more seminal influences originating in the mysterious East.

In this period, too, European culture was shaken and shaped by another novelty. The invention of the "German art" of printing seemed to many scholars a miraculous fulfillment of the humanist program—the "tenth muse," as a sixteenth-century poet exalted. "Movable type," as Egon Friedell remarked, "is the symbol of humanism."[36] There has been much discussion of this so-called "typographical revolution," especially in the wake of Elizabeth Eisenstein's comprehensive and controversial study, *The Printing Press as an Agent of Historical Change*; but whatever the exaggerations about the centrality of print culture, they hardly surpass humanist hyperbole and the commercial claims of the early scholar-printers and enthusiasts, for whom the "miracle" of printing was the primary vehicle of the "renaissance of arts and letters" and the guarantee of its continuance. "The invention of printing," declared Guillaume Budé, the leading figure in French humanism, "is the restitution and perpetuation of antiquity."[37]

This "restitution" was a sister concept to "institution" and of comparable intellectual scope. For philologists like Budé, *restitutio* was a technical term designating the sort of textual emendations (paleographical, grammatical, or conjectural) that restored original meaning. It was extended from its "trivial" base to the larger field of "antiquity" as a whole. The long-term goal of humanism, the achievement of wisdom (*sapientia*) through the restoration of a hypostasized *antiquitas*, was to be attained not merely through a piecemeal recovery of fragments and manuscript remains but, in many ways, through an encyclopedic "reintegration" of ancient culture as a whole.

Besides rhetoric, poetry, and the other human studies, classical myth and artistic forms were also reunited with their ancient meaning, as Jean Seznec has shown so brilliantly in his *Survival of the Pagan Gods* and, by analogy with the visual arts, Brian Vickers in his *Defense of Rhetoric*. Out of this transformed topos of "restitution" came the idea of the Renaissance, whose later fortunes have been traced in Wallace Ferguson's *Renaissance in Historical Thought*.

"How many new arts have been devised!" Vico was still marveling in the eighteenth century. "How many new sciences!"[38] If printing made possible the recovery, reintegration, and preservation of ancient learning, it also suggested ways of accommodating and promoting future change. The printed book, along with the compass and (though more debatably) gunpowder, formed another central topos of modernism, one that is enshrined most famously in the scientific rhetoric of Francis Bacon. Establishing the battlefield of the never-ending "quarrel of ancients and moderns," the printed book at the same time contributed mightily to the efforts of both parties, encouraging both "imitation" and "invention"—both the dialogues with the dead begun by Petrarch and the novel conversations provoked by encounters with the new world and awareness of the expanding universe of the sixteenth century, and so opened up not only historical but also broader geographical and scientific (though nonetheless human) horizons.

On the one hand, printing made the "renaissance of arts and letters" of the fifteenth century a permanent revival and prepared the ground for the new science of philology by making available critical editions, grammars, textbooks, dictionaries, encyclopedias, bibliographies, collections of historical sources, and other scholarly aids. Printing thus lent support to the "Republic of Letters" celebrated by Barbaro, Erasmus, and others. On the other hand, printing was also of major importance for scientific disciplines, which depended on uniform texts and data, cooperative research, and cumulative knowledge, including biology, medicine, astronomy, geography, and cartography, as well as vernacular languages and literature. As the Reformation illustrated massively, printing was the source not only of light but also of heat; for it could, in the pursuit of modern "causes," be conscripted not only by humane educators but also by the most unscrupulous and unsettling propagandists and ideologists (who likewise drew on the resources of Renaissance learning and in particular the persuasive devices of the *studia humanitatis*). Although backward-looking in the extreme, Renaissance humanism was an essential aspect of what Henri Hauser called "the modernity of the sixteenth century."[39]

Links between Renaissance humanism and the Enlightenment of the eighteenth century have no doubt been exaggerated. Lorenzo Valla was not a modern skeptic, after all; nor was Erasmus a *philosophe* before his time. Yet the eighteenth-century ideal of Humanity did have remote roots in the *humanitas*, in Barbaro's, Valla's and Erasmus' *Respublica Litterarum*, and in Renaissance learning. The very concept of "renaissance" played an important role in the program of the Enlightenment as viewed by the likes of Voltaire, Lessing, Condorcet, and Dugald Stewart.[40] The basis of these links was not, to be sure, any mystical sort "anticipation" or precursoring; rather, the *philosophes* themselves chose (as indeed some scholars still choose) to connect their intellectual pedigree not only with seventeenth-century natural philosophy but also with the best of Renaissance thought. This retrospective act of veneration, too, helped to expand the horizons of Renaissance humanism and even, in a certain sense, to merge them with our own.

# 3

# Humanism and Philosophy

Plato is praised by the greater men, Aristotle by the greater number; and both deserve to be praised by great men, even all men.

—Francesco Petrarch

The intellectual agenda of fifteenth-century humanists was to elaborate Petrarch's program, to extend it into other fields, to bring it to a wider audience and new generations, and in this way to reform education and society as a whole. They sought a purer language as a way to clearer and richer thought, a more human approach to moral philosophy, and larger social and political goals. The civic ideal preserved in Aristotle's view of the *polis* and (implicitly) in Plato's *Republic* had been ill served by traditions of speculative philosophy. Nor did the figure of the philosopher, treasured by Dante and satirized by Petrarch, suit the values and ambitions of humanism. The model of the active life was now to be found rather in the *ars oratoria* of Cicero and Quintilian. The philosopher disputed in the classroom; the orator performed in the forum and indeed was a "leader of people." Equally important, rhetoric offered a large critical and historical view of the human world that was denied to speculative philosophy. More than any of the other *studia humanitatis*, the art of rhetoric symbolized and expressed the humanist ideal, and more than any other it was the humanist Lorenzo Valla who explored the intellectual—as well as the professional, "scientific," and indeed philosophical—potential of this discipline.

## Lorenzo Valla and the Challenge of Rhetoric

Valla was one of the most arrogant and argumentative scholars of modern times, combining pedantry with polemical tendencies to an extraordinary degree. He possessed humanist prejudices against the learning of the schools—and celebrated the intellectual virtues of humanism—to an exaggerated extent. He was not only the most wide-ranging but also perhaps the most influential of all humanist scholars. Valla moved in the literary circles of Rome and Naples as well as Florence; and at different times he served both the papal and the antipapal parties, alternately attacking and defending the Church, writing on behalf of Alfonso the Magnanimous and ending his life at the papal court. Yet he did so without qualms because his intellectual loyalties remained constant, bound as they were not to particular political or theological causes but only to his discipline, which was the art of oratory and the "profession" of rhetoric.

In his numerous writings Valla attacked all the sacred cows of scholarship—including Aristotle (and in this connection his translator Boethius), the Stoics, the Vulgate translation of the Bible, Scholastic jurisprudence (in the person of Bartolus), various contemporaries (including his colleague Poggio Bracciolini), and even classical authors such as Livy and Cicero. His focus was at all times on questions of language and discourse, which is to say on the liberal arts of grammar, rhetoric, and what would later be celebrated as the science of "philology." For Valla, understanding and wisdom were inseparable from language, and attempts to transcend this medium of humanity were illusory. It was in these terms that Valla established a philosophy—or perhaps it would be better to say an antiphilosophy—of humanism.

In the time-honored style of Petrarch, Valla began with the ideal of antiquity, defined by the virtual synonyms *Romanitas, humanitas, civilitas* (and in the seventeenth century *socialitas* and *sociabilitas*). In his *Elegancies of the Latin Language* (1444) Valla identified himself and his intellectual projects directly with this classical canon and with "the sacramental power of the Latin language."[1] In his resounding rhetorical style he celebrated the deeds of his "ancestors," who, "as they surpassed other men in military affairs, so by extension of their language they indeed surpassed themselves," referring to the afterlife of Roman culture and the imperial triumphs of the Latin language in the lands of those "barbarians" who had themselves overrun the Empire. The revival of this ideal Valla described in much the same terms as did Petrarch and Bruni, but he saw larger implications than they had, both for criticism and for the reformation of thought.

In many ways the *Elegantiae*, which tried to restore classical Latin in the most concrete lexicographical ways, was Valla's key work. But more revealing for his attitudes toward philosophy was his *Dialectical Disputations* (1435). This work not only mounted a full-scale assault on scholasticism but also suggested a new approach to human understanding based on rhetoric. For Valla, the science of sciences, the royal road to understanding and participating in the world, was not the *ars dialectica* but the *ars rhetorica*. As always, Valla's arguments were formulated in terms of good classical usage—based not on a simple-minded aping of Cicero, however, but on a broader conception of the "authority of antiquity" (an ironic and subversive conjoining of two literary abstractions) and "the consensus of the erudite" in general.

In these disputations, Valla's first target was Boethius (in a sense, the first "Scholastic"), whose bad grammar and other linguistic abuses had led to lamentable confusions. Not Aristotle but Boethius was responsible for those imaginary "categories" (thing, quantity, relation, time, place, and the like) and "transcendentals" ("being," "the good," "the true," and so on), by which barbaric modern logicians had tried to classify knowledge.[2] Valla cut the Gordian knot by drastically reducing this cumbersome and indeed meaningless apparatus, keeping only one of the categories (thing) and three of the transcendentals (substance, action, and quality). For Valla, these are the only "categories" needed to understand the world. It should come as no surprise that the category of "thing" (*res*) is equivalent to humanly perceived "reality" and that the three transcendentals correspond to the major parts of speech (noun, verb, and adjective or adverb). In short, the categories of grammar sufficed for human understanding, and the abstractions of "that peripatetic tribe, destroyers of natural meaning," served only to confuse and to corrupt.

This sort of grammatical "realism" reinforced the humanist appreciation of the study of history. Aristotle had famously declared that poetry, because of its "philosophical" qualities, was superior to history, but Valla rejected this view. "History is more robust than poetry because it is more truthful," he declared. "It is oriented not toward abstraction [universality] but toward concrete truth."[3] And further, "The discourse of historians exhibits more substance, more practical knowledge, more political wisdom . . . , more customs, and more learning of every sort than all the precepts of all the philosophers. Thus we show that historians are superior to philosophers." And historians were superior for moral as well as epistemological reasons, for like its "mother," rhetoric, history moved men to virtue not through precepts but through human examples to imitate.

For Valla, then, the rhetorician is the one who can best understand reality. His vision is not clouded by ungrammatical philosophical fictions, and—even more important—his profession leads him into active participation in civil life, which is the only basis for true philosophy. The orator does not merely speculate but moves people to ideals and thus changes reality. The moral dimension of Valla's humanism likewise depended on an appreciation of human experience. In his dialogue on "the true good" (*de vero bono*), Valla staged a three-cornered debate on the varieties of moral philosophy—Stoic, Epicurean, and Christian—and he emphasized, in the words of one of the interlocutors, the value of pleasure and earthly rewards over the ethics of self-denial.[4] If Valla can be pinned down to a single notion in this rhetorical and dialogical exercise, it is probably a Christian synthesis of all these views in terms of human values and limitations, relegating transcendent claims and concerns to faith—and to silence.

Most enduring, perhaps, have been Valla's contributions to historical criticism in areas of classical scholarship, of biblical studies, of canon law, and of Roman law, which he regarded as central to the classical tradition.[5] His corrections of the text of Livy carried on a project begun by Petrarch, and his annotations on the New Testament were seminal in the higher criticism of the Bible. His criticisms of the *Digest* (the authoritative anthology of classical jurisprudence assembled by the Emperor Justinian in the sixth century), though made in the spirit of a grammarian rather than a jurist, were likewise a model for "legal humanism" and what would later be termed "elegant jurisprudence." Of Valla's work in these areas of pure scholarship, his critique of the famous eighth-century fabrication, the Donation of Constantine, is most famous (though it was anticipated in its methods by Petrarch's exposure of the false Habsburg donation). On the basis of logical, linguistic, historical, geographical, and paleographical arguments and exposures of contradictions and anachronisms, Valla denounced the alleged transfer of territory and authority from Constantine to Pope Sylvester as an ecclesiastical fraud characteristic of the later canonist tradition.

The combination of grammatical acumen and rhetorical excess—of aesthetic and historical criticism—that made up Valla's philological method is vividly expressed in his denunciation of this forgery. "What shall I censure the more, the stupidity of the ideas, or of the words?" he asked, turning in particular to the quoted threat of Constantine that any who questioned the document would "be burned in the lower hell and . . . perish with the devil and all the impious."[6] Nonsense, Valla protested. "This terrible threat is the usual one, not of a secular ruler, but of the earthly priests and flamens and, nowadays, of ecclesiastics. And so," he concluded, "this is not the utterance of Constantine, but of some fool of a priest who, stuffed and pudgy, knew neither what to say nor how to say it, and, gorged with eating and heated with wine, belched out these wordy sentences which convey nothing to another, but turn the author against himself."

Valla's philological rigor drew him also into theological problems, and in his *Dialectical Disputations* he took up the most sensitive of all aspects of Christian belief, the doctrine of the Trinity. For Valla, this was in effect another result of the linguistic abuses of scholastic (Boethian) Latin. The Deity might indeed exhibit three "persons," Valla acknowledged; but the word *persona* (like its Greek equivalent *hypostasis*), which classically had signified a mask, referred only to an aspect or "quality" of God, not to some polytheistic construction of philosophers resulting from bad language, bad thinking, and bad theology.[7] A similar line of argument appears in Valla's treatment of the problem of free will and foreknowledge, concepts irreconcilable in ordinary language, if not (as Augustine had long before argued) in faith. Valla also attacked the moral qualities of ecclesiastical culture, especially as expressed in the abominable institution of monasticism, which affected to scorn earthly rewards such as wealth and sex but in fact, by renouncing them, overly prized them. Valla denounced "the profession of the religious" as a divisive "sect" founded on abstract, prescriptive, and inhuman values and inclined perhaps to heresy.[8] (*Haeresis* was the Greek for "sect.")

In general, Valla situated human knowledge within the horizons of everyday experience, action, memory, language, judgment, and communication. The fabrications of philosophy, the fictions of law, and the speculations of theology fell outside these horizons; and human understanding was a product of literary and historical learning, especially as it was preserved in classical tradition. Valla's influence was apparent in Erasmus' biblical studies, in Budé's critique of the classical texts of Roman law, and in Luther's indignation at the Donation of Constantine and other forgeries found in "Romanist" tradition. But above all the antiphilosophical thrust of Valla's criticism was present in the new science of philology, which would be developed by following generations of humanist scholars and, in a longer perspective, in that attitude of mind which was later to be called "historicism." As the invention of printing operated to fix and to further the accomplishments of Renaissance humanism, so it turned the most characteristic representative of humanism into one of the most popular authors of the sixteenth century.

## Florentine Platonism and the Contemplative Life

Although initially limited to the lower reaches of the liberal arts (the actual area covered by the *studia humanitatis*), the humanist movement after Petrarch impinged upon other branches of learning as well, including philosophy and the "sciences" of law and theology. One of the crucial problems in the interpretation of Renaissance humanism is whether it possessed or acquired any philosophical or ideological significance itself (the view taken by Hans Baron, Eugenio Garin, and philosophers like Ernesto Grassi), or whether it merely converged with the older disciplines in a formal way (the opinion of Kristeller and many of his students). Renaissance humanism can hardly be identified with modern varieties of humanism, but it seems clear that many champions of the humanist cultural program developed particular methods and ways of understanding the human condition, even if they did not enroll in particular doctrinal schools. Central in any case to the understanding of Renaissance humanism is the question of the relationship between the ideas, attitudes, and prejudices of Petrarch's followers and the formal doctrines of ancient philosophy and scholastic tradition.

Valla had remained within the territory of the *studia humanitatis*, although he carried his "trivial" (grammatical and rhetorical) criticism into the domains of law, theology, and philosophy. Other members of the intellectual tradition of Petrarch, however, looked more tolerantly—or imperialistically—on other aspects of the *Studium*, and especially on the riches of Greek science, which had been in the process of rediscovery since the "twelfth-century renaissance," centering primarily on Aristotle. This "second" Greek revival was signaled especially in Florence from 1397 by the teaching of Manuel Chrysoloras, from whom Bruni learned Greek. Like Petrarch, Bruni had been committed to the study of law; but he "was actually of two minds when Chrysoloras arrived," driven especially by the thought that "for seven hundred years no one in Italy has been able to read Greeks, and yet we admit that it is from the Greeks that we get all our systems of knowledge. Overcome by such arguments," Bruni concluded, "I took myself to Chrysoloras, with such an ardor to study that what I learned in my waking hours during the day, I would be working over at night even in my sleep."[9] On this basis and in the context of his program of civic humanism, Bruni turned to the translation of the "practical" (as distinguished from the "theoretical") philosophy of Aristotle—that is, his works on politics and ethics and the pseudo-Aristotelian economics (although Bruni apparently planned also to translate some of Plato).

The renewed interest in formal philosophy in the fifteenth century was reinforced by a significant change in the climate of opinion. By the time of Bruni's death in 1444, the civic ideal seemed to be entering eclipse, and by the time of Valla's death in 1457, philosophy was returning to intellectual fashion. The Medici family had established its unofficial hegemony in Florence; and while Guelf "liberty" continued to be celebrated, some critics thought Florence was falling from republican grace into despotism. This political transformation was accompanied by a parallel shift from practical to speculative philosophy. Produced by a new enthusiasm for the works of Plato, the shift to speculative philosophy was encouraged by contact with Byzantine scholars, especially at the Council of Ferrara-Florence, and more especially after the exodus following the conquest of Constantinople by the Turks in 1453.

Byzantine scholars began an extraordinary debate over the relative merits of Plato and Aristotle, and their relationship and reconcilability with Christianity. The most significant entrants in this debate were George Gemistos Pletho, who argued that "those who had a taste of Plato greatly prefer him to Aristotle"; George Trapezuntius, who resisted the "Platonic contagion"; and Bessarion, who, in his statesmanlike representation of Conciliar "concord," tried to reconcile Plato and Aristotle with one another and both with Christian doctrine.[10] Bessarion remained in the West after the Turkish conquest and became a cardinal of the Western Church, a great collector of books, a patron of scholarship, and a sponsor of the Medici Academy. Instituted on the model of the ancient Academy, the Medici Academy was devoted to the study of Platonic and Neoplatonic philosophy, with its curious admixture of Hermetic, pseudo-Dionysian, Cabalistic, and other occult ideas, and its eclectic hope of reconciling Platonism and Aristotelianism. The Greek phase of humanism involved not only the quest for literary texts, such as the "lost" books of Livy and the works of Plato, but also the search for esoteric (and perhaps forbidden) knowledge and deeper meanings, and this also broadened the horizons of humanism.

One of the first Western enthusiasts for Neoplatonic harmony—though he was much more than this—was Nicolas of Cusa, also cardinal and well on his way to becoming Pope before his death in 1464. Cusanus was the first original systematic philosopher after the thirteenth century, assembling an extraordinary compound of Platonic, Terminist, mystical, and humanist ideas with the idea of reconciling contradictions on all levels—scientific, metaphysical, theological, ecclesiastical ("Conciliar theory"), and political. According to Ernst Cassirer, Cusanus' major significance was in making what was in effect an epistemological "turn" (analogous to the ancient "Socratic revolution," endorsed also by Petrarch) that shifted philosophical priorities from nature to the question of the means and limits of human knowledge.[11] For Cusanus, mankind seeks understanding only through particulars (empirical investigation) and reaches it only approximately (as analogously, an infinite-sided polygon approaches a perfect circle). This was the pattern of Cusanus' key idea, informing his theology as well as his philosophy, of "learned ignorance" (*docta ignorantia*), which was an inspiration for the fideistic ideas of the next century.

On this basis, Cusanus developed an evolutionary and dialectical system of thought in which the world appeared as a dual process of unfolding (*explicatio*) and enfolding (*complicatio*)—divine creation and Neoplatonic reascension to God, whether in the sense of rethinking creation or in the sense of salvation. For Cusanus, this evolutionary process is, again, a way of resolving contradictions, since all opposites are resolved in God. In some ways Cusanus' thought seems more suited to the tradition of systematic philosophy associated with Scholasticism, and yet his ideas and intellectual priorities were in accord with humanism—above all (as Cassirer argued) because of his fundamental concern with the "problem of knowledge"—the conditions, limits, and aims of human learning (and "ignorance") with respect to the transcendental questions of philosophy and theology. In the next century Cusanus' "learned ignorance" (*docta ignorantia*) reinforced the parallel intellectual thrust of modern versions of skeptical philosophy.

Western Neoplatonism found its institutional base in the Academy founded by Cosimo de' Medici in 1462. In the work of Marsilio Ficino and younger colleagues such as Giovanni Pico della Mirandola and Cristoforo Landino, philosophy and to some extent the humanist program turned from public to private concerns. The center of this school was the arch-Platonist Marsilio Ficino, who had studied medicine at Bologna and had taken priestly orders before being called to Florence by Cosimo in 1462. Unlike Bruni, who lived an active life as Florentine chancellor, Ficino was a priest and Platonist who prized above all the contemplative life. His first major work (not extant) was a textbook (*Institutiones*) of Platonic doctrine, and much of his life was devoted to his translation of the corpus of Plato's writings.[12] By 1469 this was completed, and in 1472 Ficino published his own *Platonic Theology*, which tried to reconcile Platonic philosophy with Christian doctrine (as Thomas Aquinas had tried to reconcile Aristotelian philosophy with Christian doctrine).

Ficino's aim, like that of Cusanus, was to bring together the concerns of theology and epistemology, and he drew eclectically on Scholastic, Hermetic, and occult sources as well as on Plato himself. What Ficino produced was a picture of the universe from a human point of view, a conception of the microcosm as a recapitulation of the macrocosm, structured hierarchically and given coherence by the dynamic principle of Platonic love—"so that," as Ficino described the process of Platonic (and Hermetic) comprehension, "the soul in its own way will become the whole universe."[13] In general, Ficino sang not of arms and the man, not of the Commonwealth and the citizen, but rather of God and the Soul. "Clearly . . . Plato placed as the highest good in the soul, not acting but contemplating the pure intelligence of truth," he wrote, and elsewhere, in a tone reminiscent of Petrarch rather than Bruni, "Whoever desires to attain God, avoids large numbers and movement as much as he can."[14]

In Platonic terms, too, Ficino celebrated the humanist revival of ancient wisdom—the recovery of that "age of gold" suggested in Plato's *Republic*. "For like a golden age," Ficino wrote, "this century has restored to light the liberal arts, which were almost extinct: grammar, poetry, rhetoric, painting, sculpture, architecture, music, the ancient singing of songs to the Orphic lyre, and all this in Florence."[15] Wisdom has been joined to eloquence, Ficino added; astronomy has been perfected (alluding to the astrolabe); and the German art of printing has arrived likewise in a most timely fashion to reinforce the humanist—and Neoplatonic—program of enlightenment. That such enlightenment depended as much on occult philosophy, natural magic, and especially the *Corpus Hermeticum* (part of which Ficino also translated) as on Plato reminds us of the broader horizons (and obscurer depths) of the humanist program in its encounters with philosophical tradition.

Ficino's younger colleague Pico della Mirandola carried on this Platonizing line of investigation and interpretation but in a still more eclectic fashion. In a famous exchange with the Venetian humanist Ermolao Barbaro in 1485, Pico—without denying the value of the *studia humanitatis*—defended the study as well of formal philosophies and theologies, and by inference the notion of a wisdom beyond language. The Scholastic philosophers were not "barbarians," he argued, but sources of at least partial truth—as indeed were the poets. "We have lived as famous men, Ermolao, and we shall live in times to come, not in the schools of the grammarians and pedagogues, but in the circles of philosophers, in gatherings of sages . . . ," who are concerned "not about light nothings, but about the reasons of things human and divine."[16] Wisdom transcended the faculties of memory and reason, for Pico also celebrated the enhancing powers of imagination—though again only with divine assistance.

Pico was a prodigy and a polyglot (as well as, to some, a crackpot) and, like Valla, "was pledged to the doctrines of no man." Unlike Valla, however, Pico's ambitions and expertise went beyond the bounds of the Western tradition, especially into Hebrew and Arabic scholarship. Conventional Western wisdom (*sapientia*) should be joined to eloquence, and both to the occult traditions beyond the horizons of European culture—for, as he remarked, "all wisdom has flowed from the East to the Greeks and from the Greeks to us."[17] If Ficino was the arch-Platonist, Pico was the arch-syncretist. His controversial "900 theses" proposed to reconcile not only Plato and Aristotle but, beyond that fashionable project, an enormous range of learning, Eastern as well as Western, occult as well as rational. On that basis he intended to demonstrate the essential unity (despite the vast range of cultural differences) of wisdom, human and divine—a sort of "perennial philosophy," as it would later be called. As Ficino had thought that the human mind could in effect become the whole universe, so Pico thought that the Socratic (and Zoroastrian) exhortation "Know thyself!" could be achieved only by the critical and comparative study of all human philosophies, all facets of civilization across time.

In his "Oration on the Dignity of Man" (which served as an introduction to the 900 theses) Pico expressed, with characteristic rhetorical hyperbole, his paraphilosophical confession of faith. Like Ficino, Pico began with the conventional "great chain of being," in which man supposedly occupied a central position, uniquely situated between the natural and supernatural worlds to rise from sense experience (shared with the rest of the animate world) to rational reflection and the world of ideas. But Pico went beyond this conventional hierarchy to a Platonically inspired and Neoplatonically sustained conception of man's mobility down as well as up this ladder of creation. Thus, Pico arrived at a vision of man's fundamentally "self-transforming nature" and the process of human self-creation.[18] In this way, he concluded, "we can become what we will"—if only we devote ourselves to the riches of philosophy, science, and religion as well as to the conventional program of humanist learning. It may well be that Pico's originality has been exaggerated, but the force of his rhetoric made an extraordinary impression on generations of readers.

In this and other ways, philosophy was added to the humanist "encyclopedia." Platonism (which is to say Neoplatonism) in particular had an extraordinary impact on Renaissance thought, not only as a more elegant and sensitive alternative to the modernized Aristotle that prevailed in the schools but also as a heaven-storming and mystery-probing source of enlightenment in many areas of human conceptualization. To many humanists Plato, in apparent contrast to Aristotle, seemed more easily adaptable to Christian belief in providential Creation, immortality, and spiritual values in general. What is more, Platonic and Neoplatonic writings set a number of themes on which Renaissance authors would provide innovative and seminal variations. Among these were the theory of knowledge, the philosophy of religion, ideas of "Platonic love" (especially in poetry and art), the crucial role of mathematics (especially in natural science), "utopian" political thought, and above all and related to these, the "Renaissance philosophy of man" and the foundations of what, from the sixteenth century on would be called "anthropology."

## Humanist Anthropology

In the major features of the "Renaissance philosophy of man," there was in fact little novelty. Scholastic philosophers as well as humanists had long sung the praises of the "great chain of being," the twofold nature of the human soul, and the correlation between microcosm and macrocosm. In the thirteenth century, for example, the encyclopedist Vincent of Beauvais had marveled that "Man, this miracle-compendium of creation, this universal creature made in the image and likeness of God, should become by himself, by his thoughts and by his wisdom, the living image of the universe, the great universal mirror in which should be reflected God, the world, and humanity."[19] Not only was man "made in God's image" (and woman, as most thought, not), he also shared some of God's capacities, especially his creativity. Dante had expressed man's unique nature in Aristotelian terms, arguing that humanity possessed all four of the levels of earthly existence—not only the simple being of the elements, the animated being of the vegetable world, and the sensitive being of animals, but "apprehension by means of the potential intellect."[20] This twofold positioning between the world of sense experience and that of thought allowed man to form ideas on the basis of sense impressions (as well as to attain immortality), and it distinguished him from spiritual as well as other earthly creatures. To such arguments, Platonizing and Hermeticizing philosophers like Ficino and Pico added an emphasis on factors of freedom, learning, and especially Promethean creativity, which made man (in the words of Ficino) "able to become in a sense all things, and even to become a god."

There was of course a dark side to Renaissance anthropology. Man's "dignity" or rank in the scale of creation was a complex one, involving consideration of human sin and misfortune as well as human happiness and glory. Medieval proverbs and religious lamentations reflected this negative aspect, as more famously did Innocent III's treatise *De contemptu mundi*, which was a classic portrayal of the "misery of the human condition" and which, from Petrarch to

Gianozzo Manetti, inspired optimistic humanist responses.[21] But Renaissance authors, too, could be "nay-sayers"—they could envision a "world upside down" as well as a golden age and a bright future, and they could appreciate man's potential to become not only a god but a thief, a liar, a beast, a monster, and (always) a fool.[22] Philosophy offered not only a way to the understanding of nature and the good life but also a "preparation for death"; and these themes figure centrally in the work of many Christian humanists. Budé, for example, despite his love of philology, did not overlook the sinful and evil aspect of humanity, especially in his last major work, written in a state of anxiety over Protestant infiltrations in France and devoted, significantly, to *The Transition from Hellenism to Christianity* (1535).

Renaissance "anthropology" (the word itself was a sixteenth-century coinage) focused on two basic and interrelated questions, one religious and one philosophical, or psychological. The first was the problem of free will, and the second was the problem of knowledge. The "triumph of the will" was one of the themes of Italian humanism derived from classical—especially Stoic—sources; and it fit in particularly well with the glorification of the "dignity of man" featured in the writings of Manetti, Ficino, Pico, Vives, and others. Yet in its exaggerated form the notion of free will also suggested the old Pelagian heresy denounced by Augustine. Following Augustine, Christian humanists (as well as Protestant reformers) made great efforts to reconcile the experience of human free will with the doctrine of God's "fore-knowledge." In effect, Valla resolved the question by denying that such theological concepts as "fore-knowledge" were intelligible within the limits of human language and that, consequently, the question was a matter of faith.[23] In this "humanist" argument Valla was followed, in different ways, by Erasmus, Luther, and Calvin.

"Anthropology" signified, more specifically, human psychology; and the thrust of the "Renaissance philosophy of man" was directed above all to the question of knowledge—its possibility, conditions, limits, purpose, and values. On the most practical level, this referred to ideas and systems of "liberal education," exemplified in the writings of Renaissance pedagogues like Vittorino, Guarino, and Vergerio, which constituted one of the primary aims of the humanist program. The encyclopedic pursuit of wisdom began with the acquisition of letters, and all Renaissance pedagogical treatises emphasized the crucial and central role of elementary—

especially Latin but often also Greek—"letters" forming the "trivial" subjects of grammar, rhetoric, and dialectic. Literacy was inseparable from civility, eloquence from true learning, and rationality from the highest ideal of humanity. Other disciplines were important only as they built on these foundations—the encyclopedic "circle of arts," the *studia humanitatis*.

The more technical problem was that of epistemology, formulated in terms of the dual nature of man and celebrated in political as well as psychological terms by Dante. The distinguishing and higher second nature of man was the subject of Aristotle's treatise on the soul (*De anima*), which for centuries, along with a large accumulation of commentaries, formed the basis of the discipline of psychology. The essential point was that, although human understanding was grounded in sense perception, it was capable of rising to the heights of universal reason (*nous, intellectus*). A classic discussion is Pietro Pomponazzi's treatise *On the Immortality of the Soul*, which offered philosophical (that is, Aristotelian) grounds for rejecting the idea of personal immortality. In this controversial work Pomponazzi showed how the "intellective soul" made it possible for man to ascend from his sensitive (animal) nature into the realm of ideas and rational understanding. At least through his intellect, man was "placed as a mean between mortal and immortal things," and thus enjoyed a psychological and relative sort of immortality, if not a theological and absolute one.[24] In this naturalistic context Pomponazzi also suggested (as had Valla, on rather different grounds) that a human and practical sort of "virtue" was preferable to religious concepts of morality, which depended on assumptions of immortality and heavenly rewards—not that, according to Pomponazzi, this philosophical analysis was an obstacle to a proper belief in a personal immortality or other doctrines of Christian faith.

By contrast, Platonism seemed confined to a more abstract and "theoretical" or "contemplative" sort of knowledge suitable to a disembodied "mind," which (according to Ficino) strove to escape from its earthly form, "reaching beyond any temporal change to its end and good in eternity." Yet Renaissance Neoplatonism—especially under the impulse to "harmonize" the doctrines of Plato and Aristotle—recognized the natural source and condition of learning. For Cusanus, the human mind was a "divine seed" that, in order to bear fruit, "must be planted in the soil of the sensible world." The fruit to which Cusanus referred is nothing less than a conceptual recapitulation of God's own creation—in Ficino's formula, suggesting a secular sort of immortality, the soul's potential to *become* the whole universe. For Ernst Cassirer the psychology of the Renaissance, focusing on "the subject-object problem," marked "the beginning from which was to emerge the newer, deeper concept of 'subjectivity.' "[25] What emerged, more remotely, from the Renaissance notion of man the microcosm were modern conceptions of individuality—the autonomous and eventually sovereign self, the thinking and creating agent, and eventually what has been called the "maker's theory of knowledge," which reached its culmination in the posthumanist philosophy of Giambattista Vico.

Renaissance fascination with the problem of knowledge was intensified by the revival of ancient skeptical philosophy—first the academic variety, represented by Cicero, and in the sixteenth century the radical Pyrrhonism associated with the work of Sextus Empiricus. The habits of epistemological (if not religious) doubt, already evident in Petrarch, were reinforced by the "crisis of belief" attendant on the Protestant Reformation; and critiques of the "vanity of arts and sciences," such as the work published by Henry Cornelius Agrippa under that title, highlighted this problem by casting doubt on the humanist program in the most fundamental way. For Agrippa, writing in 1531, "there is nothing more pernicious, nothing more destructive of man's well-being, nothing more damaging to the salvation of his soul than these very arts and sciences."[26]

Over the next generation or two, humanist learning, having resurrected ancient skepticism and provided a scholarly basis for modern skeptical philosophy, was employed—paradoxically and contrary to the intentions of Petrarch and many of his followers—to enhance such pious anti-intellectualism. In the name of faith, learned doubt turned "letters" on their heads and, drawing on humanistic learning to illustrate the weakness of human intelligence, turned wisdom against itself. In this way it contributed to a line of argument that reached high points first in Montaigne's bookish relativism, then in the learned free-thought (*libertinisme érudit*) of the seventeenth century, and later in Rousseau's broader indictment of the negative and unnatural aspects of civilization. In general, early modern skepticism provided rational arguments not only to reinforce unfocused doubt, moral confusion, and cultural relativism but also to sharpen the tools of criticism in various fields of scientific inquiry, humanistic scholarship, and modern "critical" philosophy. But this leads to some of the more indirect repercussions of

Renaissance humanism and to attitudes and ideas remote from the intentions and certainly the moral and social values of its founders.

## Humanism and Political Thought

The rise of civic humanism and the recovery of Greek science prepared the ground for the cultivation of modern political thought. The lawyers who were so important in "starting the Renaissance," according to Roberto Weiss, also rationalized its political foundations. Of first importance was declaring the city-state independent of the Empire, which marked the triumph, in Florence, of the Guelf program of civic "liberty" over Dante's old Ghibelline ideal of world empire. This was the significance of the famous formula of the Florentine jurist Bartolus of Sassoferrato, giving the city de facto imperial sovereignty (*civitas sibi princeps*—"the city itself is the prince") against the antiquated de jure rule of the Holy Roman Emperor. Humanists such as Salutati and Bruni, who opposed the Ghibelline "tyranny" of states like Milan, cojoined this juridical principle with classical republican ideals in the formulation of a modern "civic humanism."[27]

But the political thought of humanism, like its anthropology, had deeper foundations. The *Corpus juris civilis*, the *Politics* and *Nicomachaean Ethics* of Aristotle, classical historical works (especially those of Livy, Tacitus, and Thucydides, first translated by Valla), humanist discussions of the polities of their own city-states (especially Florence and Venice), and rhetoric more generally (as a form of public discourse)—these were the major ingredients in this new, or renewed, discipline devoted to the study of man as a civil, or "social and political animal" (as Aristotle's *zoon politikon* was rendered in the scholastic translation of William of Moerbeke and *animale civile* by Dante). In his more elegant translation Bruni advertised Aristotle's *Politics* as "a summa of the whole science of ruling and governing people."[28] For Bruni, the Athenian *polis* was the prototype of the ancient Roman and the modern Florentine *civitas*, and his translations of Aristotle marked both this essential identification of ancient and modern political experience and the humanist contributions to the vocabulary of politics, which has passed into all the modern languages.

The basic institution of humanist political thought, and indeed of civic life in general, was the family, which was set at the boundaries between culture and nature—production and reproduction, creation and procreation—and between the public and private spheres. The family, as portrayed in Leon Battista Alberti's treatise, was the vehicle of wealth, education, and the civilizing values of the new age; and the male head of family—the modern counterpart of the Roman *paterfamilias*—embodied, ideally, all the virtues of the republican citizen of antiquity. The family was not only the scene of gender and generational relations but also the fundamental locus of the interplay between "fortune" and "virtue"; and on it the fortune of the state likewise depended. The national monarchies in the north also depended on their "great families," and the property and values accruing thereto. Jean Bodin was only one of many who recognized the foundational position of that "small republic" that was the family.[29]

But the larger "republic" of political government affected to absorb familial and other social groups; and it was in this context that the terminology of Greek political science was adapted to modern social conditions. It was conflated with the "civil science" of late medieval jurists and more generally with the "civil"-izing force of Ciceronian rhetoric to express the Renaissance ideal of the "political man" (*homo politicus*), whether referring to the active citizen (*civis*), to the expert judge (*jurista*), or to the statesman (*politicus*), maker of policy and of polities. The *politiques* of the French wars of religion—regarded alternatively as irreligious and "Machiavellian" atheists or as humane peacemakers—were the direct descendants of these fourteenth- and fifteenth-century denizens, shakers, and movers of the public realm of Italian "politics," with its mottos of "liberty" and "virtue" (armed as well as civic virtue, be it noted). To Aristotelian conventions, the fifteenth century added the utopian vision of Plato's *Laws* and *Republic* (*Politeia*), and this confrontation contributed mightily to the tradition of modern statecraft—monarchical and constitutional as well as republican and democratic.

One of the political genres of humanism, derived from the ancient Aristotelian protreptic, was the treatise on the education of the prince, overlapping with the handbook of political counsel. Before the Renaissance "institutions of the prince" written by Erasmus, Budé, and others, there had been dozens of such political "mirrors" (*speculum principis, lunette des princes, Fürstenspiegel,* and the like) of the prince, which summarized the qualities, learning, and responsibilities of an ideal ruler.[30] The most notorious member of this literary species was of course *The Prince* of Machiavelli, which asked the same questions as the orthodox "mirrors": What studies should the prince take up? Is it better to be feared or loved? How important is religion in princely counsel? What are the roles of religion, liberality, cruelty? To these and other sensitive topics, Machiavelli gave very different answers from his predecessors. Worlds away from the utopian visions of Erasmus, More, and others who had followed the line of Platonic idealism, Machiavelli embraced a political sphere quite divorced from the conventions of private morality, one that featured the more beastly aspects of human nature, including the distasteful way of the fox and the fearful one of the lion.

Machiavelli, too, had a humanist face—a "civic humanist" face—and he displayed it especially in his *Discourses on Livy,* which he delivered as lectures for a serious scholarly circle. This work proposed to seek the political lessons of antiquity, as other scholars had recovered its moral wisdom. Despite the enormous respect that was commonly bestowed on antiquity, Machiavelli wrote in a famous passage, it was astounding that "in setting up states, in maintaining governments, in ruling kingdoms, in organizing armies and managing war, in executing laws among subjects, in expanding an empire, not a single prince or republic now resorts to the examples of the ancients."[31] This was to be the "new path" opened up by Machiavelli's critical analysis of Roman political experience—and one amplified later by examination of Florentine history. "Wise men say, and not without reason," Machiavelli wrote in his *Discourses,* "that whoever wishes to foresee the future must consult the past; for human events ever resemble those of preceding times." Machiavelli's notion of human psychology (the uniformity of motivation over time) transformed the conventional humanist view of the lessons to be drawn from history as the "mistress of life" into a veritable "science" of politics. In his *Florentine Histories* Machiavelli applied a similar sort of political analysis to the tragic history of his own city.

Machiavelli's version of political humanism was given a philosophical twist by its association with his assumptions about human nature and the long-term patterns of history. These assumptions Machiavelli drew from the Greek historian Polybius' famous theory of cycles (*anacyclosis*), or revolutions (*conversiones*), as some commentators regarded the process.[32] According to this scheme, adapted from the Aristotelian division of constitutions, each of the three forms of government—monarchy, aristocracy, and democracy—

tended to degenerate from a healthy into a corrupt state because of the instability of people, the succession of generations, and the inevitable defeat of "virtue" by "fortune." Here again, the humanist perspective was given a "philosophical" form and a utilitarian function, and this, too, was an important ingredient in the spectacular posthumous fortune of Machiavelli.

Some of Machiavelli's afterlives have been well chronicled—especially the evil, "atheistic," and "tyrannical" counselor of princes and, more recently, the virtuous "republican" embodying the "Machiavellian moment." But at least one other aspect of his influence deserves attention, too; and that is in the tradition of political science. Most notable in following Machiavelli's "new path," perhaps, was Jean Bodin, who set out on the same voyage with even more impressive classical baggage to discuss the nature of governments—first in his *Method for the Easy Comprehension of History* of 1566, then ten years later in his compendious *Republic*. The latter work brought the traditions of Roman law, Aristotelian political thought, and civic humanism into contact with modern historical and comparative studies, and it established, on the basis of ancient authority, the modern idea of political absolutism.[33] Bodin furnished perhaps the most direct link between the Renaissance encyclopedia and the study of public law, constitutional thought, and eventually modern political science and sociology.

From its humanist inception, the career of modern political thought continued to be torn between the extremes of private and public values symbolized by More and Machiavelli—between the moral obligations of the individual, founded in the "economic" sphere of the family, and the political necessities of government, pushed toward very different human (or perhaps not so human) values. From Petrarch to Erasmus, most humanists refused to yield to this paradox—or even to the evidence of their political perceptions. "O most fortunate prince," exclaimed a speaker in Alberti's dialogue *Della famiglia*, "who should thus desire to win affection and to be less feared than loved."[34] It was Machiavelli who insisted on facing up to the human political condition and who concluded that a wise (and indeed "virtuous") prince must ultimately rely on fear rather than love, seeing "that men love at their own free will but fear at the will of the prince"—and in that period of political "calamity," it was clearly not love but the "will of the prince" that was law.

In the sixteenth century there was a "civil" as well as a "civic" humanism, since "civil science," the modern discipline based on Roman law, continued to be a major force, especially in political thought. As in other fields, there was a division between "ancients," who wanted to study the Roman legal tradition historically, and the "moderns," who wanted to modernize the ancient legal heritage and adapt it to contemporary problems; and the latter predominated both in the universities and in the courts. As the Roman Empire (*imperium*) was a model for the national monarchs of Europe, each of whom claimed to be "emperor in his kingdom," so Roman law was a source of ideas and institutions essential to modern civil society—liberty, property, contract, representation, and resistance. Most especially, the "law of nations" (*jus gentium*) furnished the basis not only for the study of comparative law and institutions but also for the modern field of international law. Within the profession, the learned jurist was regarded as the consummate "political man" (*homo politicus*), and indeed the "perfect jurisconsult" represented one variation on the theme of the "universal man of the Renaissance."[35]

Two qualifications must be made about the rhetorical tradition of "civic humanism" and the idealized tradition of "civil humanism" celebrated by contemporary scholars. One is the tendency to neglect the darker side of civic humanism (as it seemed to Erasmus and others), which is the exaltation of military virtue. Bruni himself made this clear in his own essay *De militia,* and of course Machiavelli's *Art of War* was an important companion-piece to his *Prince*—the ways of the lion being a necessary alternative to the ways of the fox. For Erasmus, the Christian Prince ought to study history and literature to find examples of moral excellence and achievements for the public good and the maintenance of peace; for Machiavelli, "the prince ought to read history and study the actions of eminent men, see how they acted in warfare, examine the causes of their victories and defeats in order to imitate the former and avoid the latter."[36] The Perfect Warrior—this was another face of the *uomo universale* of the Renaissance.

The second qualification is the attitude often found among humanists that entails withdrawal from the active life. Petrarch and Ficino each illustrate in different ways this passive and moralistic outlook on the human tradition, as indeed does Erasmus, for whom social and religious reform was based on properly educated and motivated individuals. A more critical and self-conscious rejection of the public sphere is represented by the moral philosophy of later humanists like Montaigne (at least in his periods and moods of withdrawal from political involvement) and his lamented friend Étienne de la Boétie, for whom the larger horizons of politics—and warfare—signaled illusions and distractions from moral excellence.[37] This may serve to remind us that there was also a tradition of what might be called "uncivic" humanism, which qualifies the Renaissance ideal and which has its own place (however neglected) in political philosophy.

# 4

# Humanism and the World of Nations

I am led to a confident hope that not only morality and Christian piety, but also a genuine and purer literature, may come to renewed or greater splendor . . . in parts of the world.

—Desiderius Erasmus

Florentine humanism reached its high point—philosophically if not politically—under Lorenzo the Magnificent, when the great works of Ficino, Pico, Poliziano, and other scholars made the Medici state the cynosure of European culture. The "chorus of muses" begun by Petrarch reached a crescendo in the last quarter of the fifteenth century. Then fortune—the descent of French and Spanish troops after 1494—brought collapse (*la calamità*), or so many observers judged. Ermolao Barbaro died in 1493, Pico and Poliziano in 1494, Ficino in 1499. Lorenzo himself had died in 1492 (thus ending the Florentine golden age, as Machiavelli suggested in his *Florentine Histories*); and two years later, after his son Piero was chased out, a short-lived republic was installed under the millennialist aegis of Savonarola, under whose influence even Pico came. By 1500, one observer, Pietro Crinito, had perceived a "secession of the muses"; Machiavelli was only one of those who looked back on the Medici rule as a golden age of learning and virtue. And what to Machiavelli seemed another invasion of "barbarians" signaled, for northern scholars, a veritable "translation of studies" from Italy across the Alps to the states of Europe.[1]

In fact, humanism was becoming an international phenomenon, the basis of a "Republic of Letters," as humanists had been calling it since the early fifteenth century. This cosmopolitan forum was populated by itinerant scholars—whether Italians traveling abroad or Europeans making their Italian voyage (which was becoming an intellectual pilgrimage essential in the formation of a scholar). This network was reinforced, too, by scholarly correspondence, by the foundation of new schools, by the invasion of the universities by humanists, and especially by the reading public being created and shaped through the new "German" art of printing. Yet while it was being diffused internationally, humanism was at the same time in the process of being nationalized, as northern scholars sought to celebrate their own cultural past in order to emulate, or even surpass, the imperious Italians and their Roman pedigree. At the same time, the old conflict between "Athens and Jerusalem," reflected in Petrarch and his disciples, was intensified and even politicized, and the balance shifted from a largely classical to a largely "Christian humanism." Indeed the "new learning" of the sixteenth century was associated less with the program of the *studia humanitatis* than with the fundamentalist and schismatic activities of the Protestant Reformation—which became no less an international phenomenon.

## The German Nation

Eager to exploit the cultural riches of the Italian heritage, German humanists were nevertheless careful to revere and to exalt their own national tradition. Rudolf Agricola, "father of German humanism," attached himself to the Italian tradition by defending the *studia humanitatis* and by writing a life of Petrarch, but his style was more characteristic of northern humanism.[2] In other words, Agricola emphasized the devotional side of humanism—*philosophia Christi* was the term that he used and that Erasmus later made famous—and he tried to bring dialectic back to intellectual credit by joining it to rhetoric and showing its social value. Among Agricola's students was Alexander Hegius, who was himself among Erasmus' teachers. Later on, in the sixteenth century, the so-called "new rhetoric" of Agricola was elaborated by Philip Melanchthon, Peter Ramus, and other Protestant pedagogues, who turned the resources of humanism toward the goals of religious reform.

Another major link with Italian humanism was provided by Pico's former student Johann Reuchlin, a Christian pioneer in Hebraic scholarship, including Cabalism as well as Old Testament studies. For Reuchlin as for many Renaissance linguistic scholars, Hebrew was the original human tongue; but for many opponents of the new learning—and protectors of the old—the Judaic tradition led not only into occultism but also into heresy. Pico had escaped serious retribution for his wanderings into unorthodox fields, but Reuchlin, writing in less propitious times, was not so lucky, and he came under official censure for his Judaizing work. The Reuchlin affair eventually merged with the controversies provoked by Erasmus' controversial translation of the New Testament in 1516 and more especially by the Lutheran "scandal" that began with Luther's *Ninety-five Theses* of 1517. Both of these issues were extensions in a sense of the "new learning" as it was received and transformed in the context of "true religion" and what Luther called the "German Nation" of the early sixteenth century.

Luther himself was an impressive scholar, and he displayed many of the values and prejudices of humanism—a distaste for Aristotle, lawyers, and Scholastic theologians, and a considerable respect for the liberal arts, including history, as a preparation for confessional indoctrination. In his epoch-making and provoking translation of the Bible, Luther drew not only on the work of Erasmus but also on humanist interpretation. In some ways, indeed, Luther's fundamentalist attitude toward the holy scriptures ("the gospel alone") carried on the logocentric views of philologists like Valla, Budé, and Erasmus.

Yet as Erasmus came to realize—especially during their public controversy over the freedom of the will in 1524—Luther's mentality was far from the attitudes associated with the liberal arts. The great champion of the *studia humanitatis* among the followers of Luther was Philip Melanchthon, one of whose aims was the "reformation" of the Lutheran system of education. Like Luther, Melanchthon rejected Aristotelian philosophy and praised "elegant literature," arguing that "whoever desires to undertake anything distinguished, either in the sacred cults or in the affairs of state, will achieve but very little unless he has previously exercised his mind prudently and sufficiently with humane discipline."[3] Melanchthon recommended the study of history in particular for benefits, sacred as well as secular, and its role in legitimizing the traditions both of true religion and of the German fatherland.

By the time Lutheranism was established, German humanism had found its classical author in Tacitus—the Tacitus of the *Germania*. This work, which had been miraculously discovered in the fifteenth century, inspired a veritable *Kulturkampf* between descendants of the Romans and descendants of the barbarians who had resisted and, occasionally, overrun Rome. The *Germania* presented an idealized picture of the ancient Germans—simple, incorrupt, liberty-loving, and full of military virtues—and his many commentators drew upon this portrait and various associated legends to create an extraordinary national mythology to rival that of Rome herself. Through the Latin language, Rome had reconquered the world, Valla boasted: "Ours is Italy, ours Gaul, Spain, Germany," and so on. But German humanists contradicted this claim in cultural as well as political terms. Not the Romans', argued the German historian Beatus Rhenanus, but "ours are the victories of the Goths, Vandals, and Franks. Ours is the glory attached to the kingdoms which their peoples founded in the most illustrious provinces of the Romans, in Italy, and in the queen of cities, Rome herself."[4] And German achievements in the sixteenth century would carry these victories over into the fields of religion and culture as well, for humanists like Beatus Rhenanus and Melanchthon naturally regarded Martin Luther's revivalist program as the culmination and fulfillment of the "new learning" of Renaissance humanism.

Before the emergence of Luther, German humanists had already been contrasting the virtues of Germanic tradition with the degeneracy of Rome—modern papal as well as ancient imperial Rome. Imitating (and inverting) the humanist theme in praise of Italian culture (*Italia illustrata*), German scholars like the "arch-humanist" Conrad Celtis had established the new, though derivative, genre of *Germania illustrata*. Again it was the topos of the "translation of empire": the heyday of the Italians had passed, according to Celtis, and now it was the German's turn. Not only political and military skill, argued Celtis, but also literary culture (*litterarum splendor*) had passed to the Germans. As one fifteenth-century German author wrote, "Germany today is not only equal to other nations but it surpasses self-promoting Greece, proud Rome, and quarrelsome France."[5]

According to the Germanist myth reinforced by Renaissance Tacitism, the central national—cultural or ethnic—qualities that distinguished Germans, modern as well as ancient, included their racial and religious purity, their innocence of usury, fraud, and trickery, and above all the "liberty" that led them again and again to resist Roman "tyranny." On the very eve of Luther's stand Ulrich von Hutten began to associate this ancient *libertas Germaniae* with the *libertas Christiana* celebrated by evangelical reformers; and in this connection, too, the authority of Tacitus was invoked and extended. The secular freedom of the ancient Franks—the "free French" (*die freyen Francken, hoc est liberi franci*), as they were celebrated in the sixteenth century by their French as well as their German descendants—thus merged with the spiritual, Pauline freedom from the Judaic (and of course ecclesiastical) law that Luther preached in his tract on "The Freedom of a Christian Man" of 1520. Although at odds theoretically, the "liberty" of the Protestant professions and that of humanist anthropology were in various political ways mutually reinforcing. In other ways, too—especially through exploitation of the printing press and the reform of education—the Lutheran movement represented a continuation and an expansion of humanist tendencies in an increasingly vernacular mode.

Or did it? Behind the rhetoric of "Christian liberty," there lurked a narrow confessionalism and an equally narrow nationalism that seems hard to reconcile with the values represented by Petrarch and Erasmus. To many classicists, Lutheranism has seemed a betrayal of Renaissance humanism. "The German Reformation cut us off from the ancient world," argued Burckhardt's friend Nietzsche; "it was a victory over the same culture that was defeated in Christianity's beginnings."[6] And the debate continues not only over the relation of Renaissance and Reformation to one another but over the relation of each to the modern world. Was the Reformation a betrayal or an extension of the Renaissance? And was the Renaissance itself a surrender to authoritarian book-learning, or was it the birth of modernity—"the discovery of man and the universe"?

## The French Monarchy

In France, humanism Italian style had also been received and in various ways naturalized. Devotion to classical scholarship had preceded France's invasion of Italy in 1494 by at least a generation, and again it was closely associated with the printing press, which had been brought to the University of Paris in 1469 by Guillaume Fichet and Jean Heynlin. The humanist movement was associated, too, with the "evangelical revolution" in France contemporaneous with the Lutheran uproar. Here the pioneer was Erasmus' friend and rival Jacques Lefèvre d'Etaples, who produced the first French version of the New Testament and who has been claimed by Protestants as a founder of what used to be called "pre-Reform." Like Erasmus, Lefèvre looked forward to a "golden age" based, for individuals, on the "imitation of Christ" and, for society as a whole, on efforts to "see our age restored to the likeness of the primitive church."[7]

Like their German counterparts, French humanists displayed considerable ambivalence toward their Italian antecedents. On the one hand, they tried to outdo them in classicist enthusiasm, but on the other hand, they resented their attitudes of national priority and superiority. They took up the convenient and self-flattering theme of a transalpine "translation of studies" from Italy to France and soon developed an acute historical awareness of the revival and advancement of learning in Europe since the time of Petrarch. In the late fifteenth century Robert Gaguin (to whom Erasmus dedicated his first book) and especially Paolo Emilio, Italian immigrant and royal historiographer, brought the Brunian tradition of national history to France; and their celebration of the career of the monarchy from Frankish times, cultural as well as political, critical as well as mythological, became the basis for the official image of French history.

The leading figure in French humanism was Guillaume Budé, whom contemporaries regarded as Erasmus' equal or even superior as a Hellenist, especially for his *Commentaries on the Greek Language* of 1529, which was the starting point of modern Greek lexicography. In his praise of the humanist "encyclopedia," Budé followed Valla in regarding "eloquence" as the principle that "binds together this cycle of learning like a living body"; but his own preferred term for the modern incarnation of humanist scholarship was "philology." Of this new "science," Budé wrote: "Once an ornament, philology is now the means of revival and restoration."[8] His own special efforts, complementing those of Erasmus in biblical scholarship, was the study of Justinian's *Digest*, the anthology of classical jurisprudence that was in effect the Bible of Roman law. In this task, too, *philologia* was essential, for without it (in Valla's words), "learning is blind, especially in civil law." With Valla and Poliziano, Budé was one of the founders of what has been called "legal humanism," a tradition that was centered in France after Budé's death in 1540.[9]

But despite his enthusiasm for antiquity and for his "other wife," philology, Budé sided with the "moderns" in their quarrel with the "ancients," at least in part because of his devotion to French national tradition. "Since in our age we see letters restored to life," he asked rhetorically, "what prevents us from seeing among us new Demosthenes, Platos, Thucydides, Ciceros, etc. . . . , not only imitators but emulators of these?"[10] Such emulation had to be achieved, of course, within a Christian framework, and Budé was constant in his attachment to an orthodox (though Gallican) faith. In his later years especially he was drawn to the study of "sacred letters" and from the historical meaning of texts to their higher spiritual meaning—from *philologia,* in his words, to *philotheoria*—as suggested especially by his last major publication, his *Transition from Hellenism to Christianity* (1535), which was in part directed against the new evangelical doctrines associated with Luther, and very soon with Calvin.[11]

Jean Calvin, at least in his early years, shared the enthusiasm of Petrarch and his disciples for the Latin classics, and in particular he followed Erasmus in commenting on Seneca—"second only to Cicero," he wrote, "a veritable pillar of Roman philosophy and literature; for Brutus, and the men of his time, have been lost to us."[12] Shortly after publishing this Senecan commentary (1532), however, Calvin made his own "transition" from classicism to Christianity in what he called his "sudden conversion" to evangelical religion and his discovery of his evangelical calling in Strasbourg and especially Geneva. Turning from classical antiquity, Calvin—in the successive editions of his *Institutes of Christian Religion,* originally dedicated to King Francis I—idealized and celebrated the "primitive church" as the model of things human as well as divine. The Christian revivalism of Calvin (like that of Luther before him) represents a sort of sublimated—or consecrated—version of the revival celebrated by their scholarly sources of inspiration, including most notably Valla, Erasmus, and Budé. And French Calvinists, like German Lutherans, made full use of the weapons and resources of classical rhetoric and philology in their own enterprises of testifying to and spreading the "Word."

A more orthodox exponent of French humanism was Budé's biographer, Louis Le Roy, later regius professor of Greek in the "trilingual" college (later Collège Royal, now Collège de France) that Budé had urged Francis I to establish. Le Roy carried on Budé's campaign for "philology"—and carried it over into the vernacular, especially through his pioneering translations of Plato and Aristotle. In 1575, Le Roy published his *Vicissitude or Variety of Things in the Universe,* which was not only a glorification of *philologia* but also a comparative history of civilization. As a history, it particularly sang the praises of the modern scholars from Petrarch's time who were responsible for the most recent of the "heroic ages" of culture and for what he called "the restitution of all languages and of all disciplines," with specific reference to Petrarch, Bruni, Valla, Guarino, Poggio, Vittorino, Biondo, the Hellenist Chrysoloras, and many others. The result was that "this our age can be compared to the most learned times there ever were."[13] For Le Roy, Budé's "encyclopedia" became the very substance of history and the basis of what seemed to be a limitless future. To Budé's rhetorical question, Le Roy's answer was positive: "Nothing," he declared, "prevents us from seeing new Demosthenes and Platos," and moreover, "It is necessary to do for posterity what antiquity has done for us."[14]

In many areas, French humanists built on Italian foundations—in scholarly inquiry, in literary forms, in the reconstruction of a national tradition, and in the extension of civic humanist attitudes into a new conception of politics. In France, "vernacular humanism" was given a significant impulse by the translations of classical authors, beginning with Claude de Seyssel's rendering of the works of Herodotus and Thucydides (based on Valla's Latin) and other Greek historians, and it flourished in national literature of the sixteenth century that not only "imitated" but aspired to surpass its classical models.[15] The encyclopedic work of La Croix du Maine, published in 1583, concluded that by that time French authors had far exceeded their Italian rivals both in quantity and in quality—certainly to judge by the works of Le Roy, Rabelais, Ronsard, Montaigne, and other men who, said La Croix, "brought honor and praise to France (and consequently to the king and sovereign prince thereof) for her wealth of men learned not only on Hebrew, Greek, and Latin but also in French."[16]

The golden age of literature celebrated by La Croix was also a period of devastating civil war, and this too had its impact on the humanist tradition. Suffering through this political turmoil, Michel de Montaigne turned against the civic spirit during the French wars of religion, but he nevertheless continued to look to ancient wisdom for the foundations of his moral philosophy. Like Petrarch, Montaigne set as his goal the understanding and cultivation of his many-formed self, beginning (like Petrarch) with conventional Socratic self-doubt and irony but carrying his skepticism into the extremes of Pyrrhonism, derived from the newly printed work of Sextus Empiricus and reinforced by his bitter experiences with the religiously divided humanity of his own age. In many ways Montaigne represented the high point of French humanism before its eclipse by the forces of science and rationalism in the seventeenth century. Terence's famous "nothing human is alien to me" (*humanum nihil a me alienum puto*) was one of the classical mottos (still) carved in the ceiling above Montaigne's writing table, and Montaigne indeed inquired into all the dimensions of man's (and some of woman's) nature, from the angelic to the animal. If his emphasis fell on the latter, that was at least in part because the "humanism" of his age was overwhelmed by the forces of religious fanaticism, political propaganda, social upheaval, and military conflict; and the "encyclopedia" was preserved mainly in learning, education, and—in Montaigne's case—moral philosophy.[17]

## The English Variant

English humanism also drew upon Italian precedents, beginning especially in the fifteenth century with the contacts afforded by the patronage and the remarkable collection of Humphrey, Duke of Gloucester (including works of Petrarch, Boccaccio, Salutati, and others). Equally important was the scholarly interchange. Humanists like Poggio hunted manuscripts in English libraries, for example, while Polydore Vergil immigrated to write his seminal history of England and his popular encyclopedia, *On the Inventors of Things*, which was a summary of humanist views of their cultural heritage. At this time, too, Englishmen were making their "Italian voyage" and attending, many of them, Italian universities. By 1475, Caxton's press had given some impetus to humanism, and by the end of the century humanist scholarship had found an institutional base in the universities of Oxford and Cambridge and expression in the work of William Grocyn, Thomas Linacre, and John Colet, and later of Colet's younger associates, Thomas More and Erasmus. In contrast to Italian humanism, as Roberto Weiss judges, the English variety, when it developed its own national character in the sixteenth century, was more utilitarian, more accommodated to religious purposes, and (while inclined to be resolutely anti-Scholastic) more favorably disposed to medieval culture.[18]

Following the lead of Ficino and Pico, Colet adopted a Neo-platonic (and neo-Dionysian) conception of human nature as a microcosm of the natural world, tempering this with the dualistic vision of Saint Paul, on whose doctrines Colet based his hopes for Christian revival, in the sense of education and social reform as well as personal conversion. For More, St. Paul's School, founded by Colet in 1510, was the Trojan horse by which the new barbarism of Scholasticism would be invaded and overthrown. These pedagogical aspirations were soon joined by hopes of religious reformation as well. In Paul's words, which served as a text for Colet's famous Convocation sermon of 1512, man was not to be "conformed to the world" but rather "reformed in the newness of [his] mind"—and so was the English monarchy and Church. Colet also, along with Grocyn and Linacre, helped turn Erasmus to Greek and biblical studies and to the fulfillment of Christian humanism.

Thomas More was, at least in the early years of the Reformation, the leading figure of the English humanist movement. Although trained as a lawyer and committed to, and distracted by, a life of public service culminating in the lord chancellorship, More was also devoted to "the renaissance of good letters" (*bonae renasci litterae*) and especially to Hellenic studies. Before Luther complicated and, for many, discredited the ideal of reformation, More followed Colet and Erasmus in hoping that the new learning would bring a golden age of peace and piety; and before he turned his attention to the pursuit of heresy in the 1520s, he applied his literary talents to these Erasmian—and "utopian"—aspirations.

Like Erasmus and Colet, More wanted to put humanism into the service of religious and social reform; at least in part, this was the purpose of his famous *Utopia*. More immediately sent his work to Erasmus (whom some even regarded as its author), and Erasmus recommended it to various friends, including Budé, who wrote a preface to the Basel edition. The debate over the final meaning of More's little masterpiece is endless and ultimately unresolvable. Was it medieval or modern? Serious or frivolous? Idealistic or practical? Basically Platonic or basically Aristotelian? Or all of the above? Contemporaries may have had the best insights into the meaning of the book. According to Erasmus, More "wrote his *Utopia* for the purpose of showing what are the things that occasion mischief in commonwealths." A more thoughtful estimate was that of Guillaume Budé, for whom the basic premise of *Utopia* was to consider society in the light of reason and natural law unaided by revelation and, "blessed in its innocence," unencumbered by the weight of Western tradition.[19] *Utopia* was thus not only an ingenious (if controversial and cryptic) vehicle for social criticism, it was also a complex portrait of a community as it might be if, all at once and without the benefit of revelation, equality prevailed, peace were assured, and wealth were despised.

More and Erasmus became lifelong friends after Erasmus' visits to England beginning in 1499, and in many ways they were comrades in arms in the same peaceful battles for learning and reform—and indeed reform through learning. As Erasmus praised More and his work, so More took up the defense of Erasmus and his subversive publications against hostile critics, including Erasmus' translation of the New Testament as well as the *Praise of Folly,* which honored More himself (its Latin title, *Encomium Moriae,* being a pun on More's name). To the complaints of Martin Dorp, More responded that "you carp at *Folly,* inveigh at the poets, snarl at the grammarians, disapprove of his annotations on scripture, or judge that training in Greek literature is simply irrelevant."[20] In More's view, to attack the work of Erasmus was to reject the whole program of humanism, secular (*seculares disciplinae*) as well as sacred (*doctrina Christi*).

Another associate of More and Erasmus was Juan Luis Vives, who, after studies in Paris and the Netherlands, came to England in 1518. Vives likewise carried on the fight against Scholasticism, becoming what R. S. Chambers called "third in the great triumvirate of scholarship" (with Erasmus and Budé, not More).[21] As Erasmus devoted himself to editing the works of Jerome, so Vives became the editor of Jerome's colleague Augustine in order to promote the cause of Christian humanism. Vives also contributed to the "Renaissance philosophy of man" in his pioneering studies of psychology and education, and in his *Fable of Man,* he carried on Pico's views of the quasi-divine nature of humankind. Vives devoted his life to the pursuit of the Ciceronian and Augustinian goal of "wisdom" (*sapientia*)—whose key, he wrote, following the advice of Augustine and Petrarch, "is that most celebrated axiom among the ancients, 'Know Thyself.' "[22] The attainment of erudition and virtue, through education, was the fruit of this self-knowledge; and to Vives, as to Erasmus if not to More, larger problems of religious reform and pacification were attendant on such moral improvement. This hope was at once the strength and the weakness of Christian humanism.

## Erasmus and Cosmopolitan Humanism

The central figure in the Christian humanist movement was of course Erasmus himself, and again the point of departure was Italian learning. Like Petrarch, Erasmus was a self-conscious and self-advertising intellectual, reverent of antiquity yet deploying modern wit, style, and irony in the same characteristic genres of epistle and dialogue. Erasmus also took up the weapons and the war aims of Lorenzo Valla, but he applied them more specifically to the "philosophy of Christ" and the reformation of Christian society as a whole. Unlike many of his colleagues, however, Erasmus was not attached to a national—or indeed to a confessional—tradition or party. "My own wish is to be a citizen of the world," wrote Erasmus to Ulrich Zwingli in 1522, after an invitation to settle in Zurich, "to be a fellow-citizen to all men—a pilgrim better still."[23] Educated in Deventer with the Brothers of the Common Life, Erasmus started out as illegitimate and continued throughout his life to be rootless and Latinate, traveling across Europe (England, France, Italy, and finally Switzerland), trying vainly to avoid conflict, personal as well as political and ecclesiastical, but remaining at all times a center of attention and controversy and pursuing at all costs his scholarly and literary fame. A coward to some and a hero of moderation and an antecedent of the Enlightenment to others, Erasmus was the first modern "author"—the first exploiter of the new medium of print.

Erasmus was a humanist in the "elegant" mold of Petrarch and Valla, seeking like them a way to reconcile classical learning and Christian doctrine. Like Valla, too, he despised monasticism and the inhuman mentality it entailed. Erasmus began his literary career, in his youthful *Antibarbarus*, by defending the *studia humanitatis*—those "humanities without which all learning is blind"—against the very same enemies whom Boccaccio had targeted, namely, "those who want the Republic of Letters to be destroyed root and branch."[24] Concerning the Scholastic "pseudotheologians" in particular, he complained to an English friend, "There is nothing more rotten than their brains, nothing more barbaric than their tongues, nothing more stupid than their wit, nothing more thorny than their teaching, nothing more crude than their conduct, nothing more counterfeit than their lives, nothing more virulent than their language, nothing blacker than their hearts."[25] And on the papal tradition in general, Erasmus' position was clear: "Do not infect that heavenly philosophy of Christ with human decrees."[26]

He was reinforced in these sentiments through conversations with Colet and his reading of Valla, and by 1500 he had moved from polemical complaints to a more constructive philosophical assault on the Christian tradition which had become so corrupt (culminating later in an edition of the works of Saint Jerome, author of the Vulgate translation of the Bible). In 1505 Erasmus' scholarly ambitions were raised higher, again by an encounter with the seminal work of Valla. On one of his manuscript hunts (at a monastery near Louvain), Erasmus reported to another English friend that "an unusual quarry accidentally fell into my snare: Lorenzo Valla's *Annotations on the New Testament.*"[27] Erasmus went on to defend Valla against the charges of Scholastic critics, who "will say it is an intolerable act of rashness for a grammarian, after plaguing all the other disciplines, to apply his peevish pen to sacred learning. . . . But then what crime was it for Lorenzo to collate some ancient, emended Greek manuscripts and to annotate the New Testament, which unquestionably has its source in those Greek texts?" Erasmus asked. "I do not think that even Theology herself, the queen of all the sciences, will consider it beneath her dignity to be handled and be given due attention by her maid, Grammar."

From this time, Erasmus gloried in the epithet "grammarian" (although he actually took a doctorate in theology at Turin in 1506), and he launched himself into the study of Greek in order, following Valla's lead, to restore a correct understanding of the New Testament.[28] Erasmus associated this encyclopedic discipline with the larger project of restoring Christian thought and piety—that "philosophy of Christ," as he called it in his *Handbook of a Christian Soldier* of 1503—which coincided with and reinforced that larger "reformation" preached by Colet. "I brought it about," Erasmus boasted, "that humanism [*bonae litterae*], which among the Italians and especially among the Romans savored of nothing but pure paganism, began nobly to celebrate Christ." Through "good letters," sacred scriptures could be grasped; through scriptures, piety; and through piety, a general reform of Christian society.

The end product was Erasmus' monumental, seminal, and controversial translation of the New Testament, published in 1516. His achievement—and the temporary respite that was then being enjoyed by the European powers during the Italian wars—led Erasmus to express the hope that the golden age begun by Petrarch (and foreseen by Vergil) would carry over into the Church and into Christian society as a whole. "I congratulate this our age—which bids fair to be a golden age, if ever such there was," Erasmus wrote to Pope Leo X, "wherein I see, under your holy counsels, three of the chief blessings of humanity are about to be restored to her. I mean, first, that truly Christian piety, which has in many ways fallen into decay; secondly, learning of the best sort, hitherto partly neglected and partly corrupted; and thirdly, the public and lasting concord of Christendom, the source and parent of piety and erudition"[29]— *pietas litterata*, or *philosophia Christi*, being the motto of Erasmian humanism.

Erasmus pretended not to understand why his scholarly work disturbed his orthodox critics, but the source of the trouble was not far to seek. The worst offense was that Erasmus had presumed to correct the Vulgate (which was conventionally monopolized by licensed theologians) primarily as a "grammarian," thus stirring up a variety of implicitly theological (though explicitly only philological) questions. To many critics, it seemed subversive to humanize ecclesiastical vocabulary by speaking of the "supper" (instead of Eucharist) and "elders" (instead of priests) and especially to reject Scholastic and canonist interpretations of key scriptural passages concerning papal authority and even sacraments such as penance. "Do penance" was not the correct reading of Matthew 4:17, Erasmus said, but "feel repentance" (as Valla would have construed the passage—that is, read the Greek); indeed, it was on just these grounds that Luther based the first and most explosive of his *Ninety-five Theses*. What made matters worse for Erasmus (and what seemed to bring him nearer to Luther) was that he had also proclaimed that his humanized Word should be disseminated even to the intellectual dregs of humanity. "I wish that even the weakest woman should read the gospel . . . ," Erasmus wrote. "And I wish that these were translated into all languages, so that they might be read and understood, not only by Scots and Irishmen, but also by Turks and Saracens."[30]

Like Valla and More (and unlike Colet and Luther), Erasmus had other weapons in his humanist arsenal as well. These were displayed in his satirical *Colloquies*, in his devastating satire of the former Pope Julius II (*Julius Excluded*—from heaven), and especially in the *Praise of Folly*. "Why not tell the truth with a smile?" Erasmus asked. Yet his aim remained the same as before.

> The purpose in my *Folly* is exactly the same as in my other writings, though the approach is different. In my *Enchiridion* I presented in a straightforward manner a plan for Chris-

tian living. In my *Education of a Prince* I openly offer advice as to the type of training a prince should receive. In my *Panegyric* the praise is only a cloak for treating indirectly the same theme I treated in the previous work in a straightforward manner. In my *Folly* I am ostensibly joking, but my real purpose is the same as in the *Enchiridion*. My aim has been to advise, not to pain; to promote human conduct, not to thwart it.[31]

Again Erasmus pretended not to understand the objections of his detractors. The Pope had thanked him for the book, Erasmus reported, and had even laughed at it.

At the same time Erasmus was cautious enough to conceal his authorship of *Julius exclusus,* which viciously satirized the late warrior-Pope Julius II. Saint Peter mistakes the Pope, who is banging at the gates of heaven for admittance, for "Julian the Apostate back from hell." Julius—"a Ligurian and not a Jew like you," as he describes himself to Peter—boasts of his military victories, his fiscal management, and his patronage of art but admits to neglecting his spiritual office. "Times have changed," he answers when questioned about the disparity between his pretensions and the primitive Church. Julius wins the debate, but he is finally excluded from Paradise anyway for his betrayal of both "humanity" and "divinity." Like Colet, More, and Vives (the Spanish humanist who spent much of his career in England), Erasmus embraced the moral ideal of pacifism and rejected combat on every level except the inner struggle—fighting the good fight—carried on by the Christian soldier for spiritual victory over the flesh. He despised the practice and the institutions of war, especially wars among the European states, which showed modern Christians to be worse than the Turks and even animals. "Only reflect on what kind of men fight wars," he observed: "murderers, debauchers, dicers, rapists, filthy mercenaries for whom a little money is more precious than life."[32] Luther, too, was too aggressive for Erasmus' taste, although Erasmus at first sympathized with his protest; and this, perhaps even more than theological disagreement, brought about their final rupture in 1524.

By this time, Erasmus' project—and indeed the whole social program of Christian humanism—had been lost in the confessional maelstrom created by Luther (despite Luther's own employment of humanist methods of scholarship). Like Luther, Erasmus took his (finally anti-Lutheran) stand on the principle of "conscience" (though others called it cowardice). As Erasmus remarked to Melanchthon in 1524, "I have separated the cause of good learning from the cause of Luther."[33] But others did not accept this distinction, whence the famous aphorism quoted by Erasmus, "I laid the egg; Luther hatched it." Not that Erasmus himself accepted this neat metaphor, for he objected, "What I laid was a hen's egg; the bird Luther hatched was altogether different." Yet the charge, and the image, has remained.[34]

Perhaps the idealism and pacifism of Erasmus and his humanist friends were too personal, too grounded in optimistic conceptions of the power of moral philosophy, education, and pure intellectual qualities of humanism, to have any reality in the age of a deeply "divided Europe." Erasmus himself sensed this: "Unless precaution is taken," he wrote in 1520, "there may be a danger that this tragedy will have a very disastrous conclusion for the Christian religion"— and just a decade later: "No one will undo this universal chaotic tragedy except God, not even ten councils, so I could not possibly settle it."[35] Yet Erasmianism, whether or not it deserves to be regarded as a "second Reformation," continued to inform attempts at confessional reconciliation and political pacification for generations to come. And Erasmian skepticism, especially as applied to theology, whether a Scholastic or a Lutheran variety, served to recall controversy from dogma to more human and practical concerns.

The Reformation marks both a culmination of and a divergence from the humanist movement. It adopted and adapted humanism's educational and scholarly program but shifted emphasis not only from Italian civic culture to the transalpine nations of northern Europe, but also from the study of humanity to the study of divinity and from the positive aspects of the human condition back to its "misery" and subordinate character. It was in this context, nevertheless, that humanism invaded the universities, turned the heads of younger students, produced modern philological and historical criticism, entered the arena of theological and political controversy, and became a force in the enlightening and the inflaming of public opinion down to the present. Although the "new learning" of the sixteenth century was assaulted and reshaped by the "new philosophy" of the seventeenth century, the "humanism" created by Renaissance culture has continued in many ways to inform the assumptions and attitudes of the modern world, and in such terms it invites consideration in a more analytical mode in the following chapter.

## Mundus Novus

In 1503, in the early years of the republic in which Machiavelli served, Amerigo Vespucci—fellow Florentine, world traveler, and minor humanist—wrote a letter to a member of the famous banking house of de' Medici, describing his recent travels on the far side of the globe. Vespucci placed himself in the great tradition of Florentine intellectuals by invoking the names of both Dante, who had mistakenly thought the "Ocean sea" devoid of inhabitants, and Petrarch. Referring to his study of grammar with a monk of Saint Mark, Vespucci opened with a familiar humility topos, declaring his unworthiness and lamenting his straying into secular pursuits. "Would to God I had followed his advice and teaching," he remarked of his pious teacher, for "as Petrarch says, I should be a different man from that which I am."[36] Yet he had no regrets, Vespucci continued, and at this point, having served literary convention, he launched into his celebration of the "new world" (*mundus novus*) discovered by Columbus a decade before, recently observed by himself, and so promising for the "fortune" of European enterprisers like the Medici (for "commerce" was ever the first motive of such discoveries). Vespucci's work became one of the best-sellers of the century, and his reward—recompense for the criticism of contemporaries—was to have a hemisphere named after him.

As Vespucci's testimony began to show, the horizons of humanism in the sixteenth century were being expanded not only temporally and intellectually but also geographically, and the very discovery of a new world to set beside the old produced an "ideological revolution." Or was it a "discovery"? Edmundo O'Gorman prefers to call it an "invention," because "America" was in fact fashioned out of the traditions, prejudices, and expectations of European observers and interpreters.[37] Whatever it was that Columbus "found," the continents that Europeans came to understand were the product of an extraordinary mixture of observation, imagination, and judgment according to the myths, assumption, values, and hopes of Renaissance Europe. To begin with, the inhabitants of the Indies were regarded as "barbarians," as Vespucci had declared, and "barbarian" was a classical and basically linguistic epithet applied to presumably uncivilized aliens. These Indians indeed represented an "other"—an extraclassical and extra-Christian set of cultures—that could be fitted only with difficulty into the categories of Western thought, experience, and presumptions about what "humanity" really meant.

Yet many humanists were more than ready to cope with such novelty, and the New World soon took its place in their cultural program alongside their pioneering investigations of ancient civilization. To a scholar like Louis Le Roy, who was the first to lecture in French on Greek literature, the "ancients" and the "moderns" were allies. There was nothing more honorable to the new age, he wrote in 1575, than "the invention of the printing press and the discovery of the new world," both of which brightened the future of civilization.[38] Thus Columbus took his place among the great modern "inventors of things," whose ancient counterparts had been celebrated and classified by Polydore Vergil. Reports from the Indies reinforced and supplemented the utopian hopes and dreams—and the social and cultural self-criticism—of European scholars, and to the inherited conceptions of classical, Christian, and Eastern traditions were added the novelties, both inspiring and unsettling, of a specifically American mythology going beyond the cultural world of humanism.

Aside from the incorporation of the discoveries into humanist rhetoric, how did these new experiences and knowledge affect the humanist program? To limit this question to the nucleus of the encyclopedia, the *studia humanitatis,* there are three obvious areas of impact.[39] First, conceptions of language were expanded, and the conventions and structures of classical grammar were applied to the speech of cultures that were truly oral and unlettered beyond even the ancient German described by Tacitus. Second, the New World had to be accommodated to Western ideas of history, with the result again of subverting the supposedly "universal" history inherited from Eurocentric classical and Christian tradition. Third and most fundamental, descriptions of Indian manners and customs had an extraordinarily subverting as well as broadening effect on humanist moral philosophy, psychology, and anthropology. From the first "raw" observations to Francisco de Lopez de Gomara's *History of the Indies* to Montaigne's reflections on the relativity of customs, Renaissance conceptions of human nature were expanded far beyond the limits of the "Renaissance philosophy of man."

Nevertheless, the unclassifiable novelties of the *mundus novus* had to be translated into Western terms—that is, those of the classical and Judaeo-Christian heritages. In general and most systematically, the new barbarism was interpreted in terms of Aristotelian psychology and social philosophy and the European legal tradition—civil and canon law and especially the "law of nations" and the "natural law" associated with this tradition. Fundamental questions of human nature and human rights provoked by encounters with the Indians and by colonial policy were debated largely in the domain of the "new" law of nations derived from the ancient Roman *jus gentium*. Among the results of such debates were both modern international law and the beginnings of the modern human sciences, especially comparative ethnology and anthropology in a modern sense. At this point, however, we have gone beyond the horizons of Renaissance humanism. Now it is time to leave the larger human stage, the "world of nations" as Vico called it, and return to the original base and intellectual content of this movement—that is, the disciplines making up the *studia humanitatis*.

# 5

# The Structure of Humanism

"*Gram* loquitur, *Dia* vera docet, *Rhet* verba colorat,
*Mus* canet, *Ar* numerat, *Ge* ponderat, *Ast* colit astra."
   Grammar speaks, Logic teaches truth,
      Rhetoric colors discourse,
   Music sings, Arithmetic counts, Geometry measures,
      Astronomy watches the stars.
                    —Nicolas Orbellis (fifteenth century)

Humanism had a "trivial" origin, although in its Renaissance form it was an imperialistic as well as a revolutionary movement. In general, Renaissance humanism, looking back to the learning and ideals of classical antiquity, took its name from the original "humanities" (*studia humanitatis*), including grammar, rhetoric, history, poetry, and moral philosophy. It was originally identified with these literary arts, especially the first two, which, along with dialectic, formed the medieval *trivium*. In the Scholastic curriculum, these subjects had been estranged from the mathematical disciplines that made up the complementary *quadrivium* (arithmetic, geometry, music, and astronomy), and so the coherence of the conventional "seven liberal arts"—the basis of the ancient "encyclopedia"—was to a large extent lost.

Yet from the time of Petrarch, humanists, harking back to Cic-

Representation of History, Rhetoric, and Dialect, supported by Grammar, accompanying Latin poem (from Joannes Sambucus, *Emblemata, et aliquot nummi antiqui operis*, Antwerp, 1616, fol. 121f.).

ero and Quintilian, had a strong sense of the integrity of the liberal arts. A vivid illustration of this appears in a poem dedicated to the sixteenth-century historian of Rome, Carlo Sigonio, which, commenting on a Renaissance emblem, explains "The Difference between Grammar, Dialectic, Rhetoric, and History" in these allegorical terms:

Here are three fine maidens in different dress,
standing on a young girl serving as a pedestal.
History is simple, illuminating and preserving time,
mother of truth, bringing glory to good men.
She shows no favor, admits no preference;
she judges not, but leaves judgment to others.
She simply tells, from the beginning, what was done.
Rhetoric, who follows her, is more eloquent,
laying before the judge endless disputes.
She walks about in a long gown
and tries to win her case in careful poses,
displaying herself in jeweled finery.
One hand is open, the other carries a spear,
holding it softly, without threatening offense.
Dialectic comes next, rude and careless in dress,
bringing hidden Truth into the light.
She goes forth to seize and hold her opponent
and never allows escape from her grasp.

She taunts, ensnares, rules through reason,
and binds her quarry with strong chains.
Variously she appears in Appollo's light.
But little can she do without Grammar,
for Grammar is the base of every good work,
and those who know her not do nothing lasting.
Compare history with a flying dog, Rhetoric with a Chimaera,
Logic with a sphinx, but Grammar with a firm foundation.[1]

Though occupying separate spheres, these disciplines all depend on the art of language—indeed, they represent different forms of linguistic communication—and this is the ultimate source of the intellectual integrity of the humanist program.

But modern humanists went beyond their ancient models in appreciating the deeper implications and potentials of the *studia humanitatis*. For as many scholars from Petrarch's time suspected and some argued, the five original "humanities" were associated with alternative ways of perceiving, understanding, and evaluating the human condition and indeed the natural environment. This association is only indirectly apparent in the early stages of the humanist movement, but from the fifteenth century on, the conceptual significance of humanism became increasingly obvious as the meaning and methods of the literary arts were extended and illustrated by the "encyclopedic" labors of Renaissance scholars, who began to turn back even to "quadrivial," physical, philosophical, and theological questions. A broad understanding of Renaissance humanism must consider not only the original status of the liberal arts composing this program but also later extensions, transformations, and conquests leading to the restoration of the ancient "encyclopedia."[2]

## Ars Grammatica

In coming to terms with Renaissance humanism, a good beginning is offered by Polydore Vergil's popular encyclopedia, *On the Inventors of Things* (1496), which considers all of the arts and sciences in terms of their historical, or mythical, origin and civilizing function. After the discovery of letters, wrote Vergil, came grammar, both because it took the name "letters" (*gramma, litterae*) and because it was the sole foundation of all knowledge (*reliquarum artium unicum est fundamentum*).[3] The ancient art of grammar was, according to the conventional definition, "the knowledge of how to speak correctly and write correctly, the origin and basis of all the liberal arts." In its broadest sense, it was equivalent to "literature" (*literatura*), which was defined in Thomas Cooper's Latin dictionary (1565) as "Grammar: learning: writing: cunning." In the tenuous tradition of medieval humanism, John of Salisbury, writing in the twelfth century, had already praised grammar not only as "the fountain of all the liberal arts" but also as "the cradle of philosophy." Needless to say, this meant the study primarily of the Latin language, including reading as well as oral and written forms, and it involved linguistic analysis on the most elementary level, the first two of the three traditional "Rs."

The medieval approach to grammar had been highly abstract and analytical—*grammatica speculativa,* as it was called—and it was founded on the theoretical distinction between various "modes of signification," which in turn depended on the Aristotelian scheme of four causes. The humanists shifted to a commonsense and semantic approach, however, and rejected the artificialities of Scholastic analysis. "No one," wrote Hegius, "is denied the title of grammarian because he does not know which *modi significandi* are essential and which accidental, which material and which formal, which absolute and which representative of the parts of a sentence, but he is unworthy of the name grammarian who does not know how to speak and write correctly no matter how many words he may write about the *modi significandi.*"[4] In general, humanist grammar represented a shift from the formal and structural approach of the Scholastic "modists" (*modisti*) to a more semantic, historical, and relativist conception.

Most essential to the humanist conception of grammar was the faculty of memory, for as Guarino recalled (from Quintilian), the two aspects of grammar were first descriptive or historical (*historice*), learning the terms and conventions, and then structural or methodological (*methodice*), treating the parts of speech and their arrangement.[5] Technically, grammar's primary divisions were orthography, prosody, etymology, and syntax (especially the last two), corresponding to the study of letters, syllables, words, and sentences: "For example, the letter *V,*" wrote Guarino, "the syllable *Vi,* the word *Victor,* and the sentence, *Victor loves Andrea.*"[6] These elements had to be mastered before proceeding to the higher levels of rhetorical, poetical, and logical expression, and interpretation—and then on to the various "sciences." The foundational position of grammar made Renaissance humanism "logocentric" in the most primordial and ineradicable sense.

For Dante, the distinguishing feature of Latin had been that it was subject to the rules of grammar, while the *volgare* was governed by common usage (though it was, to be sure, a potentially "illustrious" medium of expression). But scholars of a later generation came to regard Latin, too, as the product of usage, or custom—though this meant, finally, the "custom of the learned." Juan Luis Vives, very much a disciple of Valla in such matters, summed it up in this way: "We do not speak Latin in a certain way because grammar commands it; rather the contrary: grammar commands it because that is how the Latins speak."[7] Grammar was thus an essentially conventional rather than a rational discipline, which meant that it was based on custom, authority, and memory rather than on nature, reason, and logic. As Johannes Dullardus observed, "The better you are as a grammarian, the worse you will be as a logician" (*Quanto eris melior grammaticus, tanto peior dialecticus*).[8]

The basis of grammar was "not reason but example," as Lorenzo Valla put it, "not a rule of speech but observation [or] custom." For Valla, needless to say, this custom and these examples were to be drawn not from ordinary current speech but from the authority of the ancient masters. Indeed, he made a careful distinction between speech that was classical (*Latine*) and that which was merely grammatical (*grammatice*) in a Scholastic sense, the first producing elegant "elocution" and the second simply "locution."[9] Usage was the basis of proper speech and writing (*consuetudo certissima magistra loquendi*, in the famous formula of Quintilian cited by Valla), but again this had to be expert usage (*consuetudo peritorum*). What was more, all the higher sciences, including philosophy and even theology, had to return to these conventional foundations, which were pre-, extra-, or even non-rational, but which had acquired legitimacy and authority through the force of time and popular acceptance.

Grammar is concerned above all with the meaning of terms, and in this connection it depended on a fundamental distinction between the letter and the spirit of a word. A word's spirit (*spiritus, mens, sententia*, and the like) might designate the original intention of the author, the reason or rationale of a text, or a variety of figurative meanings (allegorical, moral, or tropological, according to the standard medieval theory of exegesis). But only grammatical construction referred to literal or, in this sense, "historical" signification. For many humanists, this focus was a healthy shift of attention from fanciful allegorizing and foolish "moralizing" (although they pursued their own kind of figurative and mystical meanings) to the human and, in a modern sense, "historical" construction. In later stages of humanist scholarship, this literal approach could be turned to the narrower purposes of editing and criticizing classical texts or to the excesses of biblical fundamentalism; but in any case the emphasis fell on the primacy not of rational argument but of textual authority and the conventions of ordinary language—whether Latin, Greek, or even vernacular.

On the level of elementary education, grammatical instruction was a simple matter of recalling dictionary meanings. But for humanist scholarship the task of recovering literal signification became increasingly entangled in problems of translating from one language to another, especially from Greek to Latin—and of recovering meanings of texts by authors alien in culture or remote in time. The inclination of humanists was against paraphrase and toward what Bruni called "word for word" rendering.[10] In this connection, classical and biblical scholars were confronted with questions of anachronism, the instability of meaning, cultural context, and various kinds of linguistic relativity. Glossary-making was transformed into the delicate and demanding art of historical lexicography, which was further expanded by the demands and possibilities of print culture. Increasingly, grammar broadened its semantic field by reaching out to the sister arts of rhetoric and poetry. The "grammarian" was no longer an elementary schoolteacher but the philological ideal of Valla, Poliziano, Erasmus, and the legal scholar Jacques Cujas, who were all more than proud to bear this title. "When they wanted to humiliate M. Cujas, they called him 'grammarian,' " remarked the great J. J. Scaliger, "but he laughed and said that such people should be ashamed not to be such."[11]

In the wake of Renaissance humanism, the image of the "grammarian" oscillated between the heroic ideal of polyhistors, "Critics," and *érudits* in the mold of Cujas, Scaliger, Selden, Bentley, Wolf, and Housman, and the grinding pedantry of the inhuman Dryasdust—between the seventeenth-century Huguenot scholar Isaac Casaubon, and his pathetic namesake recreated two centuries later in George Eliot's *Middlemarch*. The extremes meet in the portrait of the crabbed scholar satirized—and eulogized—in Browning's poem "The Grammarian's Funeral":

> Dead from the waist down,
> . . . bald, too—eyes like lead,

the grammarian

> . . . decided not to live but Know.

And yet:

> He was a man born with thy face and throat,
> Lyric Apollo!

Though concentrating on the "deadening letter" of texts, he also sought the life-giving spirit; though "Ground he at grammar," he aspired to the heights of human erudition and the depths of historical understanding.

In a similar way, the old art of grammar aspired to more than teaching children their ABCs. It ventured into fields of technical scholarship—into what was variously called modern historical criticism (*ars critica*), hermeneutics (*ars hermeneutica*), and philology. Following classical usage, Poliziano concluded, the modern *grammaticus* should be identified with the ancient *criticus*. This potential had in a sense been recognized from the beginning. As Aeneas Sylvius declared in his treatise on the *ars grammatica*, "Grammar . . . is the portal to all knowledge whatsoever. As a subject of study it is more complex and more fruitful than its name would imply, and it yields its full profit only to such as enter early and zealously upon its pursuit. The greatest minds have not been ashamed to shew themselves earnest in the study of Grammar."[12] Ultimately, as Hegius wrote, grammar was concerned with reality, not language (*res non verba*); and his former pupil Erasmus defended his own grammatical calling by invoking this same classical topos. The foundational status of grammar was described by Poliziano in this way: "It is the office of the 'grammatici' to expose and develop every kind of writers; poets, historians, orators, philosophers, doctors, and lawyers."[13] The point was that, following the Creator himself, man's science began as a naming process and never ceased to be a search for proper terminology.

The end product of this expansion of the elementary art of grammar was the emergence of the modern science of "philology," celebrated by Guillaume Budé as the very essence of the ancient encyclopedia in its modern form. For Budé, *philologia* made possible the "restitution" not only of particular words and texts but also of ancient culture—*antiquitas*—in a more general sense. In the sixteenth century, philology extended itself from narrow textual concerns to the outer reaches and inner depths of universal history, producing such ground-breaking works as Scaliger's *De emendatione temporum* (1583) and the great works of erudition of the following century. The expansive thrust of philology was explained in a more sophisticated fashion two centuries after Erasmus by one of the last products of Renaissance humanism. "Philology is the study of speech . . . ," wrote Giambattista Vico in his work on *Universal Law,* "but since words represent the idea of things, philology must first treat the history of things . . . , i.e., human governments, customs, laws, institutions, intellectual disciplines, and the mechanical arts."[14] Thus philology was identified with the whole encyclopedia of Renaissance arts and sciences.

In this connection, humanists began to take an interest in the historical dimension of language. They continued to play the old etymological games that Isidore of Seville had made famous, and they continued to distinguish between a spiritual and a literal aspect of word derivations. Medieval etymologists had been usually more interested in the essence, the "quiddity," of terms than with their historical relations or transformations. The idea that law was derived from justice (*jus a justitia*), or king from rulership (*rex a regendo*), was clearly a linguistic impossibility even if it was in keeping with logical or philosophical assumptions. Such etymological license permitted more speculative associations (though not always entirely serious, one suspects), such as the famous derivation of testament (*testamentum*) from a "testifying of the mind" (*testium mentis* and "parlament" (*parlamentum*) from "speaking one's mind" or even "peers' lament" (*parium lamentum*). The science of philology, however, shifted attention to linguistic origins and genetic relationships, especially with growing interest in the development of vernacular languages—either autonomously or by degeneration from classical Latin. This interest culminated in the ingenious and speculative use of etymology, on the basis of which Vico erected his "new science."

Central to humanist conceptions from the beginning was the problem of modern vernacular speech and its relation to the ancient languages. Inevitably, the two fundamental issues of Renaissance logomachy—the *questione della lingua* and *querelle des anciens et des modernes*—became entangled. The discovery of new languages from the sixteenth century intensified humanist interests in historical, comparative, and finally "general" linguistics and led to the conviction—reflected, for example, in the pioneering work of Conrad Gesner—that all languages whatsoever could be reduced to writing and to rules of "grammar."[15] In this way Babel was, as it were, rediscovered and was made the target of scholarly investigation—and of efforts to find universal linguistic structures (or "innate ideas") behind the cultural diversity revealed by expanding temporal and geographical horizons. In this way "grammar" became a way of defining the human condition—not only *homo sapiens* but also *homo loquens* and *homo scribens*. Such was the character of the taproot of contemporary "grammatology," with its own grounding in *écriture*, formulated in recent times by Jacques Derrida.

## Ars Rhetorica

Man (and, in his company, woman) was thus the speaking and writing creature, but in civilized discourse grammar, though fundamental, was only a beginning. In the conventional ladder of learning, the next step after grammar was the more social art of rhetoric. According to Polydore Vergil, rhetoric was "invented" by men when, having received the gift of speech, they realized that some words were useful and others injurious.[16] If the *ars grammatica* was the gateway to knowledge for humanists, the *ars rhetorica* represented the high road to true wisdom. "For," as Salutati wrote in his praise of the *studia humanitatis*, "if intelligence and reason, by which the human race has some common property with superior beings, are a source of beauty, if men are clearly distinguished from other living creatures because they can use words; how much more excellent than other men is he who, relying on his reason, stands forth with brilliant eloquence."[17] In many ways indeed the master of rhetoric fulfilled the ideal of the *uomo universale* in moral and political as well as in literary and philosophical terms. The Orator, in other words, was the very prototype and paradigm of the Renaissance man.

Rhetoric stood high on the humanist agenda of cultural restoration and educational utility. In the early fifteenth century it was still "well nigh a lost art," wrote Vergerio in his defense of liberal studies (ca. 1404). "Oratory, in which our forefathers gained so great a glory

Philosophy, holding a book and scepter, nursing the seven liberal arts, including the armed figure of Rhetoric (School of Strasbourg, twelfth century).

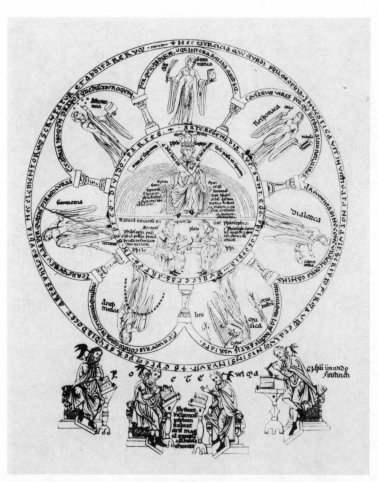

Harrad of Landsberg's *Hortus Deliciarum* (Garden of Delights), fol. 32, in the form of a rose window. Philosophy is in the center, with its forms (ethics, logic, physics) above, Socrates and Plato underfoot, the seven liberal arts surrounding and represented as established by the Holy Spirit, and four poets underneath (twelfth century).

Philosophy, with book and scepter, presiding over the seven liberal arts, with the church fathers above, representing divine philosophy, and Aristotle and Seneca below, representing natural and moral philosophy (from Gregor Reisch's encyclopedia, *Margarita philosophica* [Strasbourg, 1504]).

Symbolic tree, rooted in enthroned Philosophy and branching out into the seven liberal arts, with God the Father, Christ, the Virgin, and the church fathers overhead (woodcut, 1508, by "Master D. S.").

Elaborate allegory of Grammar, with all of its parts from letters and syllables to syntax and prose style (engraving attributed to Vogtherr, from *Margarita philosophica*, edition of 1548).

for themselves and for their language, is despised; but our youth, if they would earn the reputation of true education, must emulate their ancestors in this accomplishment."[18] Over the next several generations, indeed, literary "eloquence" was cultivated and even codified, especially in Lorenzo Valla's *Elegances of the Latin Language*. The great "triumvirate" of sixteenth-century learning—Erasmus, Budé, and Vives—were all Valla's disciples in one way or another. It was Valla in particular, according to Erasmus, who "summoned from the grave and restored to their former splendor Latin letters, corrupted, crushed, and extinguished by barbarian ignorance"; and in his various recommendations for the correct "method of study," Erasmus insisted that pupils "should diligently study Lorenzo Valla, the extremely elegant arbiter of elegant Latin."[19]

Renaissance rhetoric drew upon a rich Greek as well as Latin heritage, but it had to be reassembled after centuries of medieval "fragmentation," during which it had been divided into three separate "arts"—the *ars dictaminis*, the *ars arengandi*, and the *ars praedicandi*, referring respectively to the drafting of documents, the writing of private letters, and the delivering of sermons. From the time of Petrarch, there began to occur what Brian Vickers has called the "reintegration" of rhetoric in the context of the encyclopedic program of the *studia humanitatis*. As ancient gods and heroes were restored to their proper classical forms, so the meaning of ancient discourse was resurrected, and with it the understanding of the resources and functions of language. The declared aim of rhetoric and the "art of oratory" was the achievement of "eloquence," or "elegance," but these qualities did not refer merely to ornamentation or verbal virtuosity. They implied also, and more importantly, conditions of human understanding, virtue, and social life; and the enormous literature devoted to rhetoric in the Renaissance ("One Thousand Neglected Authors," marvels James Murphy) elaborated on all these philosophical and cultural themes.

As in humanist views of grammar, the key to humanist rhetoric lay in the shift from logic to language, from *ratio* to *oratio*, as the distinguishing feature of humanity—not abstract "thought," in other words, but human use of the "tongue" (or pen), which is to say communication. In medieval discussions *oratio* had signified merely the grammatical unit of the sentence, but for humanists it meant connected discourse, or even speech, in a more general sense, which was the defining trait of human nature. As Rudolf Agricola put it, "Oratory, for whatever reason it was instituted, and every act of discourse with which we reveal the thoughts of our minds, is observed to perform and hold this principal and appropriate office: to teach something to him who is listening to it. Is it not obvious to whomever takes stock of this fact that God, the parent and author of all things, endowed man alone of all animals, who is capable of rational instruction, with the gift of speaking and of oration?"[20] Man had the ability not only to think God's thoughts after him but also, through linguistic representation, to create his own world of culture and likewise, through education, to maintain it over time.

This way of conceiving the *logos* as discourse rather than as concept was the basis of Erasmus' method, both of translating and of expressing his own thoughts. "I have learned from Galen," he wrote, "that what differentiates man from the animals, or brutes [*alogi*], as they are called, is not reason, but speech" (*non ratione sed oratione*).[21] The understanding of human nature, therefore, depended not on rational analysis but rather on reading the great authorities of literature—not merely on the skeletal *artes* of medieval schools but on the rich *auctores* of classical tradition. It is this attitude to which Ernst Cassirer was referring when he remarked that "it was precisely the 'philologists' of the Renaissance who, on the basis of their deepened understanding of language, demanded a new 'theory of thought.' They argued that the scholastics had seen only the outward, grammatical structure of language, while its real kernel, which is to be sought not in grammar but in stylistics, had remained closed to them."[22]

Although linked to oratory, Renaissance rhetoric in practice marked a shift from oral to scribal—and so typographical—culture. Writing—*scriptura, écriture*—defined the world of humanism according to the Petrarchian vision and furnished the conditions of literary fame that promised an earthly immortality. The communications and persuasions made possible by rhetoric were extended over time not only in projections of writing toward a concerned posterity but also in furthering a discourse begun many centuries before—"dialogues with the dead." The "Republic of Letters" was thus extended in time as well as in space, and it found its most concrete expression in the books that preserved traditional and "authoritative" discourse. In the logocentric world of self-conscious humanist authors, as in the ingenious neorhetorical arguments of Derrida, writing asserted primacy over speech, especially the spoken words of those educated in the formal tradition of "letters."

Rhetoric implied both imitation and originality—if such a distinction is meaningful within rhetorical convention. An elegant literary style depended not merely on learning linguistic precepts but on following the practice of the great authors. At times, this could result in the ludicrous literalness of those "apes of Cicero" whom Erasmus denounced in his *Ciceronianus,* but at best it meant exploiting the resources of ancient Latin by determining what Valla had called "the consensus of the erudite." What is more, modern authors had to develop their own style, and here the usual analogy was with the art of painting—*ut pictura rhetorica.* No wonder these arts, as Valla proclaimed, should have been restored together. This celebration of a cultural renaissance was itself a central topos in the work of humanists like Valla and Erasmus. To the old questions formerly debated by historians—Was there a Renaissance?—the answer must be: yes, obviously, if only in the eyes, and in the "rhetoric," of humanists.

From Petrarch to Erasmus, the humanist celebration of rhetoric was accompanied by contempt for conventional dialectic and disputation. Petrarch's sarcastic contrast between his own liberal "ignorance" and the pretentious and disputatious "wisdom" of contemporary logicians began this polemical tradition; the campaign was continued even more vigorously in the anti-Aristotelian assaults mounted by Valla in his *Dialectical Disputations,* by Erasmus in his *Antibarbarus,* and by Vives in *Against the Pseudodialecticians.* All were intended to clear the way for the new and integral art of rhetoric by exposing the fallacies of Scholastic method. Like dialectic, rhetoric emphasized "invention" and the discovery of "topics," but convention outweighed reason in the sense that such topoi were rhetorical rather than dialectical "arguments" and designed for affective and civilizing persuasion rather than syllogistic and uncivil demonstration. The aim was, in the Ciceronian formula, to "delight, move, and teach" (*delectare, movere, docere*) humanly rather than to argue logically—a sublimated form of warfare, Erasmus thought. Not "disputation" but civilized conversation was the humanist aim, and it is only natural that—from Petrarch to Erasmus—humanists should have cultivated so reverently the conversational dialogue form that Plato had created and that Cicero has imported into the Latin tradition.

One result of these attitudes was to reignite the old conflicts between rhetoric and philosophy that had been initiated by Plato's attacks on the Sophists (even though Socrates himself was regarded as such), and in this effort Valla was a veritable intellectual pyromaniac. "But look at the difference," Valla exclaimed: "the dialectician uses so to speak a nude syllogism, the orator uses one which is clothed and armed and decorated with gold and purple and precious gems."[23] And in his treatise on the "true good" (*De vero bono*), Valla puts into the mouth of the Milanese humanist Maffeo Vegio these words: "I have been initiated, not into the rites of philosophy, but into the more significant and lofty ones of oratory and poetry. Truly, philosophy is like a soldier or lower officer at the orders of oratory, his commander and (as a great writer of tragedies [Euripides] calls her) his queen."[24]

The classic confrontation between rhetoric and philosophy in the Renaissance appeared in the famous exchange between Pico della Mirandola and Ermolao Barbaro in 1485. Responding to Ermolao's attack on philosophy, Pico admitted—rhetorically—the disparity between these ancient disciplines. "So great is the conflict between the orator and the philosopher that there can be no conflicting greater than theirs," he wrote, referring to the alleged lies and entrapments of sophists.[25] For Pico, philosophy sought the life-giving spirit, as it were, while rhetoric was satisfied with the deadening letter. Yet in his conclusion Pico called for a union—or rather a reunion—between eloquence and philosophy as the only way to achieve true wisdom. Two generations later (in 1558), Philip Melanchthon added his own *opinio* to the debate, agreeing that eloquence should be joined to wisdom but denying that Scholastic philosophy qualified as wisdom, and concluding with a defense of the active life.

For Melanchthon, who himself was involved in the reformation of higher education in the German universities, "the orators bring into writing the best experience, which exercises and sharpens their thinking. That is why they transfer philosophy aptly to use and to common life."[26] According to Bruni, "It is the orators who teach us to praise the good deeds and to hate the bad; it is they who teach us how to soothe, encourage, stimulate, or deter. All these things the philosophers do, it is true, but in some special way anger, mercy and the arousal and pacification of mind are completely within the power of the orator."[27] Or as Vives put it, "the more corrupt men generally are, so much the more ought the good and intelligent men to cultivate carefully the art of Rhetoric, which holds sway over the mind, so that they may lead others from misdeeds and errings to, at least, some care for virtue."[28]

In this way rhetoric became a source not only of moral improvement but also of social cohesion. In the words of Stefano Guazzo, "Nature has given man the power of speech. But certainly not in order that he converse with himself. . . . It was given to him that he could use it as a means of communication with others. You can see that we are using this tool in order to teach, question, negotiate, deliberate, improve, discuss and judge. Also, in order to express the emotions of the soul. All these are means by which men come together and love one another."[29] Indeed, rhetoric was a primary cause of the emergence of society in the first place. As Melanchthon wrote, "It has been said, with good reason, that when men were still dispersed and nomadic they were gathered together by eloquence, and that by it states were founded; by it rights, religions, legitimate marriage, and the other bonds of human society were constituted. In fact, it is by eloquence [*oratio*] that these things are maintained in commonwealths."[30]

Rhetoric aspired to be more than an introduction to "letters." "Those who teach rhetoric immediately after grammar," declared one English teacher of rhetoric, "are wrong to do so because the practice of rhetoric depends upon knowledge of the great arts, and upon practical judgment of public life."[31] Rhetoric had long been tied to public service and political engagement, as Dante's predecessor, Brunetto Latini, had suggested when he declared, "The art of speaking well and of ruling is the noblest art in the world."[32] "Orator" was the term applied to the new office of the Renaissance diplomat, and judicial oratory enjoyed a great revival in the later sixteenth century. For Guarino, "eloquence" was part of "civil science" (*civilis scientia*), which was also the name given by professional jurists to their discipline.

The close affiliation between rhetoric and civil law is explained in part by the fact that before the twelfth-century revival of Roman jurisprudence, law had in effect taken refuge in the teaching of rhetoric, in part by their common reliance on persuasion (the "judicial" aspect of oratory) and claims to social and political utility. The jurist regarded himself as the quintessential "political man" (*homo politicus*), but in the human community the orator had even grander pretensions—claiming to be not only a citizen but a "leader of the people" (*dux populi*). According to Valla, "Even in our own time, although the philosophers may call themselves leaders, it is the orators—as events show us—who may be designated the leaders of others" (*rectores alii*).[33] Out of the *ars rhetorica*, in short, there emerged not only the idea of the "renaissance" but also that equally controversial abstraction called "civic humanism."

To this civic ideal there was a religious counterpart; for if Jerome represented the Christian grammarian, Augustine represented the Christian Orator—and as Erasmus modeled himself after the first, so Luther (among many others) followed the second.[34] The preacher was not only the messenger delivering the Word of God but also, as Erasmus said, the "savior" (*soter*) of the people. In Protestant education, especially that intended for the ministry, the place of rhetoric, was correspondingly elevated in practice as well as theory. The old *ars praedicandi* reached new heights in the age of Erasmus—and contributed in many ways to the religious controversies and logomachies so deplored by Erasmus. Dialectic and rhetoric were traditionally represented by the images of the closed fist and the open hand. In the "new dialectic" developed by Peter Ramus, the rigor of the first was joined to the persuasive power of the second.[35] This alliance between elegance and rigor suggests one of the ways in which rhetoric was extended into what amounted to a theory of propaganda in the period of religious reform—and of the religious wars.

Here we can begin to see a negative aspect of "rhetoric"—a term that, in the Renaissance as today, had pejorative connotations. "A rhetorician of times past," remarked Montaigne, "said that his trade was to make little matters appear and be thought great"; and in politics the results could be momentous, as history had shown. As Montaigne also wrote, "Eloquence flourished most at Rome when affairs were in the worst state and agitated by the storm of civil wars, as a free and untamed field bears the lustiest weeds. From that it seems that monarchical governments need it less than others."[36] Writing almost contemporaneously, Davy Du Perron seconded Montaigne's opinion: "Rhetoric is a tool invented to manipulate a mob and disorderly commoners, and is a tool used only in sick states, like medicine, in those where the vulgar, the ignorant, where all were in power, as in Athens, Rhodes and Rome, and where things were in perpetual tempest, these orators thronged. . . . Eloquence flourished best in Rome where things were in their worst state and when the storm of civil wars agitated them."[37]

Du Perron went on to explain the reasons for this deplorable connection—and in effect the negative aspect of "civic humanism."

---

The places where eloquence has always reigned and triumphed more have been in Republics and popular governments, for the reason that, in those states where deliberations depend on the multitude, the first particular that must be sought is that the people, who are, as they say, a many-headed animal, agree on a self-same intention; otherwise, as long as the people are divided amongst themselves, there will be no progress toward the execution of what is useful and necessary. . . . [F]or it is eloquence that manages whole assemblies of men by the spoken word, which makes itself mistress of their affections, shapes their wills as it suits these affections, and withdraws them from whatever it does not please to see them inclined to.

Such criticisms, however, apply rather to the persons who apply the weapons of rhetoric than to the *ars rhetorica* itself, which—despite attacks from skeptics and devotees of the new science—was preserved as a literary, educational, and social ideal. Although Bacon prized reason above memory and especially above imagination and had to "descend from reason to reach rhetoric," he did acknowledge that "Eloquence prevaileth in the active life," and he admitted the importance of the orator's role, which was to apply reason to the imagination for the better moving of the will.[38] In general, and more than any of the other liberal arts, rhetoric was identified with the encyclopedic and public ideals of the Renaissance—the Orator as the universal man, the master not only of himself but also of his society and of his cultural tradition, including all the liberal arts and sciences. It was one of the orator's skills that he should also be an accomplished historian; and this brings us to the third of the *studia humanitatis*, the daughter of oratory (as Valla argued)—the art of history.[39]

## Ars Historica

Of all the arts, Polydore Vergil wrote, history was the most admirable because of its moral, commemorative, and potential political value.[40] In general "history" was associated with the *studia humanitatis* in several ways. In the first place, the word referred to the the levels of linguistic meaning—designating (with *methodus*) one of the two parts of grammar and literal understanding (*sensus his-*

*toricus*), as distinguished from various kinds of figurative interpretation. According to Guarino, the second stage of grammar, which he called *Historice,* is itself "concerned with the study of continuous prose authors, more particularly the Historians. . . . By their aid [the scholar] will learn to understand the varying fortunes of individuals and states, the sources of their success and failure, their strength and their weakness."[41] At this point the transition has already been made to the field of rhetoric—"continuous prose," in Guarino's phrase, treating what had actually happened in the past. As Leonardo Bruni remarked in the introduction to his history of Florence, "History . . . involves at the same time a long continuous narrative, causal explanation of each particular event, and appropriately placed judgments on certain issues."[42]

Through its form and purposes, history was linked not only to the first two members of the *trivium,* grammar and rhetoric, but also to moral philosophy, in the sense that it provided a repository of examples to be imitated or avoided. History was also linked to poetry, in the sense that the poets were often regarded—historically—as the first historians, more primitive and credulous but (like Homer) concerned nevertheless with the past of their society. In both connections, history was seen as appealing to human emotions rather than to logical propriety, and as following the sequence of human experience rather than argument. It was revered as a repository—or a "mirror"—of the cultural past that formed the foundations of humanist learning. But most directly and "literally" history constituted a literary genre and an "art"—analogous to the arts of grammar, rhetoric, and poetry. Like these sister arts, history also had encyclopedic and intellectually imperialistic aspirations, and in a variety of contexts in the Renaissance, it became a dominant mode of inquiry, understanding, organization, and expression.

An interest in history furnished an original impetus to the humanist movement in the sense that it represented Petrarch's emotional point of departure for exploring the classical past. Yet while the study of history represented a search for his intellectual, moral, and national ancestors, Petrarch also acknowledged, following the prescription of Cicero, that the "first law" of history, in contrast to the functions of rhetoric and poetry, was to tell the truth and nothing but the truth. For humanism, then, history represented the reality principle—that is, the *res gestae* of the moral, political, and cultural past—or rather the recovery and recounting (*narratio rerum gestarum*) of this past. In all of its forms, history also had to be employed for the larger goals represented by moral and perhaps political philosophy.

In this connection it is important to recall that humanists in the Petrarchian mode tended to place themselves not in the Scholastic world of thought and propositional argument but in the universe of the written word—not in the scholastic classroom but in the "Republic of Letters," which spanned many centuries and many cultures. In sum, grammar taught words, whereas rhetoric mainly taught written discourse, and history represented the written formulation of human thoughts and deeds that had themselves been preserved in earlier writing. Though in some ways this is an exaggeration and an undervaluing of oral and artistic culture, it seems a fair appraisal of the humanist movement in the historical perspective of several centuries—which is the only one available to us in any practical and "historical" sense.

The assumption that history is not what happened but what can be—rhetorically—recaptured and represented in retrospect is altogether in keeping with the conventional definition of history drawn from Cicero. According to this endlessly repeated rhetorical formula, history is "the witness of time, the light of truth, the life of memory, the mistress of life, and the messenger of antiquity" (*testis temporum, lux veritatis, vita memoriae, magistra vitae, nuncius antiquitatis*).[43] This set of topoi suggests all the central qualities of history, including its commemorative function, its fixation on the significant past, its identification with truthfulness and accuracy, its value for moral philosophy, and its association with the faculty not of reason or imagination but rather of memory. Another implication was that, in contrast to the universalistic claims of philosophy, history afforded access to the "local knowledge" associated with a "usable past," for elsewhere Cicero had recognized the value of history in commemorating and in celebrating the national past, and Renaissance humanists likewise pursued the cultural and political applications of history.

Like rhetoric, history put itself into competition with philosophy. In opposition to the old canard of Aristotle that poetry was superior to history because it was more "philosophical," Valla offered ingenious counter-arguments for the value of the humanities. "History is more robust than poetry because it is more truthful," he declared. "It is directed not to abstraction but to concrete truth . . . , teaching by example."[44] Consequently, "We assert that historians are superior to philosophers; and with respect to divine things we may mention Moses . . . and the evangelists . . . , who are no more than historians." And further, "To be adept in history one must be superior in knowledge, acumen, judgment . . . , accuracy, sagacity, memory . . . etc." The historian had always to consider his audience as well as his intellectual office, for as Guillaume Budé wrote, "History cannot long keep its authority if it is not written by a man who is eloquent, who knows how to join the grace and gravity essential to history to veracity and verisimilitude, and who can formulate it in a pleasing way to a worthy assembly."[45]

The moral uses of history became a central theme in humanist pedagogical literature praising the liberal arts. "Among these," declared Vergerio,

> I accord first place to History, on grounds both of its attractiveness and of its utility, qualities which appeal equally to the scholar and to the statesman. Next in importance ranks Moral Philosophy, which indeed is, in a peculiar sense, a "Liberal Art," in that its purpose is to teach men the secret of true freedom. History, then, gives us the examples of the precepts inculcated by philosophy. The one shows what men should do, the other what men have said and done in the past, and what practical lessons we may draw therefrom for the present day.[46]

In the famous phrase of Dionysius of Halicarnassus, endlessly repeated between the Renaissance and the Enlightenment, history was "philosophy teaching by example."[47]

Such exemplaristic "philosophy" could have a public as well as a private application, and indeed this was why Bruni argued that history "is a subject no scholar should neglect."[48] In particular, "It is a fit and seemly thing to be familiar with the origins and progress of one's own nation, and with the deeds in peace and in war of great kings and free peoples. Knowledge of the past gives guidance to our counsels and our practical judgment, and the consequence of similar undertakings [in the past] will encourage or deter us according to our circumstances in the present." Machiavelli followed Bruni's civic conviction in both *Florentine Histories* and his *Discourses on Livy*, which likewise looked to the past as a guide to the future. Indeed, Machiavelli pushed the utilitarian conception of history to an extreme, if not an absurdity, by suggesting that it was possible "by diligent study of the past to foresee what is likely to happen in the future in any republic, and to apply those remedies that were used by the ancients . . . or to devise new ones from the similarity of the events."[49] For Machiavelli, this view of history opened up a "new route" to a practical science of politics and statecraft—a route that would be followed by many other practical- or policy-minded scholars down to the present.

As a literary practice, humanist historical writing did not entirely conform to the rhetorical ideal, but it did attempt to follow classical forms. Leonardo Bruni himself had chosen the Livian kind of national history in his own history of Florence, and this model was imitated by historians throughout Italy and, in the next century, across Europe—Paolo Emilio for French history, for example, Polydore Vergil for English, Beatus Rhenanus for German, and many others. Equally influential was Flavio Biondo's works on the antiquities of Rome (*Roma triumphans* and *Roma instaurata* and especially his magisterial survey of medieval history (*Historiarum ab inclinatione romanorum imperii decades*), which also became a source and a model for the study of the medieval heritage of other national traditions. While these works hardly fulfilled the Ciceronian formula, they did try to found historical narrative on critical erudition and to reconstruct various aspects of post-Roman history. In a sense the emergence of humanist historiography represents one aspect of the adaptation of the *studia humanitatis* to European culture and another chapter in the story of the endless "quarrel" between the "ancients" and the "moderns"—and perhaps also suggested a means of reconciliation.

The humanist conception of history was taken up, and considerably modified, by Protestant authors, who were likewise concerned with reconstructing and legitimizing a tradition that was modern and yet in accord with the values of—in this case Christian—antiquity. In both cases, history was a bridge not only between ancients and moderns but also between pagans and Christians. Luther praised the secular uses of history in conventionally Ciceronian terms, while at the same time engaged in a wholesale revision of the history of Christianity; so, more learnedly and systematically, did his chief collaborator, Philip Melanchthon, whose own contribution to the "art of history" appeared as his introduction to the Lutheranized world chronicle of Johann Cario. Melanchthon's veneration for history was displayed, too, in his educational reforms (aimed at installing a humanist curriculum in the Lutheran universities) and in his efforts to give Lutheranism legitimacy and an ancient genealogy through a continuous spiritual link with the "primitive church."[50] Moreover,

Johann Sleidan, official historiographer of the Lutheran party, followed humanist models in his pioneering history of the Reformation, amplifying these conventions by joining sacred with secular—ecclesiastical with political—narrative and by placing modern history (down to 1556) within the framework of Christian "universal" history.[51] Responding to critics of this work, Sleidan also praised the *ars historica* in an apologia that again invoked the famous formula of Cicero and that protested his absolute devotion to historical truth, accuracy, and—disingenuously but quite in keeping with rhetorical convention—"impartiality."

From the work of Sleidan and other confessional and national authors, it is obvious that the Ciceronian "first law of history" was by no means an obstacle to partisan commitment. This is clear, too, from the pedagogical writings of Melanchthon. An enthusiastic champion of the *studia humanitatis*, Melanchthon celebrated history both for its central role in liberal education and for its value in supporting national—and confessional—tradition. "To be ignorant of history is forever to be a child," he quoted from Cicero (as Valla and many others had done), but more specifically, "It is shameful to ignore the history of one's *patria*," and "it is an act of piety to study the antiquities of one's country."[52] Like the great *Monumenta Germaniae historica* of the nineteenth century, Melanchthon's impulse to the investigation of history was a "love of the fatherland"—reinforced, of course, by a commitment to the Lutheran faith and to its own sort of "German liberty."

Like grammar and rhetoric, history had its own darker face as well, and skeptics criticized not only particular historical works but also the historiographical enterprise in general. If Herodotus was the father of history, he was also, as Vives charged, the "father of lies." According to Henry Cornelius Agrippa of Nettesheim, history was not the mistress of life but the great deceiver of men.[53] No less than philosophers were historians able to agree on the truth, and in fact many of them were mercenaries and liars. Moreover, Agrippa added, "Many write histories not so much for the truth's sake as to delight the reader." It should be added, however, that such skepticism was not necessarily destructive; it also might be employed for the benefit of historical criticism, and so indeed it was in the later sixteenth and seventeenth centuries, both in the practice and in the theory of history.

The humanist genre of *ars historica*—analogous to the *ars rhetorica* and the Horatian *ars poetica*—was pursued well into the seventeenth century in letters, educational works, prefaces to historical works, and translations, and especially in treatises and dialogues devoted to questions of the nature of history: Is it an "art" or a "science"? What are its divisions, standards, rules, and uses? In the context of the Reformation and the Counter-Reformation and polemics over Christian tradition, the Italianate "art of history" was increasingly superseded by the French "methods of history," which shifted emphasis from the writing of narrative to the reading, criticism, and employment of sources. The shift in effect from "art" to "science" is most famously exemplified by Jean Bodin's *Method for the Easy Comprehension of History* (1566). In this work, the ancestor of handbooks of historical method down to the present century, Bodin did for history what Valla had in effect tried to do for rhetoric and Poliziano perhaps for "grammar"—that is, to place it, in Bodin's words, "above all other disciplines."[54]

Nor was this claim "mere rhetoric," for in fact in the context of the humanist movement, history was becoming a distinctive mode of understanding and indeed a way of organizing the entire "encyclopedia" of learning. Other examples, besides the aforecited *Inventors of Things* by Polydore Vergil, include Vives's *Transmission of Knowledge* (including a discussion of the "causes of the corruption of the arts"); the encyclopedic *ars historica* of Christophe Milieu, *On Writing the History of the Universe of Things* (1551), which surveyed the whole range of human "wisdom" (*sapientia*), from the mechanical arts to "literature" in the widest sense of written books in general; Louis Le Roy's *Vicissitude or Variety of Things in the Universe* (1575), which traced "the concurrence of arms and letters . . . since civilization began until the present"; Étienne Pasquier's *Researches of France* (1560–96), which treated, among other things, the history of the universities and all the arts, sciences, and professions in French intellectual tradition; and Henri de la Popelinière's *History of History and the Idea of Perfect History* (1599), which subjected historiography itself to historical interpretation—that is, it traced the art back to its poetical origins and down to his own encyclopedic and "contemplative" form. As Bodin's disciple Pierre Droit de Gaillard summed it up in his own "method of history," "in a word, all disciplines take their source and principles wholly from history, as from an overflowing fountain."[55] More than that, as Gaillard declared, the humanist fulfillment of the "most remarkable" of ancient aphorisms—"Know thyself"—"depends upon history, sacred as well as profane, universal as well as particular."

In the sixteenth century historians had a choice of ancient models, and this devolved essentially upon the examples set by Herodotus and by Thucydides, both of whose works had been translated by Valla. Thucydides, who eschewed "archaeology," focused on recent events and employed sharp political and "pragmatic" analysis (like the narratives of Machiavelli and Guicciardini), while Herodotus, a traveler as well as a writer, carried on his "inquiry" (*historia* in his original coinage) with broader concerns for antiquities, customs, and cultural matters. "Herodotus seems to us so much more human than Thucydides," Arnaldo Momigliano has remarked,[56] and, despite the canard that represented him as the father not only of "history" but also, as Vives said, of lies, so too did many humanists—and precisely because of his interest in remote antiquity, ethnography, and the world of the "barbarians." The Herodotian conception of history was especially consonant with the expanding "world of nations," including the New World as well as medieval Europe, which had to be accommodated to the Renaissance view of the cultural past.

The fortunes of the term and concept of "history" were extraordinarily complex and ambivalent from the later sixteenth century on. "History" might also refer to experience and data quite apart from considerations of chronology, perspective, and self-knowledge; Baconian usage recognized not only civil and ecclesiastical history but also "natural history." For other champions of the "new science" (rhetorically not unlike conventional skeptics), "history" became actually pejorative. Thus Galileo, in defending his "mathematical philosophy," regarded "historians" as mere "memory-experts," poles apart from true philosophers; and in expounding his analytical "method," Descartes came to much the same conclusion. The prejudice against history—on the grounds that it was itself a repository of "prejudice"—became a commonplace among champions of the "new philosophy that puts all in doubt." It was one of the aims of the "new science" of that last of humanists, Giambattista Vico, to resurrect the faculty of memory and the conceptual value of history—and to reassert the authority of humanist tradition—in the face of such naturalistic and scientistic challenges.

From the Renaissance, too, the larger implications of a "sense of history" began to emerge. To begin with, this was expressed in the form of discriminating taste and in the topos (invoked by Valla in his *Elegances*) blaming ignorance and barbarism "on the times rather than the men" (*non hominum sed temporum culpa*), and it was most famously expressed in Valla's exposure of the false Donation of Constantine (and before him in Petrarch's exposure of the Habsburg donation). In a similar vein, Erasmus remarked about the study of mythology, "After Hesiod, Boccaccio dealt with the genealogy [of the gods] with more eloquence than one would expect from the age in which he lived."[57] In the following generations such an aesthetically based sense of anachronism was elevated into the techniques of "historical criticism" in a modern sense.

In general, Clio—muse, teacher, truth-teller, curator of cultural tradition—never ceased to be celebrated in some circles of conventional (and, in Vico's case, unconventional) learning. Neo-Ciceronian hyperbole was preserved, the polemical uses of history continued to inform the massive antiquarian enterprises of the seventeenth century, and the classical and Christian perspectives constructed by humanists still provided the larger framework of human knowledge, values, and goals. Through the study of history, wrote, Galileo's contemporary Daniel Heinsius, "that fretful animal we call man . . . would be free from the limits of time and space. . . . He would gather into one focus the immeasurably great vastness of ages and generations." Finally, Heinsius concluded in his highly rhetorical fashion, "History renders man contemporaneous with the universe."[58]

## Ars Poetica

According to Polydore Vergil (with usual "rhetorical" hyperbole), poetry was distinguished in two ways—because it surpassed the other sciences (*reliquas antecedit disciplinas*) and because it was the product of divine inspiration.[59] Poetry, with its critical companion, poetics, represented a sister art to history and rhetoric that had negative as well as positive links to them. On the one hand, poetry was distinguished from history by its relative indifference to the problem of truth; on the other hand, it was related to it by the fact that historically (as many humanists noted) "the poets were the first historians"—a judgment based on the example not only of Homer but also of the Pentateuch, presumably written by Moses. On the one hand, poetry was distinguished from rhetoric by its identification with verse (rather than prose) forms; on the other hand, it resembled rhetoric in its commitment to the same humanist—that is, aesthetic and utilitarian—goals. In France, indeed, it was regarded as a "second rhetoric" because it was likewise devoted to invention, disposition, and elocution. And again, the art of poetry emulated both rhetoric and history in the imperialistic impulse to encompass—and even to rule over—the entire humanist encyclopedia.

The classic humanist defense of poetry appears in the later books of the encyclopedic *Genealogy of the Gods*, written by Petrarch's first disciple, Giovanni Boccaccio, in the fourteenth century. Building on the poetics of Aristotle and Horace, Boccaccio celebrated poetry as a civilizing and edifying as well as an entertaining form of discourse. According to one admirer of Boccaccio, "His arguments are convincing, approximating today's anthropological explanation of myths."[60] Defending ancient learning against the ignorant, the Scholastics, and the jurists, Boccaccio celebrated poetry not only as a true science—"founded upon things eternal, and confirmed by eternal principles"—but as a form of theology. For Boccaccio poetry "is a sort of fervid and exquisite invention, with fervid expression, in speech or writing, of that which the mind has invented"—and, he added, "It proceeds from the bosom of God."[61] When combined with the precepts of the other liberal arts, it produces wonderful effects on the mind—more wonderful indeed, though inspired by imagination and covered by a veil of fiction, than the other disciplines—certainly more than the discourse of the lawyers, whom Boccaccio had singled out as the particular enemies of poetry, and as always the "noisy sophists" of the schools.

For Boccaccio poetry was a form of theology and hence of religion. This gave poets, pagan as well as Christian, profound (if subversive) insights about the "nature" of man in the sense of his physical and historical genesis. In book 12 of his *Genealogy of the Gods* he summarized the Vitruvian—ultimately Epicurean—evolutionist view of what Erwin Panofsky called "the early history of mankind," in which Vulcan is represented (as he was in paintings) as being brought up by "apes." Boccaccio read this allegory as man, the "imitative" animal, nurturing fire and being led then to human discourse. More than three centuries later, such unorthodox "anthropological" speculation would be elaborated more systematically and ingeniously by Giambattista Vico in his search for "poetic wisdom."[62]

Far from being liars or the "apes of philosophers" (as Vico also believed), the pagan poets had been the first theologians (*vates*). They were also *musici*—inspired by the Muses—and their genius and divine frenzy (*ingenium, furor poeticus, enthusiasmos*) gave them direct contact with divine wisdom. The role of *poeta-theologus*—and the function of poetry as *altera philosophia*—had been filled not only by Homer and Vergil but also, in modern times, by Dante and Petrarch. Cristoforo Landino and Marsilio Ficino emphasized the philosophical and theological dimension of the art of poetry and hence its exalted place in the circle of human wisdom. "But that the origins of poetry are more noble than the other human arts is proved by the fact that the divine frenzy by which poetry is generated is more excellent than the human skills by which the other arts are generated."[63] Like Salutati, Landino concluded that "the subject matter of poetry is much more divine than that of the other arts, since it embraces all of them."

"Side by side with the study of history a careful reading of the poets will be taken in hand," wrote Guarino. "The true significance of poetry . . . consists, as Cicero says, in the exhibition of realities of our own life under the form of imaginary persons and situations."[64] For him, Vergil was no less valuable than Cicero, and indeed Guarino permitted himself to "transfer the words of Cicero from the orator to the poet and say with him, 'In my opinion no one can reach the highest rank as a poet unless he has mastered all the highest arts and sciences.' " According to Salutati, "the art of Poetry presupposes the whole *Trivium* and *Quadrivium*, all philosophy, things divine and human, and in short all knowledge."[65] Poetry was, according to Bartolommeo della Fonte, "the mother of all doctrines." It was another, and higher, representation of the humanist encyclopedia.

Nor did Christians have reason to fear pagan poetry any longer. Against the strictures of canon law, Salutati defended Vergil on the basis not only of literary elegance but also of "the profundity of his thought and ideas drawn from the depths of ancient learning and from the loftiest heights of philosophy." Poetry in general, beneath its ostensibly trivial exterior, contained not lies (as critics since Plato had charged) but "marvelous hidden truths" and prophecies. In this connection and following a continuous medieval tradition, Salutati invoked Vergil's famous fourth eclogue, which foretold a "new-born time" that Christian exegetes associated with the coming of Christ. "Do you not see," Salutati wrote elsewhere, "that sacred literature, the whole body of Holy Scripture, is, rightly considered, nothing else in its method of expression, than poetry?"[66]

Boccaccio complained that poetry, unlike philosophy and law, lacked a tradition of commentary, but this deficiency had been overcome with a vengeance by the sixteenth century.[67] By then, the *ars poetica,* vernacular as well as classical, had generated even more discussion than the parallel *artes historica, grammatica,* and even *rheto-rica.* The result was a vast new scholasticism, replete with disputes over the origin and nature of poetry and the value of particular poets, ancient and modern. In these discussions the work of Horace was important, as was the Latin rhetorical tradition; but the center of the debate was occupied by the authoritative works of Plato and Aristotle, which inspired endless commentaries and criticisms. In Horace, who had emphasized "universal utility and pleasure," the rhetorical connection was most evident. Aristotle was invoked on many topics, including his analogies between poetry, painting, and music and his elevation of poetry above history, but especially his philosophical rationalizations. The influence of Plato was more am-biguous, for his authority could be invoked either for or against the value of the poetic function: the poet for Plato on the one hand was divinely inspired and on the other was the liar expelled from the Republic.

For Aristotle and many practitioners as well as theorists of Renaissance poetics, poetry was superior to history because it was more universal—that is, more philosophical. Torquato Tasso put it this way:

> But because that which principally constitutes and deter-mines the nature of the poetry and makes it different from history in the consideration of things not as they have been but as they should have been, having regard to the probable in universals rather than to the truth in particulars, the poet should investigate, before he does anything else, to see whether any event in the material he has chosen to treat would give greater delight if it had happened otherwise . . . [and] he should at his will reshape and reduce the quantity of accidents in the material in the manner he believes to be better, paralleling what is entirely feigned with truth that is altered.[68]

The opposite pole is well represented by Lodovico Castelvetro, for whom history, as the representation of truth, was prior to poetry, as the representation of verisimilitude. Castelvetro thought it unfortu-nate that Aristotle had never written a treatise on the art of history as he had for rhetoric, but he surely would have disagreed with this view. "For poetry borrows its light from history," Castelvetro wrote, "a light that does not yet burn or at least not as brightly as it should, and, unable to borrow it, poetry must wander in great darkness."[69]

An equally important question in Renaissance poetics was that of imitation (Aristotelian *mimesis*), especially in its relation to poetic "invention" and with the psychological faculty of "imagination." The orthodox view, expressed by Alessandro Lionardi, was that the poet's task was simply, though with artifice and artistry, to represent reality. "Poetry," he declared, "consists in imitation, which is either of things or of persons, and of all that pertains to body and mind, in regard to their qualities, operations, conditions, and states. A poet should therefore studiously, diligently, and artfully represent speech, actions, manners, and emotions, painting all as well as he can with words as a painter would with colors."[70] The Horatian motto *ut pictura poesis* (and the analogous *ut pictura rhetorica*) was quite appropriate, but like the painter the poet was obliged to imitate nature as carefully as possible to achieve creative perfection.

In other ways, too, poetry was accommodated to Aristotelian philosophy, with its divisions into species (genres), its analysis of literary qualities, and its enumeration of rules—which, though originally drawn from nature, as critics argued, had in modern times become matters of authority. Poetry was also linked to the complex tradition of Aristotelian psychology and theory of imagination. For pleasure is an effect produced on the soul in a sound body, wrote J. C. Scaliger: "The cause of this effect is what the philosophers call an object commensurate with the desire for it. By poetry the soul is sent back on itself, and it draws forth from its celestial force whatever there is within it of divinity, which part indeed cannot be exhausted even by perpetual drawings off."[71] The link between Aristotle's *Poetics* and his *De Anima* was explained in this way by Francesco Robortello: "There is a certain force in men which the Greeks call *phantasian;* we call it 'the power of reflecting' [*cogitandi vim*]. The force receives and retains images coming to it from the sense and transmits them to pure mind, which they call intellect. These, when the pure and simple mind has received them and distinguished them, are called *ennoiai* or *ennoemata*, by us 'notions.' "[72] According to this psychologistic conception, poetry was one product of the natural process of intellection.

By the midsixteenth century a reaction against Aristotelian theory—the "lying rules of Aristotle," as Tommasso Campanella called them—had been launched by the "new arts of poetry" throughout Europe. Among others, Lodovico Castelvetro and Francesco Patrizi in Italy and Joachim DuBellay in France opposed the rigidity of Aristotle's naturalistic theories. About poetry Patrizi concluded "that the most common teachings of Aristotle . . . are not true either with respect to its universal origin or with respect to many particular species; neither true, again, nor proper insofar as it is said that poetry is all imitation, or that every poet is an imitator."[73] In part, Patrizi's objection was based on the fact that poetry existed long before ideas of *mimesis:* "Therefore imitation by resemblance does not make poetry; therefore poems are not imitations; therefore the Aristotelian teaching that all poems are any more imitations than all the other writings in prose is neither good nor true."

The impact of Platonism reinforced these criticisms, especially by considering the poetic process in its own terms rather than in rhetorical or philosophical terms. When the poet invoked his muse, he was not setting out to copy God's own creation as carefully as possible; rather, he was appealing for divine inspiration—or perhaps looking into his own soul. What he was drawing on, in short, was not reason but the mythopoeic faculty of imagination—"image making"—which was not without sources, yet not without "originality" either. Similarly, the poet's aim was not fidelity to history nor perhaps even to nature but rather a sense of wonder and the "marvelous"; and so Patrizi could observe that "all poetry must have as its object the incredible because this is the true foundation of the marvelous." Philosophically understood, poetry involved not the Aristotelian categories and conceptualizations but the pursuit of the aesthetic and affective ideals of beauty and love. In general, the upshot of such Platonizing was to establish the independence of the art of poetry from both history and philosophy—though it could indeed, as Sir Philip Sidney wrote in his *Art of Poesie,* employ both of these disciplines in an auxiliary way.

"Poetry is a form of power," writes Elizabeth Sewell, and no one has ever pushed this sort of artistic chauvinism further than the humanists. Renaissance theorists revived—or preserved—earlier notions of the philosopher- (or theologian-) poet, the demiurge who created another, more human world. As Sidney put it, "Onely the poet disdeining to be tied to any such subjection, lifted up with the vigor of his own invention, doth grow in effect into another nature: in making things either better then nature bringeth foorth, or quite a new, . . . so as he goeth hand in hand with nature."[74] In other words, Renaissance poetics contributed indirectly, but in the most concrete way, to what has been termed the "maker's knowledge tradition," which proposed that what humankind made, and therefore could understand, was not God's creation but its own—not nature but "second nature."[75] It was in this sense that the poet could claim to be "another God" (*alter Deus*).

Tommasso Campanella was one of those who defended this approach to understanding—as indeed the best of ancient authorities had understood. For, he wrote,

> the ancients never submitted to rules set up in advance for them, except those set by God, by whom the good ones are inspired, and by nature, which must be imitated; for in truth these pedantic rules darken and deaden the pure and lucid spirit of the poet, which easily transmutes itself into every thing and which speaks of every thing, imitating the passion which it expresses. Therefore to follow minutely the rules of writers according to somebody else's judgment and not according to what is seen to happen in nature, always makes a man less admirable and of lesser fame than other men who are not so subjected.[76]

One reason for this, Campanella suggested, invoking another central theme of Renaissance poetics, was the divine function of poetry. Campanella acknowledged that "all the sciences of language speak about everything, as history, logic, oratory, and poetics," but the latter, in its encyclopedic hubris, claimed a special connection with the study not only of humanity but also of divinity. Thus, the poet became a model not only of the universal man of the Renaissance but—rhetorically and poetically if not historically—*alter deus.*

What made this heaven-storming program possible? It was not merely the power of reason but rather the faculty of imagination, empowered by human will, that underlay this quasi-divine creativity. But in Campanella's time, the heyday of the new science, such notions seemed dubious and even destructive of the rational process. What the imagination needed was "weights, not wings," declared Bacon, who surely knew Sidney's apology, and in his influential scheme of learning, imagination was marginalized in favor of the other two faculties, memory and reason, which formed the basis of the Baconian method. "Poesie," he wrote,

> is a part of learning in measure of words for the most part restrained, but in all other points extremely licensed, and

doth truly refer to the Imagination, which, being not tyed to the Lawes of matter, may at pleasure joyne that which Nature hath severed, & sever that which Nature hath joyned, and so make all unlawful Matches & divorses of things. It is taken in two senses in respect of Wordes or Matter. In the first sense it is but *Character* of stile, and belongeth to Arts of speeche. In the later, it is, as hath beene said, one of the principall Portions of learning, and is nothing else but Fained *History,* which may be stiled as well in Prose as in Verse.[77]

Bacon's undervaluation of imagination became a virtually unquestioned premise of the "new philosophy that called all into doubt," but it did not go unchallenged within the humanist tradition. The best example of this was the still-newer "new science" of Giambattista Vico, which was predicated on the belief that imagination and its conceptual twin history (*memorare* = *imaginare* was one of his etymological linkages)[78] were prior to and in a way more fundamental than reason not only in the education of the young but also in the development of civilization. Yet despite his claims of innovation, Vico was in many ways only following the ideas of Renaissance poetics, which likewise saw poetry as an original form of human wisdom (*sapienza umana*), an imaginative form rather than a rational one. As Francesco Patrizi wrote in 1586, poetry had its roots in myth and so in religion, especially in hymns, paeans, songs in praise of heroic figures, and epic.[79] Only later had it assumed more "civilized" functions, displaying

a usefulness for life and a glorifying of others, and this took many ways: now blaming the misdeeds or the defects of others, or exhorting to virtue, by means of precepts and warnings, showing the way to live well; and now on the stage putting before men's eyes the inconstancy of human affairs and the variety of fortunate and unfortunate adventures which befall others; and in part giving instruction about natural things, both in heaven and on earth, so that they might be of value for civil living.

Vico's "new science" built on these humanist insights and gave them more systematic historical form. For Vico—adapting the old Aristotelian view of the philosophical character of poetry—the poets were the first philosophers, and superior to their academic successors. "The poet teaches by delighting what the philosopher teaches austerely," he wrote in his early essay in praise of the liberal arts. "Both teach moral duties; both depict human habits and behavior; both incite to virtue and deter from vice."[80] But the poet does so humanly and in particular—extending the Aristotelian view of the essentially philosophical nature of poetry—by creating "imaginary figments which are, in a way, more real than physical reality." A quarter of a century later, in his *Scienza nuova*, Vico had come to view poetry as the source and first stage of human cultural development. What he called "poetic wisdom" was divine in origin but was accessible to the historian through the techniques of philology and its modern incarnation, Vico's final philosophy of history.[81] In its almost unrecognizable form as the "new science," humanism seems to come full circle—"the circle of divine law," as Vico called it, but also the encyclopedic circle of arts, which Vico called philology, on the basis of which human language and culture might be traced back to their (for Vico providential) origins, thus recreating the process of human history from poetic beginnings to philosophical achievement—and cultural decline.

# 6

# Beyond Humanism

The *studia humanitatis* supplied the forms, methods, and goals and much of the content of Renaissance humanism. But from the fifteenth and especially the sixteenth century, the interplay of humanism with other disciplines and doctrines makes it almost impossible to identify it in any meaningful way. Renaissance learning, aglow with the ideas of various philosophical "sects" and awash with a revived scholasticism, with Hermetic, occult, and religious beliefs, and with insights from new discoveries, was becoming too eclectic and encyclopedic to fit the original framework. For this reason, despite the strictures of P. O. Kristeller, it is difficult not to associate "humanism" with the values of Renaissance "anthropology" in a general sense. Nor does it seem adequate to limit the term, as Hans Baron's investigations suggest, to the immediate context of the Italian city-state—or to banish it altogether, as has been proposed by some historians who either fear anachronism or who do not see the value of historical generalizations, or both. "Humanism," even in its expansionist phase, represents a legitimate historical judgment, for the one common feature of the original circle of humanities was the image of man (and perhaps, arguably, woman) as a creator—interpreting, shaping, in this sense "making" his world, and reshaping, in his own terms, God's creation. Such was the office of the orator, the historian, the poet, and the philosopher, and more generally the Renaissance "artist," who likewise, though dependent on the resources of the "encyclopedia," followed nature but ended up creating a second nature—a world of man's own making.

## Moral Philosophy

Moral philosophy, which defined this world and thereby set itself apart from the theoretical study of natural philosophy, was of course one of the original *studia humanitatis*, but its concerns inevitably led beyond the liberal arts to the larger arena of "practical philosophy." According to Polydore Vergil, philosophy had passed from the "barbarians" to the Greeks, but "moral philosophy" in particular was the product of that Socratic turn noted by Cicero, by which Socrates shifted attention from the cosmos to the households of men.[1] Moral philosophy, fifth member of the *studia humanitatis*, was formed initially in a literary context, associated with the writings of orators, historians, and poets; yet at the same time it established ties with the major schools of philosophy known to the Renaissance—the Peripatetics, the Academics, the Stoics, and the Epicureans. Moral philosophy joined the ethics of Aristotle with that of Cicero and other Latin authors, including Stoics and Epicureans. It claimed possession not only of political thought—and implicitly political economy—but also of the science of law and the "true philosophy" of law. In this amorphous and eclectic way moral philosophy confronted all the central themes of the Renaissance philosophy of man, including the nature of the soul, the "dignity of man," individual virtue, the management of the household, the common good, the best form of government, the purpose of human life, the relationship between the private and public spheres, and the extraordinary variations within the species *homo sapiens*.

In moral philosophy as in the other liberal arts, Petrarch was a founding and a defining figure, and his attitudes were tied especially to his fondness for the "solitary life." For Petrarch, wisdom was the product of a lonely quest for personal excellence—a "selfish" approach in more than one sense and one not necessarily joined to a social conscience. "If, however, I proposed to commend this virtue [the life of solitude] to the crowd, I should be spending my efforts in vain," Petrarch wrote. "I speak not alone of the ignorant crowd but of many who think themselves educated" but in fact were misled by pride and ambition.[2] Petrarch contrasted the "wretchedness of busy men" and of "men of action" to the pleasant and productive lot of those who retired to a life of contemplation. Indeed, in his own life he prized his quiet life in retreat in the "closed valley" (Vaucluse) above the turmoil and corruption of cities like Rome and Avignon (where, in Petrarch's day, the papacy had relocated). "Let us leave the city with no idea of returning to it. . . . Let us rather pray that we may never return to the ungrateful crowd which is undeserving of the regard of all good men."

Not that Petrarch altogether avoided political involvement, and indeed his famous sonnet "Italia mia" (quoted at the close of Machiavelli's *Prince*) suggested his latent patriotism. But in his most eloquent writings he praised the *vita contemplativa* and, in his famous letters to Cicero, criticized that author for abandoning his philosophical and literary work and for his vain political efforts. Petrarch even had some doubts, or at least anxieties, about classical learning, which in some moods he suspected to be a distraction from Christian goals. In his account of his ascent of Mount Ventoux and in his letters to his brother, who had become a monk, Petrarch displayed this ambivalence and suspicion that the straight and narrow route of simple faith might be preferable to the vain efforts of human learning.[3] "I believe," he wrote, "that a noble spirit will never find repose save in God, in whom is our end, or in his private thoughts, or in some intellect united by a close sympathy with his own." Yet he also believed that, for himself at least, the pilgrimage of life had to pass through the complexities of the *studia humanitatis* and all the human experience contained therein.

Petrarch's was a mind divided between flesh and spirit (in Pauline terms)—between the secular values of Cicero and the Christian devotion of Augustine, though ultimately he thought that the two paths to the good life might be reconciled. His predicament was the same as that of Jerome, whose famous dream defined the basic dilemma, faced again and again by Petrarch: Are you a Christian or a Ciceronian? In a sense, Petrarch's ambivalence reflected the twofold nature of man himself and the consequences of sin. In Petrarch's dialogue *The Secret*, Augustine, who had suffered similar doubts, put the matter this way: "Indeed, just as I do not deny that your soul has been well formed and of heavenly origin, so you should not doubt that it has degenerated much from its original nobility due to the contagion of this body where it is buried."[4] Humanity might strive for knowledge and virtue, but only within the Christian predicament. "Thus when the illustrious pagan philosophers refer everything to virtue," Petrarch's Augustine continues, "the philosopher of Christ [*Christi philosophus*] refers virtue itself to the author of virtue, God, and by using virtue enjoys God, nor ever stops with his mind before he has reached Him."

Another expression of this dualism appeared in the debate that ran through the whole course of Renaissance moral philosophy—the question of the "dignity of man." Petrarch entered the debate in his *Remedy for Both Kinds of Fortune*, responding characteristically in dialogue form to the famous treatise on *The Misery of the Human Condition* by Pope Innocent III. "I do not deny that the misery of the human condition is great and manifold and that some have mourned it in entire volumes," Petrarch admitted. "But if you regard the matter differently, you will see that there is also much which can render life happy and pleasant, although no one, unless I'm mistaken, has attempted to write about this previously. . . . Happiness is small and hidden and must be dug out by a more thorough investigation in order for it to be shown to the incredulous." The life of solitude and study revealed many of these positive features. "As I select the best from many, are these a small cause of joy to you: the image and similitude of God the Creator within the human soul? the mind, memory, providence, eloquence, so many inventions, so many arts, which serve the soul, or the body? so many opportunities, virtue, material pleasures . . . , for unless you have willingly submitted to the yoke of sin, you may have dominion over all things which are under heaven." This optimistic view of the human condition—and of the "dignity of man"—was pursued more systematically by authors such as Manetti, Ficino, and especially Pico.

The very non-Augustinian notion that the human will had a large role to play in attaining the good life was a continuing, though controversial, theme of moral philosophy in the Renaissance, and no one emphasized this view more than Petrarch's disciple Coluccio Salutati. "The primacy of the will" is the way Eugenio Garin characterizes Salutati's conception of human nature and the significance of the *studia humanitatis*.[5] Following the attitudes of Petrarch (and adapting those of Augustine), Salutati rejected the preoccupations and assumptions of natural philosophy—"the soul is nobler than external things." On these grounds, for example, he praised the poets above the philosophers and the jurists above the doctors of medicine. The controversy between the faculties of law and medicine was an old one, and Salutati was following good academic precedent when he urged that law was the higher "science" because it treated not only speculation but also action and so the world of human will, values, and goals.

In this way Salutati reexamined the problem first posed in Petrarch's letters to Cicero concerning the relative value of the *vita activa* and the *vita contemplativa*. As the first of a long and distinguished line of chancellors of the Florentine Republic, Salutati did not enjoy the luxury of Petrarchian retirement, and he was much more inclined to appreciate the "activist" side of Cicero (whose "familiar letters" he discovered). For Salutati, the "primacy of will" was joined with civic life and service to the state. With Petrarch, he accepted "contemplation" (though not mere "speculation") as the highest human goal, but only because it represented the "end of all actions." Leonardo Bruni, Salutati's successor as Florentine chancellor, extended these voluntarist moral views into the realm of political philosophy—which, within the framework of the *studia humanitatis*, constituted nothing more than a department of moral philosophy.

Bruni's own position was a sort of synthesis of Ciceronian moral thought and the "practical philosophy" of Aristotle, whose work on politics and ethics, along with the pseudo-Aristotelian economics, he translated. Like Petrarch and Salutati, Bruni made a basic distinction between natural philosophy, concerned with the externals of experience, and moral philosophy, which is "entirely concerned with our own affairs, so that those who neglect it and devote themselves to physics would seem, in a sense, to be minding somebody else's business and neglecting their own."[6] The end of moral philosophy was earthly "happiness" (*beatitas*), whether defined as knowledge, virtue, utility, prudence, pleasure, or some other human conception of the highest good (*summum bonum*). Of the particular virtues, Bruni wrote, "some are clearly reserved for the contemplative life of retirement, while others are more suited to the active, civic life." His conclusion was that, while both the private and the public spheres had their value, it was the latter that was "more excellent with respect to the common good." The purpose was, as it were, the greatest good (*summum bonum, agathon*), for the greatest number.

In the fifteenth century the discussion of this "greatest good" increasingly turned away from the *studia humanitatis* to the more formal theories defended by particular philosophical "sects." An introduction and critical overview of these ideas was provided by Lorenzo Valla's dialogue "On the True Good" (*De vero bono*, also entitled "On Pleasure," *De voluptate*). In this work the various philosophical positions are represented by contemporary humanists. The Stoic, and generally Aristotelian, view, for example, is represented by the great orator and historian Bruni (whom Valla calls *pater*), Epicureanism by poet Antonio Beccadelli (Panormitanus) and later by Maffeo Vegio, Stoicism by Catone Sacco, and Christian orthodoxy by Antonio da Rho. The Stoic defends the standard moral (cardinal) virtues, while the Epicurean celebrates self-interest and pleasure and the Christian insists on the priority of the love of God.

Valla's own position has been debated for centuries. One of his aims was certainly to overturn the abstract, inhuman, unreal, and even "hypocritical" ideas of the Stoics. Because of the relish and rhetorical hyperbole with which his interlocutors defended human pleasure, the dialogue has scandalized many readers—hearing, for example, that adultery was more virtuous, because it was more pleasurable, than marriage. It seems most likely that Valla's purpose was some sort of synthesis of the three positions and a remedy against the false duality of flesh and spirit—within the framework, as always, of the humanist and rhetorical view of culture. Moral philosophy needed to be humanized, not reduced to rational or authoritarian precepts, but given practical meaning through example, persuasion, and links with human emotions. "Thus nothing is rightly done without pleasure"—and most certainly not in this life.

The effort to understand the human condition posed another question fundamental to moral philosophy and so to the liberal arts: How could the mind ascend from sense experience to more general knowledge (*scientia*) and, beyond that, to true wisdom (*sapientia*, the "knowledge of things divine and human," in the famous Ciceronian—and Augustinian—formula)?[7] The humanist answer to this question would take the form of a conception of education—a process ascending, by means of memory, experience, and "practice," through the arts of grammar, rhetoric, history, and poetry to higher levels of practical and contemplative philosophy to the search for the greatest good, private and public. Here again was a convergence between humanist notions and traditions of formal philosophy, especially Aristotle's treatise on the soul (*De Anima*), which established the tradition and set the terms of medieval and modern psychology.

The story of Renaissance psychology, based largely on interpretations of Aristotle, is enormously complex. But the basic theory was that ideas were formed from sense impressions ("fantasms"), according to the assumption that nothing existed in the mind that was not previously in the sense (*nihil in intellectu quod non prius in sensu*).[8] The mind consisted of the faculties of reason, will, memory, and imagination; of these, at least for most philosophers, reason was the governing power. One of the results of humanism, however, was to question this conventional hierarchy and especially the primacy of reason. As humanists challenged the hegemony of philosophy and asserted the parity or even superiority of the liberal arts in the "encyclopedia" of learning, so they argued for the emotional integrity of the mind and its various aspects. Boccaccio's identification of poetry and philosophy, and Valla's assertion of the superior value of rhetoric and history to formal philosophy, implied a significant elevation of the faculties, respectively, of imagination, memory, and will—and their integration into the equally encyclopedic Renaissance ideal of the *uomo universale*.

The view of moral philosophy as a practical rather than a theoretical discipline, associated with all dimensions of humanity, was the message of Valla's work, and so it was for Valla's admiring disciple Erasmus. Rejecting Scholastic ethics and what he regarded as the hypocritical abstinence of monkery (which Valla had also denounced), Erasmus proposed a "philosophy of Christ" that was founded on the ideals—or at least Erasmus' idealizations—of the primitive Church.[9] These moral ideals were carried over into his ecclesiastical, social, and political criticism, including his attacks on papal corruption, contemporary monasticism, and the institution of war. Individual enlightenment and moral purity were for Erasmus the basis for reform at all levels of society.

Debates over moral philosophy were pursued in the age of the Reformation along all the traditional lines, especially Stoicism, which enjoyed a "renaissance" in the later sixteenth century, particularly in the work of Justus Lipsius and Guillaume du Vair, who sought consolation from the troubles of their age in "constancy" and other Stoic virtues. In that period, the discussion of moral philosophy was enriched and enlivened by another approach that reinforced humanist attitudes. This was the skeptical philosophy, reinforced and intensified in this period by Pyrrhonism, represented by the work of Sextus Empiricus, first published in 1562. The radical questioning not only of conventional knowledge but more fundamentally of the very possibility of knowledge sent skeptics back to practical experience, however limited and remote from the ideals of science and certainty.

The first great representative of Pyrrhonism, Michel de Montaigne, cultivated moral philosophy in both its psychological and its ethical dimensions. Psychologically, Montaigne turned back to the Petrarchian model of self-examination and withdrawal from the storm and stress of public life—although like Petrarch, Montaigne had been involved in and frustrated by political action. His lifework was the search not for Man in the abstract but for his own essential *Moi*, its immediate habitat, and its placement with respect to the rest of humanity and to history. As a "subject," he was a literary rather than a psychological construction. "I myself am the matter of my book," he wrote of his *Essays*.[10] "I hold that I exist only in myself; and as for that other life of mine that lies in the knowledge of my friends . . . , I know very well that I feel no fruit or enjoyment from it except by the vanity of a fanciful opinion." Again, "I would rather be an authority on myself than on Cicero." Like Petrarch, Montaigne subordinated natural philosophy to this human subject. "We entangle our thoughts in generalities and the causes and conduct of the universe, which conduct themselves very well without us, and we leave behind our own affairs, and Michel, who concerns us even more closely than man in general."[11]

Yet Montaigne's pursuit of self-knowledge did go beyond the private sphere to encompass not only the classical past but also the "new horizons of the Renaissance." His skeptical philosophy was given a further human dimension by his growing awareness of the enormous range of human behavior and social customs reported by historians and especially by travel accounts of the New World, which by implication enormously expanded moral philosophy. For Montaigne, an understanding of his species was to be attained not by speculations about a generalized human nature but only by a particularized investigation of a human "second nature"—which was to say, of the "habits" and "customs" that proverbially expressed that "second nature" in particular cultural contexts. Because of human imperfection and variability, Montaigne concluded, "to judge a man really properly, we must chiefly examine his ordinary actions and surprise him in his everyday habitat."[12]

The study of *coutume*, then, was the true path to an understanding of the human condition and to wisdom. "So many humors, sects, judgments, opinions, laws, and customs teach us to judge sanely of our own," Montaigne wrote, "and teach our judgment to recognize its own imperfection and natural weakness, which is no small lesson."[13] "It is for custom to give form to our life, just as it pleases; it is all-powerful in that; it is Circe's drink, which varies our nature as it sees fit." Custom was truly—in the words of Pindar, cited by Montaigne, Bacon, Hume, and many others—"the mistress of life," as, according to the famous Ciceronian formula, was history.

For Montaigne, then, skepticism and the pursuit of self-knowledge reinforced both the humanist appreciation of the faculties of memory and imagination and the humanist "turn" away from a hypostasized, essentialist Aristotelian or Stoic "Nature" to the local knowledge and cultural relativism associated with the investigation of "second nature."[14] In the context of the liberal arts and especially of moral philosophy, humanism in its extended forms laid the foundations for the modern sciences of humanity. This has never been more forcefully expressed than in the motto made famous by Pope but derived ultimately from Montaigne's fellow Pyrrhonist, Pierre Charron: "The true science and study of man is man himself."

## The Creative Arts

In the Renaissance, and especially in the context of the humanist movement, "art" (*ars, techne*) was an extraordinarily rich and suggestive term, representing an alternative and a rival to "nature" itself—Nature herself.[15] An "artist" (*artista*) could be a practitioner of the mechanical and the "fine" as well as the liberal arts, but in any case he was potentially a creator, in the context of humanist aspirations, not unlike God Himself. Beyond the circle of the *studia humanitatis*, the fine arts, linked by their common source in "design" and later by the philosophical field of aesthetics (formulated in the eighteenth century), included painting, sculpture, architecture, music, and in its "aesthetic" rather than its liberal role, poetry. All of these were represented, though more confusingly, by the nine muses of classical mythology, daughters of Jupiter and Mnemosyne (memory). In certain ways, the creative arts overlapped with the liberal arts (since poetry was included, along with music, painting, sculpture, and architecture, among the five "major arts") and with the "mechanical arts"—a classification that included architecture, music, and theater as well as more humdrum fields of agriculture, navigation, practical medicine, and the artisanal crafts and lower professions organized into guilds. For Polydore Vergil, even painting was still grouped with pottery and clay-working.[16]

Along with the more prosaic humanities, the "chorus of muses" was awakened in the age of Dante and Petrarch after having been "buried" for many centuries, as Vasari wrote, largely as the result of religious zeal and obscurantism. This ushered in the new golden age perceived by Valla, Ficino, Erasmus, and others. Valla marveled that "those arts which are most closely related to the liberal arts, the arts of painting, sculpture, modeling, and architecture . . . have been aroused and come to life again."[17] In similar terms, Ficino celebrated the simultaneous revival of liberal and fine arts, including music, as in the next century did Louis Le Roy.[18] The theme was carried on by practicing artists like Alberti and Vasari, who celebrated this renaissance and the progress toward the "high perfection" of the sixteenth century.[19] Following the lead of Bruni's explanation of Guelf cultural achievement, Vasari also pointed out the "civic" aspect of the fine arts—their support by and contributions to communal society and government—after their revival on Tuscan soil "towards 1250" and their development toward "perfection."

In painting, the counterparts of Dante and Petrarch were Cimabue and Giotto, who cast aside the old "Greek" (that is, Byzantine) mode for a newer and more natural style. In the work of Giotto and especially of his Florentine successors of the fifteenth century, *pictura* depicted not only classical figures, restored to their ancient properties, but also the richness, complexity, glory, and tragedy of modern life. At least in theory, it was reintegrated into the "encyclopedia" of classical arts and sciences. Painting had connections with poetry and especially rhetoric (*ut pictura poesis* was one topos, as we have seen, and *ut pictura rhetorica* another), since it likewise depended on narrative, "composition," and "history" (referring to the theme of the work), had intellectual content—painting more than sculpture, as Piero della Francesca remarked—and proposed to "teach, please, and move." And (as Michael Baxandall has shown) through observation, comparison, aesthetic theory, and the development of a vocabulary of description and analysis, the links between painting and rhetoric became even closer in the fifteenth and sixteenth centuries.[20]

Architecture, too, aspired to the status of a liberal art. Renaissance architecture was based on "natural" principles, but like literature, it was imitative and legitimized by classical authority, especially after the fifteenth-century "discovery" of Vitruvius' *On Architecture*, which became one of the major sources for the Renaissance idea of "encyclopedia." The Architect was not a carpenter or a joiner but "in Dignity not inferior to the most excellent," exalted Alberti. He was "the master of a true science, who, by a sure and wonderful Art and Method, is able, both with thought and invention to devise [works that can], with the greatest Beauty, be adapted to the uses of Mankind."[21] Citing Thucydides, Alberti also praised the use of impressive structures to magnify the "power" of states and to immortalize the rulers who endowed such projects. In general it was not fire or water but the creations of Architecture that represented the root of the civic principle—"the chief causes of assembling men together," first in families and then political communities—and the fulfillment of the utopian vision of the ideal City.

Renaissance art, especially painting, established a bridge between the divine and the human since the artist repeated the divine creative activity by the "imitation" of Nature herself as well as earlier masters and classical style. Yet as in the cases of poetry and rhetoric, such imitation (*mimesis*) was not to be literal or "mechanical." Rather, it was to be an effort that, though grounded in nature and conventional mastery of artistic skills, was an expression of artistic "genius" (*ingenium*) and so of novelty and originality. In this way painting and its sister arts were able to claim a more exalted, "liberal," and even "philosophical" condition, as Leonardo—though not himself a man of learning—argued. In this way, too, the artist was able to lay claim to some participation in the ideal of the universal man of the Renaissance.

The art of music—etymologically, at least, the most direct representative of the "muses"—displayed similar, and in some ways even larger, ambitions. It too had close ties with rhetoric (*musica rhetorica*), and indeed it followed this topic in Polydore Vergil's encyclopedia.[22] Music—like painting, suspended between "imitation" and "invention"—also made contributions to communal, ecclesiastical, and courtly society, and likewise, by virtue of its associations with the mechanical ("performing") arts, it was largely excluded from the formal *Studium* of learning (although formally it was a part of the *quadrivium*). Yet the art of music had encyclopedic claims, and the musical artist was encouraged to be poet and composer as well as performer. Moreover, especially because of associations with Neoplatonic and Neopythagorean thought, the art of music claimed parity even with philosophy. Socrates himself, argued Franchino Gaffurio in his *Musical Theory* of 1492, had taken up the lyre in his later years. Finally, as the visual arts had important theoretical relations with "natural" and scientific disciplines (optics and geometry), so music, through the laws of harmony, had links with mathematics, astronomy, and even political philosophy (the concept of "harmonic justice"), thus adding further to the coherence and integrity of the humanist "encyclopedia."

The end-product of this escalation of the status of these creative disciplines, it may be added in conclusion, was the emergence of (capital-A) Art, to sit beside (capital-C) Criticism (as well as [capital-H] Humanism) as creations of Renaissance humanism.[23] In a sense, it was the rhetoric and poetry of Renaissance humanism that created what Kristeller has called "the modern system of the arts"—the "fine arts"—as well as the modern discipline of aesthetics, which raised the faculty of imagination to at least the level of memory and reason and in this way emphasized the creative force and psychological integrity of humanity.

## Encyclopedia

During the long career of Renaissance humanism, the five disciplines comprising the *studia humanitatis* underwent many permutations and combinations, many interconnections and associations with other fields of learning—including law, theology, and philosophy and its various branches. In general, the tendency of humanism was to shift away from the elementary *artes* back to the standard—that is, classical—*auctores*, and thus toward an interdisciplinary orientation, neglectful of academic boundaries and methods. This was the thrust of the postmedieval idea of that elegant "circle" of arts and sciences celebrated as the "encyclopedia," which fashioned its own methods, values, and goals and swept other branches of knowledge into its orbit.

In general, as has been suggested, the humanists rejected the hierarchical structure of the medieval *Studium,* in which theology, and in its company philosophy, had enjoyed an intellectual hegemony, challenged only by the other professional fields, law and medicine. Yet the humanities, often disregarding disciplinary boundaries, displayed their own sort of imperialism, each of them presuming in effect to subsume or to absorb the other branches of knowledge in its quest for independence, or primacy. Grammar was capable of being expanded into a universal sort of "Criticism"; rhetoric established the study of language and communication as a sort of first philosophy; history represented itself as the source and vehicle of the other arts; poetry, as another and perhaps more fundamental theology or philosophy, claimed special insight into God's creation; and moral philosophy, asserting jurisdiction over law and political science as well as ethics, established itself as the governing discipline of human life on earth and a prototype of modern social science. Nor did any of them, in pursuit of their special goals and claims to represent the highest ideals of humanity, hesitate to call upon the auxiliary services of their sister arts.

Although it was based in the *studia humanitatis,* in short, Renaissance humanism did not hesitate to explore the furthest reaches of the encyclopedia. Despite the centuries-long war between rhetoric and philosophy, humanists did turn back to Platonic and Aristotelian doctrines, especially in the effort to understand them correctly—"historically"—and to provide proper Latin translations from the Greek and later to provide vernacular translations from both classical languages. This was done for Aristotle—at least his "practical" philosophy—by Bruni and for Plato by Ficino. The advent of printing had encouraged translations of all the major and most of the minor Western philosophers by the end of the sixteenth century.[24] The Latin translation of Sextus Empiricus, the locus classicus of ancient skepticism and the inspiration for modern skepticism, was one of the last of these publications (*Outlines of Pyrrhonism* first appeared in 1562). The translation of Diogenes Laertius' *Lives of the Philosophers* (by Ambrogio Traversari, around 1435) promoted the study of the history of philosophy, which became a significant literary genre from the sixteenth century onward. Indeed, it was the history of philosophical thought since the time of the "barbarians" (as Diogenes Laertius called the Near Eastern nations) and the pre-Socratics, rather than academic projects of philosophizing, that attracted humanist scholars and critics.

The connections between humanism and the science of law were extremely close; for Roman law, as Walter Ullmann wrote, "was perhaps the strongest bond holding together the ancient, medieval and modern worlds."[25] Salutati's view of the legal tradition illustrates the assumptions not only of "civic humanism" but also of professional "civil science." As he wrote, "The subject of legal science is the civic work of men directed by the laws relating to the laws and ordering human society." Moreover, civil law was itself a liberal art (*studium liberale*), according to Andrea Alciato, one of the founders of humanist jurisprudence, and more specifically a part of moral philosophy.[26] While denouncing the mercenary attitudes of the legal profession and faculties of law, Petrarch had praised the ancient Roman lawyers—"fathers of jurisprudence," he called them—as part of classical literature, and so, more self-consciously, had Valla. For Valla, civil law was a "golden science" (*aurea disciplina*) enjoying the closest ties with the master discipline of rhetoric, and he began the critical study of the canonic texts of Roman law gathered in Justinian's *Digest*. Following his and Poliziano's lead, Budé continued these scholarly efforts of "legal humanism," setting out to do for the *Digest* what, contemporaneously and also under Valla's influence, his colleague Erasmus was doing for the Bible.

A distinction must be made here between the literary study of legal sources, represented by Valla, Poliziano, and Budé, and professional scholars of the law, such as Alciato and Jacques Cujas, who worked within the conventions of "civil science," as the modern jurisprudence of civil law was called. Here, too, humanism had its impact. Alciato in particular claimed to be "the first in a thousand years to teach civil law in a Latin manner." The "method" developed by his French students at the University of Bourges, drawing on the disciplines of history, literature, and philosophy, extended and systematized Alciato's humanistic approach, but without departing from the standards of the legal profession. The aim of these humanist practitioners of the "French method of teaching law" (*mos gallicus juris docendi*) was to recover the form as well as the literary substance of the legal tradition with reference to the goals not merely of historical truth and philosophical consistency but also of human "justice," the art and science of which civil law claimed to be. From this point of view, civil science could itself aspire to be a version of the "encyclopedia" and to subsume the other arts and sciences, including the liberal arts, philosophy, and even theology.

Medicine had no less complex relations with the humanities. It was both science and art, both "a system of explanation and a set of techniques," as Nancy Siraisi writes, and as such it had ties with the "mechanical arts" and with the higher sciences.[27] Not only both art and science, it was also a "second philosophy," according to Isidore of Seville—indeed, "the philosophy of the body," and as such an integral part of Renaissance "anthropology." Yet medical theory, disputed by followers of Aristotle and of Galen, had associations with Greek and, what was worse, Arabic natural philosophy, especially at the University of Padua, and it developed dangerous attitudes that separated man's "physical" nature from his "moral" nature. From Petrarch to Salutati, humanists criticized the materialistic and mechanistic tendencies of medicine and resisted its recognition as a truly liberal study.

In general, the relationship between humanism and science was ambivalent and problematical. From the beginning humanists, in contrast to Dante, had displayed a deep prejudice against natural philosophy, associating it with inhuman ideas of naturalism, determinism, mechanism, and astrology, and especially with the degenerate version of Aristotle constructed by Scholastic and Averroist interpreters.[28] Inspired both by Augustinian and by Platonic attitudes, Petrarch made his own "Socratic revolution": he turned away from the study of nature—"the vast floods of the seas, the huge streams of the rivers, the circumference of the oceans, and the revolutions of the stars," in the words of Augustine that so moved him during his ascent of Mount Ventoux—and focused instead on self-knowledge. Humanists such as Pico, Poliziano, and Lefèvre d'Etaples did study natural philosophy, but in terms of method the investigations of Paduan Aristotelians, Oxford nominalists, and Parisian *calculatores* seemed an affront to humanist conceptions of language, cultural values, and social awareness. On such grounds Salutati had criticized the narrowness of medicine and Pico the presumptions of astrology, and such prejudices continued to inform the work of Renaissance rhetoricians and philologists.

Yet in other respects, humanist scholarship made important contributions to modern natural science. The first and most fundamental contribution was the publication and translation of classical texts, such as those of Lucretius, Pliny, and Vitruvius, but especially the works of such Greek authors as Euclid, Archimedes, Hippocrates, Galen, Ptolemy, Theophrastus, and of course Aristotle—the "historical" Aristotle—himself. Platonism not only emphasized the conceptual power of mathematics in the understanding of nature but also gave a privileged place to the sun, which contributed at least to the rhetoric of the heliocentric ideas of Copernicus, Kepler, and Galileo. Humanist attitudes placed emphasis, too, on the value of particular experience. The importance of the rhetorical tradition for Baconian "method" has long been recognized, especially its insistence on calling things by their right names and on finding a language that was nontechnical yet faithful to nature. In such ways humanism, which began with an inward turn, looked once more to the world of nature, and so God's creation assumed once again a position in the "encyclopedia" of Renaissance learning.

Magic and the occult tradition had links with humanism as well as with philosophy, science, and art.[29] Like science in the seventeenth century, magic, natural and supernatural, promised insights into and perhaps control over the environment in ways that might be reconcilable with philosophy but went beyond what orthodox religion was prepared to tolerate. As one recent scholar remarks, "occult philosophy is not so much the opposite of the humanism of Petrarch and Erasmus as it is the radical extension of certain humanist attitudes."[30] Still more radical were the conceptions of admirers of Neoplatonic, Hermetic, and Cabalistic philosophy like Ficino and Pico, for whom magic—"the noblest of the arts," as Ficino called it—was a sign not only of immortality but also of the creative, indeed godlike, power of man (reflected also in poetry and art). Establishing a connection between humanity and divinity, microcosm and macrocosm, flesh and spirit, occult philosophy extended Renaissance anthropology from the natural into the supernatural realm.

The intersection between humanism and theology came above all in the biblical scholarship of Valla and Erasmus and in the "Christian philosophy" attendant on their critical attitudes. Protestant fundamentalism represented a radicalization of Christian humanism, insisting on a "historical" interpretation of Scripture but shifting emphasis from the "learned piety" of Erasmus and the simple "imitation of Christ" to technical issues of Christological and soteriological doctrine. Luther, Zwingli, and Calvin were all "Christian humanists" in a sense, and they carried on the ideals of Renaissance pedagogy; yet their concerns, values, and goals far transcended the "Renaissance philosophy of man" and the cultural and social questions pursued by humanists.[31] Protestantism was both an extension and a violation of Renaissance humanism as represented by Petrarch, Valla, and Erasmus, and despite the continued reliance of Protestant scholars on the new science of philology, the confessional controversies and religious wars in the wake of the Reformation illustrated this fundamental divergence.

Out of the "encyclopedia" ideal of Renaissance humanism came not only a concept of the interconnections of the arts and sciences and of human society based on this ideal but also a vision of and even a theory of cultural history. Implied in the work of Valla, Erasmus, Budé, and other philologists, this ideal received comprehensive (if often commonplace) expression in educational writings, especially Vives's treatise on *The Transmission of Knowledge* (1531), which among other things provides a useful summary of the Christian humanist view of the evolution of humanity. Vives began not with creation but with the gradual emergence of humanity from a natural to a social condition. "We men are born for society," declared Vives, invoking the Aristotelian topos of man as a "political animal." This transition was accomplished by the devising of the "mechanical arts," by the social organization beyond the family, and above all by speech, the most fundamental of all civilizing forces, "for it is a bond which holds society together as well as a way for minds to reveal themselves." Giving things their proper names is the most essential of all human offices, and so "the first thing man has to learn is speech."[32]

For Vives, the civilizing process was not only a result of the "translation of studies"; it was also a recapitulation, on a macrocosmic level, of individual development. It was founded on the twofold power of the mind—experience or observation (or history), and judgment or reason (or philosophy)—and its basic mechanism was the practice and theory of "imitation." Being concerned with educational psychology and the "institution" of learning, Vives naturally described cultural history according to the conventional classification of knowledge—the *studia humanitatis* and their extensions into what he called the "higher studies." Beyond grammar and rhetoric, Vives recognized the more sophisticated field of "philology," especially as pursued by the moderns. "Francis Petrarch, little more than two hundred years ago," Vives repeated, "first opened up the closed libraries and shook the dust and dirt off the works of the greatest writers," and he was followed by scholars such as Bruni, Valla, Barbaro, Poliziano, Pico, Erasmus, Budé, Alciato, and Melanchthon.[33] In language study there had also been a movement from art to science, as reflected in the emergence of theoretical and historical linguistics (*ratio linguarum*), but the aim of study remained practical—to achieve the good, and of course the pious, life. Each of the arts and sciences, Vives insisted (in good Aristotelian fashion), was defined by its particular purpose; the purpose of the "encyclopedia"—and of civilization—as a whole was wisdom (*sapientia*).

From the Renaissance to the Enlightenment, the "encyclopedic" tradition of Renaissance humanism was preserved in classical philology, in histories of learning and "philosophy," and in the systems devised by "polyhistors" (as Vives had also called them), but it received its most comprehensive expression in the "new science" of

Giambattista Vico. His work was designed in part to repair the damage to and the neglect of the old "encyclopedia" that Descartes had encouraged. Vico's ambitions were already apparent in his early oration devoted to the correct method of study (which represented his turn back from Cartesianism to Renaissance humanism), the principle of "authority," and the faculties of memory and imagination (virtually identical for Vico) that this entailed. "In the past," Vico declared, "all arts and disciplines were interconnected and rested in the lap of philosophy; subsequently, they were sundered apart." His own solution was this: "I would suggest that all our professors should co-ordinate all disciplines into a single system so as to harmonize them with our religion and with the spirit of the political form under which we live. In this way, a coherent body of learning having been established, it will be possible to teach it according to the genius of our public polity."[34]

If Vico began his search for a "new science" by ransacking and revising the humanist "encyclopedia," he ended by transmuting it, even more radically than Vives had done, into historical terms. For Vico, "philology" was the first form his *nova scientia* took, and "wisdom" in general (Vives's *sapientia*), corresponding to the most rudimentary form of philosophy, was identified with stages of cultural development: poetic, heroic, and civilized. Most fundamental— since the "nature" of things was defined by their origins—was the first stage, and to analyze this "poetic wisdom," Vico drew on Renaissance ideas of the philosophical and theological dimensions of the art of poetry. He turned in particular to the oldest of philological and historical questions, the study of the Homeric poems.[35] What Vico did with the old *Studium* goes far beyond the limits of this discussion; suffice it to conclude that, in its premises if not in its final speculative form, Vico's "new science" represented at once a summation and a radical historicization of the "encyclopedic" vision of Renaissance humanism.

In the early eighteenth century, Vico was in many ways out of fashion. By then, the Renaissance notion of "encyclopedia" had been transformed mightily by the revolution of modern natural science, and by the end of the century this intellectual movement had become a new orthodoxy. This eclipse is illustrated by Condorcet's famous survey of the "progress of the human spirit" down to his own day (1794), in which the period of Renaissance humanism is relegated to a pre-enlightened age "from the invention of printing to the time when the sciences and philosophy threw off the yoke of authority."[36] Condorcet acknowledged the educational advances in this, the eighth period of "progress," culminating in his own age "from Descartes to the foundation of the French Republic" and characterized by the perfection of mathematics and natural philosophy and social improvement on this scientific basis. But although "reason, toleration, humanity" was Condorcet's motto, he had little to say about the value of "good letters" or the contributions of civic humanism. Despite the "perfection" attained by literature and the visual arts in the Renaissance, that age was innocent even of political economy, and before Descartes showed the way, human science (*la science de la morale*) could not yet exist.

Yet it should be remembered that humanists like Le Roy accommodated something like Condorcet's idea of modern progress in their agenda. "Besides the restoration of ancient learning, now almost complete," wrote Le Roy, "the invention of many new things . . . has been reserved to this age." He invoked here the printing-compass-gunpowder topos that Bacon later took up.[37] Echoes of the humanist view can be heard not only in Bacon's celebration of the "advancement of learning" but also among the *philosophes*. The eighteenth-century *Encyclopédie* was, as D'Alembert wrote in his *Preliminary Discourse,* "a reasoned dictionary of the sciences, arts, and trades," incorporating and extending not only the old medieval *Studium* but the humanist circle of disciplines and much of the accompanying rhetoric. For D'Alembert, these arts and sciences were "mutually supporting" with "a chain that binds them together."[38] Writing for the *Encyclopaedia Britannica* in 1815, Dugald Stewart took a more sympathetic view of learning "from the Revival of Letters to the publication of Bacon's Philosophical Works," as befitted a more empirical-minded scholar, and he pointed in particular to the anti-Aristotelianism of Valla and other humanists and to the importance of linguistic studies.[39] Stewart, too, however, looked to natural philosophy—to Baconian method, Newtonian science, Lockean psychology, and the new discipline of political economy—to restore the integrity of the "encyclopedia" and to place it more comprehensively, scientifically, and practically in the service of humanity.

The "encyclopedia" of the eighteenth century, then, was modernized in many ways. As Diderot wrote, "the aim of an *encyclopedia* is to collect all the knowledge scattered over the face of the earth, to present its general outlines and structure to the men with whom we live, and to transmit this to those who will come after us, so that the work of past centuries may be useful to the following centuries, that our children, by becoming more educated, may at the same time become virtuous and happier, and that we may not die without having deserved well of the human race." But while such an "encyclopedia" was impossible before an age of true "philosophy," historians may recognize in such rhetoric several general themes of earlier defenses of the "encyclopedia": the methodological organization of knowledge, derived in part from past centuries, employed to educate, to achieve "virtue," and to benefit future generations of humanity.

*Humanitas* (a classical abstraction), *Humanität, l'Humanité* (the vernacularized Enlightenment motto), *Humanismus* (an early nineteenth-century coinage)—these terms all express the underlying unity of the movement that took specific historical form as "Renaissance humanism" and that would survive in various ways in modern scholarship, philosophy, and the so-called human sciences. A brief word needs to be said about this afterlife and in general the legacy of humanism.

## Posthumanism

Two sorts of "humanism" have been considered in this book. One refers to the study of the humanities, the *studia humanitatis,* and the other to the study of humanity, *humanitas,* itself; both indeed are relevant to an understanding of that cultural phenomenon located in the Renaissance. However, it will not do to take the humanist movement at its own rhetorical estimate, for in fact there is, as has been suggested, a negative and as it were antihumanistic and uncivil side to the story that should not be overlooked. Within the humanist movement itself there was a perpetual tension between the call of Cicero and that of Christ, between classical exaltation of human freedom and creativity and Christian awareness of sin and evil, between the song of life and the dance of death. Not only the "dignity of man" but also the "misery of the human condition," whether expressed or not, was an integral part of Renaissance anthropology. As Montaigne recalled (from Cicero), "To philosophize is to learn to die," and as he added from personal conviction, "Our religion has no surer foundation than contempt for life." Related to this were the various forms of self-doubt, ranging from religious questioning of the power of human reason in a "fallen" condition and Cusanus' paradox of "learned ignorance" to radical doubt deriving from classical skeptical and Pyrrhonist sources. Humanist disinterment of ancient philosophy led not only to misgivings about the presumptions of metaphysics and theology but also to extremes of self-doubt and the beginnings of critical philosophy.

Nor was the classical "encyclopedia" as stable as some humanists pretended. Within the liberal arts there had already been a division, and the "quadrivial" disciplines remained in some ways alienated from the five traditional humanities. This duality was expressed on a higher level as a distinction between "natural" and "moral" philosophy—a distinction that still pertained in the eighteenth and nineteenth centuries. Most fundamentally, this separation could be resolved into the difference between a linguistic and a quantitative approach to understanding. The upshot of this can be seen in Galileo's hybrid conception of a "mathematical philosophy," his rejection of literary authority and of historians as "memory-experts" wholly innocent of a true philosophy, and his desire to read the "book of nature" in terms of number and geometrical figures. It can been seen, too, in Bacon's marginalizing of the faculty of imagination and Descartes's wholesale rejection of the faculty of memory as irrelevant to philosophical method—as well as in the general inclination to promote natural-science models in all areas of inquiry. As a result, "Nature" (formerly a goddess) has come to be mistaken for reality, when in fact it represents a marvelously rich and often contradictory tradition of human interpretation.

Most essential to Renaissance humanism in the restricted sense, perhaps, was the linguistic turn that it took, first inadvertently by proclaiming the primacy of *litterae* and then, more deliberately, by elevating rhetoric above philosophy, as in the work of Valla. The result of this was to cast suspicion and then to undermine critically the presumptions of formal philosophy and rational theology by emphasizing literal meaning over figurative interpretations and the inability of human language to express transcendental and spiritual categories and experience. Later the semantic suspicions of humanism were turned on itself, and the presumptions of rhetoric, too, were subjected to linguistic and skeptical criticism, as in the reflections of Montaigne. The seventeenth-century impulse toward mathematical philosophy and "universal grammar" opposed the conventionalist and relativistic implications of this linguistic turn, which had emphasized historical and philological specificity, and encouraged the reception of the methods of the "new philosophy that calls all into doubt" into the human sciences.

Yet despite the intellectual imperialism of natural science, the humanist tradition preserved at least a tenuous tradition down to the present. This is not the place to tell the story of the afterlives of "humanism," preserved by reading and misreading, by appropriation and misappropriation, ranging between the usual positive and negative poles (the "integral humanism" of Jacques Maritain, for example, the philosophical humanism of F.S.C. Schiller, and the "secular humanism" of fundamentalist critics). But a few concluding remarks may be in order. The spirit of humanism can still be detected—and is evoked—in a number of contemporary schools of thought, including phenomenology, especially in its existentialist form, in modern hermeneutics, in philosophical "anthropology," and in the so-called "new rhetoric." In the wake of the "linguistic turn" of our own century, twentieth-century humanists have, following the ancient path of the sophists and philologists like Valla and Vico, called for an end to naïve conceptualizing, for a critical awareness of the role of language in philosophy, and for some philosophical parity between the theoretically formulated world of Nature and the practical "lifeworld" of Second Nature.

The "new rhetoric" of Chaim Perelman and L. Obrechts-Tyteca seeks to return to this tradition most directly. Their work constitutes, they argue, a *"break with a concept of reason and reasoning due to Descartes* which has set its mark on Western philosophy for the last three centuries."[40] In direct contrast to Cartesian method, the new rhetoric emphasizes the probable, persuasive, historical, and local nature of human discourse, and social considerations of action, exchange, communication, judgment, and human values. Most crucial of all is the formative role of the audience, long recognized in the humanist tradition; and in this connection the authors cite the remark of Vico that "the end sought by eloquence always depends on the speaker's audience, and he must govern his speech in accordance with their opinions."

A different and more philosophical approach to the rehabilitation of humanism is suggested by the work of Hans-Georg Gadamer, who, in his treatise on *Truth and Method*, has emphasized what he refers to as "the significance of the humanist tradition for the human sciences."[41] Here Gadamer considers "humanism" in its larger signification and points in particular to four central concepts, all of which are related to the faculty of imagination and the discipline of aesthetics, which have risen in value in the company of the liberal and the fine arts.

The first is the foundational idea of "culture" or education in the sense of mental development or progress toward an ideal— *paideia* and *institutio* might be humanist equivalents of Gadamer's *Bildung*. This process, displaying a trajectory through memory and imagination to more universal and rational formulations, is based not on mathematics but, as Gadamer insists, on "humanistic studies," and the application of scientific methods to this arena could only, for "truth and method," be "self-annihilation." Second is the notion of "common sense"—the *sensus communis* of the ancient Romans as interpreted by Vico, other humanists, and nineteenth-century Romantics and members of the historical schools—which also is opposed to a universal and metahuman and metahistorical concept of reason. Indeed "common sense," as Gadamer suggests, calls up the old humanist linguistic and rhetorical ideal of *eloquentia* and again depends on the faculty of memory (which for Vico is virtually identical with imagination), aiming not at theoretical but at practical, human, historical, communal, and "local" knowledge (*prudentia* and *phronesis*). "For their object," as Gadamer says of the methods of the human sciences, "the moral and historical existence of man, as that takes shape in his activities, is itself largely determined by the sensus communis." Third is the concept of "judgment," or conclusions drawn on the basis of "good sense," which is the human condition of understanding also entailing "prejudgment"—"prejudice" (*praejudicium*)—in the sense of common assumption and language to make communication possible.[42] In the humanist tradition, such judgment, again, is not associated exclusively with "pure reason" or regarded as subordinate to it, as in the critiques of Kant, who in contrast to Vico, as Gadamer points out, had no use for "common sense." Rather, it leads to the fourth concept, which is the aesthetic and moral idea of "taste." From the eighteenth century onward, according to Gadamer, aesthetics emerged as the master discipline of the humanist tradition—and its chief modern progeny is modern "historicism" and philosophical hermeneutics.

Obviously, Gadamer's discussion represents not so much a historical explanation as an exercise in philosophical canon-formation, with Renaissance humanists replacing academic philosophers and Vico replacing Descartes as the spokesmen for "truth and method."

Yet this is not, ultimately, the way a history of ideas is formed. In this humanly created perspective, Renaissance humanism is linked not merely with its chroniclers and historians—Kristeller, Baron, Garin, and their many students—but also with such modern investigators of the human sciences as Wilhelm Dilthey, Benedetto Croce, Ernst Cassirer, and Gadamer himself, as well as modern practitioners of hermeneutics, philosophical anthropology, "interpretive social science," the aforementioned "new rhetoric," and perhaps people who write books like this one.

But as usual there is a negative side to this posthumous story, and it has to do with a fundamental issue about the contemporary human predicament. Certain schools of modern philosophy—among them "humanist Marxism," Edmund Husserl's phenomenology, and French existentialism—have tried to keep alive the ideals of Renaissance humanism as they are commonly understood. It was in this spirit, for example, that Jean-Paul Sartre represented his existential philosophy, which seemed to reproduce in modern terms the image of the godlike and absolutely free "chameleon" man celebrated in Pico's *Oration on the Dignity of Man*. Following the famous formula wrenched and vulgarized from Martin Heidegger's *Being and Time*—"existence precedes essence"—Sartre argued for the essential and metaphysical principle of human liberty, for the universality of the human condition (if not of human nature), and in effect for the corollary that existentialism was essentially a "humanism."[43]

Such naïve or doctrinaire efforts have not gone unchallenged and indeed have been seriously undermined by more recent criticisms based on a sort of critical "antihumanism." It was in response to Sartre's popular and literary proclamations, for example, that Heidegger issued his famous countermanifesto, his "Letter on Humanism," protesting that "existentialism is not a humanism."[44] By this, Heidegger meant to explain that his own existentialism was a philosophy of "being and time" and not just another "metaphysical" definition of the "nature" of man; and in the sense that it avoided talk of essences and human nature, Heidegger's position was nominally "antihumanistic." It has certainly contributed to the contemporary "rage against reason" and the assault on the "subject" that have been pursued by Michel Foucault, Jacques Derrida, and other (especially French) students and deconstructive critics of the human sciences.

Yet Heidegger, who was one of Gadamer's teachers, had made his own—linguistic and aesthetic—"turn" away from metaphysics toward poetry and language, particularly ancient Greek. In this sense, his quest for being seems quite in keeping with the deeper aspirations of Renaissance humanists. Montaigne also opposed metaphysics ("Philosophy is an empty and fantastic name") and an essentialist view of humanity. "Others form man," he wrote; "I expose him, and portray a particular one, whom I should make very different from what he is if I had to fashion him all over again."[45] In keeping with Heidegger's "turn," too, is the humanist attitude toward the art of poetry, that "other philosophy" (*altera philosophia*) and "theology of the world" (*theologia mundi*). So indeed Ernest Grassi, admirer of Vico and Heidegger's former student who was the first publisher of the "Letter on Humanism," has argued in two books devoted to the subject of "Renaissance humanism." In its drive to scientific status and in its self-preoccupation, philosophy has forgotten being, while history, philology, and above all poetry continue to search for meaning. To humanity and the human sciences, metaphysics offers only closure, while, as Grassi puts it—and as so many Renaissance humanists devoutly believed—"the muses 'open' the cosmos."[46]

In the final analysis, or at least in a current perspective, "humanism" may seem today a shelter for elitist conceptions that are difficult to maintain at the end of the second millennium of the modern era (as Petrarch no doubt would locate us historically). The indulgent privatism of Petrarch, the poetic fervor of Boccaccio, and the optimistic civism of Bruni hardly seem suited for what some have called the "posthumanist" world emerging as we approach the year 2000. In an age of exploding demographic growth, rampant technology, and runaway consumer culture, conventional "humanist" scholarship and education may well seem irrelevant and unworthy of the sort of patronage they attracted in former centuries. Yet the larger lessons of the humanist tradition, such as recalling what the "proper study of mankind" really is, still need reaffirming. Whether or not "the Italian Renaissance must be called the leader of modern ages," as Burckhardt concluded his book,[47] it does seem worthwhile to review some of the accumulated wisdom—private, public, and scientific—as well as some of the darker lessons that have been drawn, expressed, and transmitted by Renaissance humanism.

# Document and Commentary

Lorenzo Valla's *Elegantiae Latinae linguae libri sex* (*Elegances of the Latin Language*), written in 1444, less than a decade before the "invention" of printing, became one of the most influential and most frequently reprinted books during the first century of the new medium. An introduction to classical Latin grammar and correct style, the work displayed the two fundamental aspects both of Valla's own program and of Renaissance humanism in general: philology, the critical study of language and literary texts, and rhetoric, the theory and practice of persuasive discourse essential to civic life. The first of these was aimed at recovering the lost or forgotten culture of antiquity through the reading and historical understanding of its literary monuments; the second was the application of this knowledge to the conditions and challenges of modern society. Taken together, they defined the program of the *studia humanitatis* of Petrarch and his followers and especially its culmination in the scientific and professional formulation of this tradition in the work of Valla.

What follows is an extract from the preface to book 1 of this important work.

When I consider for myself the deeds of our ancestors and the acts of other kings and peoples, ours seems to me to have excelled all others not only in empire but even in the propagation of their language. For the Persians, the Medes, the Assyrians, the Greeks, and many other peoples have seized dominion far and wide ..., but no people has spread its language so far as ours has done, who in a short space of time has made the Roman tongue, which is called Latin from Latium where Rome is located, well-known and almost queen ... almost throughout the entire West and not a negligible part of both the North and Africa. Further, as far as the provinces are concerned, the Roman tongue was offered to mortals as a certain most excellent fruit for the sowing. Certainly this was a much more famous and splendid task than increasing the empire itself. For they who increase the extent of the empires are accustomed to be greatly honored and are called emperors; however, they who have conferred any benefices on men are celebrated not by human but by divine praise, especially when they further not so much the grandeur and glory of their own city but also the public utility and well-being of all men.

As our ancestors, winning high praises, surpassed other men in military affairs, so by the extension of their language they indeed surpassed themselves, as if, abandoning their dominion on earth, they attained to the fellowship of the gods in Paradise. If Ceres, Liber, and Minerva, who are considered the discoverers of grain, wine, oil, and many others have been placed among the gods for some benefaction of this kind, is it less beneficial to have spread among the nations the Latin language, the noblest and truly divine fruit, food not of the body but of the soul? For this language introduced those nations and all peoples to all the arts which are called liberal; it taught the best laws, prepared the way for all wisdom; and finally, made it possible for them no longer to be called barbarians.

Why would anyone who is a fair judge of things not prefer those who were distinguished for their cultivation of the sacred mysteries of literature to those who were celebrated for waging terrible wars? . . . For not by arms or bloodshed or wars was its [the Latin language's] domination achieved, but by benefits, love and concord. Of this achievement (so far as I can conjecture) the sources have been . . . first, that our ancestors perfected themselves to an incredible degree in all kinds of studies, so that no one seems to have been pre-eminent in military affairs unless he was distinguished also in letters, which was a not inconsiderable stimulus to the emulation of others; then, that they wisely offered rewards to the teachers of literature; finally, that they encouraged all provincials to become accustomed to speak, both in Rome and at home, in the Roman fashion. . . .

The Roman dominion, the peoples and nations long ago threw off as an unwelcome burden; the language of Rome they have thought sweeter than any nectar, more splendid than any silk, more precious than any gold or gems, and they have embraced it as if it were a god sent from Paradise. Great, therefore, is the sacramental power of the Latin language, truly great in its divinity, which has been preserved these many centuries with religion and holy awe, by strangers, by barbarians, by enemies, so that we Romans should not grieve but rejoice, and the whole listening earth should glory. We have lost Rome, we have lost authority, we have lost dominion, not by our own fault but by that of the times, yet we reign still, by the more splendid sovereignty, in a greater part of the world. Ours is Italy, ours Gaul, ours Spain, Germany, Panonia, Illyricum, and many other lands. For wherever the Roman tongue holds sway, there is the Roman Empire. . . .

· Who does not know that when the Latin language flourishes, all studies and disciplines thrive, as they are ruined when it perishes? For who have been the most profound philosophers, the best orators, the most distinguished jurisconsults, and finally the greatest writers, but those indeed who have been most zealous in speaking well? . . .

But when I wish to say more, sorrow hinders me and torments me, and forces me to weep as I contemplate the state which eloquence had once attained and the condition into which it has now fallen. Indeed, for many centuries not only has no one spoken in the Latin manner, but no one who has read Latin has understood it. Students of philosophy have not possessed, nor do they possess, the works of the ancient philosophers; nor do rhetoricians have the orators; nor lawyers the jurisconsults; nor teachers the known works of the ancients. . . . Many, indeed, and varied are the opinions of the wise men on how this happened. I neither accept nor reject any of these, daring only to declare soberly that those arts which are most closely related to the liberal arts, the arts of painting, sculpture, modeling, and architecture, had degenerated for so long and so greatly and had almost died with letters themselves, and that in this age they have been aroused and come to life again, so greatly increased is the number of good artists and men of letters who now flourish.

But truly, as wretched as were those former times in which no learned man was found, so much the more this our age should be congratulated, in which (if we exert ourselves a little more) I am confident that the language of Rome will shortly grow stronger than the city itself, and with it all the disciplines will be restored. Therefore, because of my devotion to my native Rome and because of the importance of the matter, I shall arouse and call forth all men who are lovers of eloquence, as if from a watch tower, and give them, as they say, the signal for battle.

In this passage Valla displays, argues, and advertises a number of fundamental premises and topics in Renaissance humanism in the second century of its career. The first premise is Valla's identification of himself and his Roman (at this time papal) patrons with the tradition of Rome—not the dilapidated "Holy Roman Empire of the German Nation" of his day, but the glorious *Imperium Romanum* of antiquity. The historical face of Renaissance humanism often expressed itself as a search for a suitable cultural pedigree (often argued in questionable linguistic and etymological terms) and as an effort to construct suitable national myths in support of modern respectability and pretensions.

In general, the discussion represents a variation on the theme of power and learning—of arms and the toga in one classical topos, or of Mars and Minerva in another. The argument centers on the assumption of the mutual dependence of political and military success and cultural supremacy, arising in part from the public patronage of art and learning (such as Valla himself enjoyed) and in part from the civic spirit expressed in each of these dimensions of national culture. This linkage is illustrated by the congruent trajectory of empire and letters in Roman history, rising in the Ciceronian republic and declining in the aftermath of Caesar. Here Valla illustrates the historical sensitivity of humanism, commenting that the subsequent loss of such cultural excellence (over some thousand years of darkness) was due not to the people but "to the times" (the humanist topos *non hominum sed temporum culpa*) and in the conventional thesis of a "translation of empire" (*translatio imperii*). The congruence of power and culture was illustrated too by the famous medieval formula, adopted by humanists, of a "translation of studies" (*translatio studii*) in the succession of the so-called Four World Monarchies (Medes, Persians, Greeks, and Romans).

An assumption that is especially characteristic of Valla (and his ancient philological and rhetorical sources) is that language—and especially "the sacramental power of the Latin language"—is the primary medium and sign of such a politico-cultural process. For this reason, too, Valla celebrated the "liberal arts"—that is, the humanities, and in their company the "fine arts"—above not only the military arts but also above the productive and "mechanical arts" and the material benefits deriving from them. For these "human studies" contained the "sacred mysteries of literature," especially the wisdom contained in poetry; they contained the basis for law (that is, classical Roman law, which Valla also celebrated in the *Elegantiae*); and they contained the gateway to true "wisdom" (Ciceronian and Augustinian *sapientia*). For Valla, the art of "speaking well" was the major way to distinguish cultivated peoples from "barbarians."

In this connection Valla declares his belief in a cultural revival that involved not only "good letters" but also the visual arts. Though he does not specifically mention the Florentine achievement, Valla does suggest here the claims of his older friend Leonardo Bruni about the simultaneous emergence of literary elegance in the work of Petrarch and his followers and the artistic genius in that of Giotto and his. Exhorting his contemporaries in characteristically rhetorical style to continue these efforts, Valla not only expresses the idea of a "renaissance of arts and letters" based on imitation and emulation of the ancients but also, implicitly, the inferred notion of future progress by their modern descendants. Not only was the famous "quarrel between the ancients and the moderns" derived in large part from the tradition of "Renaissance humanism," but so was the agenda of each of these two contending parties.

From this point of view, Valla went on in his *Elegantiae* to survey the intricacies of Latin usage in terms of classical literature and the "consensus of the learned," and in other works, to attack "barbarism" in all of its forms—in Scholastic philosophy, law, and theology—and to establish the primacy of rhetoric above these more highly regarded "sciences." In this way, Valla did much to lay the foundations for modern philological criticism, to provide justification for historical scholarship, and to establish Renaissance humanism itself on a professional and "scientific" basis.

# Chronology

| | |
|---|---|
| 1250 | Emperor Frederick II dies. First democracy in Florence. |
| 1265 | Dante Aligheri born. |
| 1274 | Thomas Aquinas dies. |
| 1276 | Giotto born. |
| 1281 | Alexander of Roes's *Translatio Imperii*. |
| 1282 | Second democracy in Florence. |
| 1293 | Ordinances of Justice in Florence. |
| 1297 | Closing of the Great Council of Venice. |
| 1300 | Dante's *Divine Comedy* opens. |
| 1302 | *Unam Sanctam*, bull of Boniface VIII. Dante expelled from Florence. |
| 1304 | Francesco Petrarch born. |
| 1305–1378 | Babylonian captivity of the Church. |
| 1309 | Bartolus of Sassoferrato born. |
| 1313 | Giovanni Boccaccio born. Emperor Henry VII dies. |
| 1314 | Cola di Rienzo (Rienzi) born. |
| 1321 | Dante dies. |
| 1327 | Baldus de Ubaldis born. |

1331    Coluccio Salutati born.

1336    Petrarch ascends Mt. Ventoux.

1337    Giotto dies.

1341    Petrarch's coronation.

1342    Petrarch's *Secret*.

1345    Petrarch discovers Cicero's *Familiar Letters*.

1347    Revolution of Rienzi.

1349    William of Ockham dies.

1352    Bartolus dies.

1354    Rienzi assassinated.

1355    Petrarch's critique of the Habsburg donation. George Gemistos Pletho born.

1370    Guarino da Verona and Pier Paolo Vergerio born.

1374    Petrarch dies.

1375    Boccaccio dies.

1378    Vittorino da Feltre born. Salutati's *Letters on Liberal Studies*.

1378–1417  Great schism.

1380    Poggio Bracciolini born.

1382    Ciompi revolt in Florence.

1392    Flavio Biondo born. Salutati discovers Cicero's *Letters to Atticus*.

1395    George Trapezuntius born.

1397    Manuel Chrysoloras teaches Greek in Florence.

1397–1402  "Crisis of the Early Italian Renaissance."

1400    Chaucer and Baldus de Ubaldis die.

1401    Nicholas of Cusa born.

1402    Vergerio's *De Ingenuis moribus*. Giangaleazzo Visconti of Milan dies.

1403    Bessarion born.

1405    Leonbattista Alberti born.

| | |
|---|---|
| 1406 | Salutati dies. |
| 1407 | Lorenzo Valla born. |
| 1409–1449 | Conciliar period. |
| 1414–1417 | Council of Constance. |
| 1415 | John Hus executed. Bruni's *History of Florence.* |
| 1415–1417 | Poggio discovers manuscripts of Cicero, Quintilian, and others. |
| 1420 | Statutes of Guelf party. |
| 1424 | Christoforo Landino born. |
| 1431 | Valla's *On the True Good.* |
| 1433 | Marsilio Ficino and Alexander Hegius born. |
| 1434–1494 | Medici rule in Florence. |
| 1435 | Alberti's *Della Famiglia* and *On Painting.* Valla's *Dialectical Disputations.* Palmieri's *De Vita civile.* |
| 1436 | Bruni's *Lives of Dante and Petrarch.* |
| 1437 | Bruni's translation of Aristotle's *Politics.* |
| 1438–1445 | Council of Ferrara-Florence. |
| 1439 | Valla's declamation on the Donation of Constantine. Bruni's *Constitution of Florence.* |
| 1440 | Nicholas of Cusa, *On Learned Ignorance.* |
| 1444 | Rudolf Agricola born. Vergerio dies. Valla's *Elegances of the Latin Language.* |
| 1446 | Vittorino da Feltre dies. |
| 1449 | Valla's Annotations on the New Testament. |
| 1450 | Claude de Seyssel born. Pletho dies. |
| 1452 | Alberti's *On Architecture.* |
| 1453 | Fall of Constantinople. Ermolao Barbaro born. |
| 1454 | Invention of printing (?). Angelo Poliziano born. |
| 1455 | Jacques Lefèvre d'Etaples and Johann Reuchlin born. |
| 1457 | Valla dies. |
| 1458–1463 | Pius II's papacy. |

1459   Flavio Biondo's *Roma Triumphans*. Poggio dies.

1460   Guarino da Verona dies.

1462   Platonic Academy founded in Florence.

1462   Pietro Pomponazzi born.

1463   Giovanni Pico della Mirandola born. Biondo dies.

1464   Nicholas of Cusa dies.

1466   Desiderius Erasmus born.

1467   John Colet and Guillaume Budé born.

1469   Ficino's translation of Plato. Machiavelli born.

1470   Polydore Vergil born.

1471   Alberti dies.

1472   Bessarion dies.

1473   Ficino's *Platonic Theology*.

1476   Caxton uses printing press.

1478   Thomas More born.

1483   Luther born.

1484   Ulrich Zwingli and J. C. Scaliger born. Trapezuntius dies.

1485   Letters between Pico and Ermolao Barbaro. Beatus Rhenanus born. Agricola dies.

1486   Pico's *Oration on the Dignity of Man*. Henry Cornelius of Nettesheim born.

1492   Lorenzo de' Medici dies. Juan Luis Vives and Andrea Alciato born.

1493   Barbaro dies.

1494   The French invade Italy. Pico and Poliziano die. François Rabelais born.

1496   Vergil's *On the Inventors of Things*.

1497   Philip Melanchthon born.

1498   Hegius dies.

1499   Ficino dies.

1503   Erasmus's *Handbook of the Christian Soldier*.

1504    Landino dies.

1505    Erasmus discovers Valla's notes on the New Testament.

1506    Johann Sleidan born.

1509    Erasmus's *Praise of Folly.* Jean Calvin born.

1510    More's life of Pico. Colet founds St. Paul's School.

1512    Colet's sermon to the Convocation.

1513    Machiavelli's *Prince* written (published 1528).

1515    Petrus Ramus born.

1516    Erasmus's translation of the New Testament and *Institution of a Christian Prince.* More's *Utopia.* Pomponazzi's *On the Immortality of the Soul.*

1517    Luther's *Ninety-five Theses.* Machievelli's *Discourses on Livy.*

1519    Budé's *Institution of the Prince.* Colet and Seyssel die.

1522    Jacques Cujas born. Reuchlin dies.

1524    Erasmus and Luther break over "free will."

1525    Pomponazzi dies.

1527    Machiavelli dies.

1528    Erasmus's *Ciceronianus.*

1529    Budé's *Commentaries on the Greek Language.* Paolo Emilio and Beatus Rhenanus die. Francesco Patrizzi and Etienne Pasquier born.

1530    Jean Bodin born.

1531    Agrippa's *Vanity of the Arts and Sciences.* Vives's *Transmission of Knowledge.* Zwingli dies.

1532    Machiavelli's *Florentine Histories* (posthumous).

1533    Michel de Montaigne born.

1535    More and Agrippa die.

1536    Calvin's *Institutes of Christian Religion.* Erasmus and Lefèvre d'Etaples die.

1540    J. J. Scaliger born. Budé and Vives die.

1543    Ramus's animadversions against Aristotle.

1546   Luther dies.

1550   Vasari's *Lives*. Alciato dies.

1553   Rabelais dies.

1555   Vergil dies.

1556   Sleidan dies.

1558   J.C. Scaliger dies.

1560   Melanchthon dies.

1561   Francis Bacon born.

1564   Calvin dies.

1566   Bodin's *Method of History*.

1568   Tommaso Campanella born.

1572   Ramus dies.

1575   Le Roy's *Vicissitude of Things*.

1576   Bodin's *Republic*.

1580   Montaigne's *Essays* (first edition).

1583   J. J. Scaliger's *De Emendatione Temporum*.

1590   Cujas dies.

1592   Montaigne dies.

1596   Bodin dies.

1597   Patrizzi dies.

1605   Bacon's *Advancement of Learning*.

1609   J. J. Scaliger dies.

1615   Pasquier dies.

1626   Bacon dies.

1639   Campanella dies.

1678   Giambattista Vico born.

1709   Vico's *Study Methods*.

1725   Vico's *New Science*.

1744   Vico dies.

# Notes and References

## 1. THE ORIGINS OF HUMANISM

1. Jacob Burckhardt, *The Civilization of the Renaissance in Italy* (New York: Phaidon, 1950), 1.

2. Dante, *De monarchia,* in *Latin Works* (London: J. M. Dent, 1904), 132.

3. Aulus Gellius, *Noctes atticae,* xvii.

4. Paul O. Kristeller, "Studies on Renaissance Humanism during the Last Twenty Years," *Studies in the Renaissance* 9 (1962): 22.

5. Dante, *Divine Comedy,* 1.4.130.

6. Augustin Renaudet, *Dante humaniste* (Paris: Les Belles Lettres, 1952).

7. Ewart Lewis, *Medieval Political Ideas* (New York: Knopf, 1954), 2:467–68.

8. Petrarch, "Letter to Posterity," in *Petrarch, the First Modern Scholar and Man of Letters,* ed. J. H. Robinson (New York: G. P. Putnam's Sons, 1898), 59ff.

9. Cited by T. E. Mommsen, *Medieval and Renaissance Studies,* ed. E. Rice (Ithaca, N.Y.: Cornell University Press, 1959), 122.

10. Petrarch, *Epistolae metricae,* 3:33 (my translation).

11. Petrarch, *Epistolae de rebus familiaribus,* 3:18.

12. Petrarch, "On His Own Ignorance and That of Many Others," in *Renaissance Philosophy of Man* (Chicago: University of Chicago Press), 47ff.

13. Ibid., 111.

14. Mario Cosenza, *Petrarch's Letters to Classical Authors* (Chicago: University of Chicago Press, 1910), 21.

15. *Renaissance Philosophy of Man*, 115.

16. Ibid., 44.

17. Edward Bulwer-Lytton, *Rienzi, the Last of the Roman Tribunes* (London, 1835).

18. Mario Cosenza, *Francesco Petrarca and the Revolution of Cola di Rienzo* (Chicago: University of Chicago Press, 1913).

19. Peter Burke, *The Renaissance Sense of the Past* (London: Edward Arnold, 1969), 50.

## 2. THE CONTEXT OF HUMANISM

1. George Holmes, *Florence, Rome and the Origins of the Renaissance* (Oxford: Clarendon Press, 1986).

2. Cited by Hans Baron, *The Crisis of the Early Italian Renaissance* (Princeton: Princeton University Press, 1956), 1:47.

3. Roberto Weiss, *The Dawn of Humanism in Italy* (London: Basil Blackwell, 1947), 5.

4. See n. 8.

5. D. R. Kelley, *The Human Measure* (Cambridge, Mass.: Harvard University Press, 1981).

6. Alberti, *The Family in Renaissance Florence: A Translation by Renée Neu Watkins of I Libri della Famiglia by Leon Battista Alberti* (Columbia: University of South Carolina Press, 1969).

7. William J. Bouwsma, *Venice and the Defense of Republican Liberty* (Berkeley: University of California Press, 1968).

8. Hans Baron, *The Crisis of the Early Italian Renaissance*, 2d ed. (Princeton: Princeton University Press, 1966), and *In Search of Florentine Civic Humanism*, 2 vols. (Princeton: Princeton University Press, 1988).

9. Benedetto Cotrugli, *On Commerce and the Perfect Merchant*, in *Medieval Trade in the Mediterranean World*, ed. Roberto S. Lopez and Irving W. Raymond (New York: Columbia University Press, 1955), 375.

10. "Preamble to the New Code of the Statutes of the Guelf Party" (1420), in *The Humanism of Leonardo Bruni*, trans. Gordon Griffiths, James Hankins, and David Thompson (Binghamton, N.Y.: Medieval and Renaissance Texts and Studies, 1987), 48.

11. Bruni, "Oration for the Funeral of Nanni Strozzi" (1427), in ibid., 124.

12. Bruni, *The New Cicero*, in ibid., 187.

13. Bruni, "Comparison of Dante and Petrarch," in ibid., 100.

14. Bruni, "An Isagogue of Moral Philosophy," in ibid., 182.

15. Bruni, "On the Study of Literature" (1424), in ibid., 245.

16. Bruni, "Life of Petrarch," in ibid., 97.

17. J.G.A. Pocock, *The Machiavellian Moment* (Princeton: Princeton University Press, 1975).

18. Anthony Grafton and Lisa Jardine, *From Humanism to the Humanities* (Cambridge, Mass.: Harvard University Press, 1986), and Paul Grendler, *Schooling in Renaissance Italy* (Baltimore: Johns Hopkins University Press, 1989).

19. George Holmes, *The Florentine Enlightenment 1400–50* (New York: Pegasus, 1969), 4.

20. Erasmus, *On the Method of Study*, in *Collected Works*, vol. 24, ed. Craig R. Thompson (Toronto: Toronto University Press, 1978), 666.

21. Bruni, "On the Study of Literature," *The Humanism of Leonardo Bruni*, 240.

22. Foster Watson, *Vives and the Renaissance Education of Women* (New York: Longmans, Green & Co., 1912).

23. Werner Gundersheimer, "Bartolommeo Goggio: A Feminist in Renaissance Ferrara," *Renaissance Quarterly* 33 (1980):175–200.

24. See *Beyond Their Sex: Learned Women of the European Past*, ed. Patricia H. Labalme (New York: New York University Press, 1980), especially the contributions by Margaret King and P. O. Kristeller.

25. Vespasiano, *Renaissance Princes, Popes, and Prelates*, trans. W. George and E. Waters (New York: Harper & Row, 1963), 411.

26. David Quint, *Origin and Originality in the Renaissance* (New Haven: Yale University Press, 1983).

27. Vico, *On the Study Methods of Our Times*, trans. E. Gianturco (Indianapolis: Bobbs-Merrill, 1965), 19, 33.

28. See n. 34, ch. 6.

29. Petrarch, *Letters to Ancient Authors*, 84.

30. Ibid., 148; Giuseppe Billanovich, "Petrarch and the Textual Tradition of Livy," *Journal of the Warburg and Courtauld Institutes* 4 (1951): 137–208.

31. Vespasiano, *Renaissance Princes*, 352.

32. *Two Renaissance Book Hunters: The Letters of Poggius Bracciolini to Nicolaus de Nicolis*, trans. Phyllis Walter Goodhart Gordan (New York: Columbia University Press, 1974), 192.

33. Ibid., 199.

34. Gibbon, *Decline and Fall of the Roman Empire*, ch. 71.

35. Roberto Weiss, *The Renaissance Discovery of Classical Antiquity* (Oxford: Basil Blackwell, 1969).

36. Egon Friedell, *A Cultural History of the Modern Age*, trans. C. Atkinson (New York: Knopf, 1920), 1:210.

37. Budé, *De l'Institution du prince* (Paris: Maistre Nicole, 1547), fol. 63.

38. Vico, *Study Methods*, 47.

39. Henri Hauser, *La modernité du seizième siècle* (Paris: Colin, 1963).

40. See n. 38, ch. 6.

## 3. HUMANISM AND PHILOSOPHY

1. Valla, *Elegantiae latinae linguae*, bk. 1, preface, in *Opera omnia*, ed. E. Garin (Turin: Bottega d'Erasmo, 1962), 1:4.

2. Valla, *Dialecticae disputationes*, in ibid., 1:646.

3. Valla, *De rebus a Ferdinando rege Hispaniarum rege et maioribus eius gestis*, in ibid., 2:6.

4. Valla, *On Pleasure*, trans. A. Kent Hieatt and Maristella Lorch (New York: Abaris, 1977).

5. See D. R. Kelley, *Foundations of Modern Historical Scholarship* (New York: Columbia University Press, 1970), ch. 2

6. *The Treatise of Lorenzo Valla on the Donation of Constantine*, trans. C. B. Coleman (New Haven: Yale University Press, 1922), 115.

7. Valla, *Disputationes dialecticae*, in *Opera*, 1:8, and *Elegantiae*, in *Opera*, 16:34.

8. Valla, *The Profession of the Religious*, trans. Olga Zorzi Pugliese (Toronto: University of Toronto Press, 1985), 22.

9. *The Humanism of Leonardo Bruni*, 24.

10. Pletho, *Difference between Plato and Aristotle;* Trapezuntius, *Comparison between Plato and Aristotle;* and Bessarion, *Against the Calumniators of Plato and Aristotle;* on this see C. M. Woodhouse, *Gemistos Plethon* (Oxford: Oxford University Press, 1986), and John Monfasani, *George of Trebizond* (Leiden: Brill, 1976).

11. Ernst Cassirer, *The Individual and the Cosmos in Renaissance Philosophy*, trans. Mario Domandi (New York: Harper & Row, 1963).

12. Arthur Field, *The Origins of the Platonic Academy of Florence* (Princeton: Princeton University Press, 1988).

13. Ficino, "Five Questions concerning the Mind," in *Renaissance Philosophy of Man*, 201.

14. *The Letters of Marsilio Facino*, vol. 1, trans. Language Department, London School of Economics (London: Shepheard-Walwyn, 1975), 51, 32.

15. Cited in *The Portable Renaissance Reader*, trans. J. Ross and M. McLaughlin (New York: Viking Press, 1953), 79.

16. Pico, "Letter to Ermolao Barbaro," in *Renaissance Philosophy* (New York: Random House, 1967), 1:107.

17. Pico, "Oration on the Dignity of Man," in *Renaissance Philosophy of Man*, 244.

18. Ibid., 225.

19. Astrik L. Gabriel, *The Educational Ideas of Vincent of Beauvais* (Notre Dame, Ind.: Medieval Institute, 1956), 8.

20. See n. 5, ch. 1.

21. *Two Views of Man: Pope Innocent III and Giannozzo Manetti*, trans. B. Murchland (New York: Ungar, 1966).

22. See Jean Delumeau, *Sin and Fear: The Emergence of a Western Guilt Culture 13th–18th Centuries*, trans. E. Nicholson (New York: St. Martin's, 1990).

23. Valla, *Dialogue on Free Will*, in *Renaissance Philosophy of Man*, 155; cf. Luther and Erasmus, *Free Will and Salvation*, ed. E. Gordon Rupp et al. (Philadelphia: Westminster Press, 1969).

24. Pomponazzi, *On the Immortality of the Soul*, in *Renaissance Philosophy of Man*, 257.

25. Ernst Cassirer, *The Individual and the Cosmos*, 141.

26. Agrippa, *On the Uncertainty of Our Knowledge*, in *Renaissance Philosophy*, 66. See Richard H. Popkin, *The History of Skepticism from Erasmus to Spinoza* (New York: Harper & Row, 1979).

27. Quentin Skinner, *The Foundations of Modern Political Thought* (Cambridge: Cambridge University Press, 1978), I. See Nicolai Rubinstein, "The History of the Word *Politicus* in Early-Modern Europe," in *The Languages of Political Theory in Early-Modern Europe*, ed. Anthony Pagden (Cambridge: Cambridge University Press, 1987), 41–56.

28. Bruni, letter to Ferdinand of Aragon (1441), *The Humanism of Leonardo Bruni*, 168.

29. Bodin, *Six Books of a Commonweale*, trans. D. Knolles (London: Impensis G. Bishop, 1606), ch. 2–5.

30. Erasmus, *The Education of a Christian Prince*, trans. Lester K. Born (New York: Columbia University Press, 1936), introduction, and Allan H. Gilbert, *Machiavelli's Prince and Its Forerunners* (Durham N.C.: Duke University Press, 1938).

31. Machiavelli, *Discourses on the First Decade of Titus Livius*, in *The Chief Works*, trans. Allan Gilbert (Durham, N.C.: Duke University Press, 1958), 1:191.

32. Ibid., 197ff.

33. Bodin, *Method for the Easy Comprehension of History*, trans. Beatrice Reynolds (New York: Columbia University Press, 1945), 153.

34. Alberti, *The Family in Renaissance Florence*, 316. See Machiavelli, *The Prince*, in *The Chief Works*, 1:61.

35. D. R. Kelley, "Law," in *Cambridge History of Political Thought 1450–1700* (Cambridge: Cambridge University Press, 1991), 66–94, and "Jurisconsultus Perfectus: The Lawyer as Renaissance Man," *Journal of the Warburg and Courtauld Institutes* 51 (1988):84–102.

36. Machiavelli, *The Prince*, ch. 14.

37. La Boétie, *Anti-Dictator: The "Discourse sur la servitude volontaire,"* trans. Harry Kurz (New York: Columbia University Press, 1942), 19.

## 4. HUMANISM AND THE WORLD OF NATIONS

1. For "Humanism beyond Italy," see Rabil, *Renaissance Humanism*, vol. 2.

2. See Lewis Spitz, *The Religious Renaissance of the German Humanists* (Cambridge, Mass.: Harvard University Press, 1963).

3. Cited by Noel L. Brann, "Humanism in Germany," in Rabil, 2:147.

4. Aventinus, *Sämtliche Werke* (Munich: C. Kaiser, 1880), 2:402.

5. Felix Fabri, *Historia Suevorum*, in M. Goldast, ed., *Suevicar. rer. scriptores* (Frankfurt: W. Richter, 1605).

6. Nietzsche, *Unmodern Observations*, trans. W. Arrowsmith (New Haven: Yale University Press, 1990), 351.

7. Lefèvre d'Etaples, in *Renaissance Reader*, 85.

8. Budé, *De Philologia*, following *De studio litterarum* (Basel: J. Walderum, 1533), 217.

9. D. R. Kelley, *Foundations of Modern Historical Scholarship*, 66ff.

10. Budé, *De asse et partibus ejus* (Lyon: S. Gryphius, 1551), fol. 141.

11. Budé, *De transitu Hellenismi ad Christianismum*, trans. Daniel F. Penham (Ph.D. diss., Columbia University, 1954).

12. Calvin, *Commentary on Seneca's De Clementia*, ed. F. Battles and A. Hugo (Leiden: Brill, 1969), 13.

13. Le Roy, in *Renaissance Reader*, 91.

14. Le Roy, *La Vivissitude ou variété des choses* (Paris: L'Huillier, 1575), fol. 255, and *Le Phedon de Platon* (Paris: S. Nyvelle, 1553), 14.

15. See D. R. Kelley, "France," in *The Renaissance in National Perspective*, ed. R. Porter and M. Teich (Cambridge: Cambridge University Press, 1991).

16. La Croix du Maine et du Verdier, *Les Bibliothèques françoises* (1584; Paris: Saillant et Noyen, 1772–73).

17. See n. 10, ch. 6.

18. Roberto Weiss, *Humanism in England during the Fifteenth Century* (Oxford: Basil Blackwell, 1957), and James Kelsey McConica, *English Humanists and Reformation Politics* (Oxford: Clarendon Press, 1963).

19. Erasmus and Budé, in *The Complete Works*, vol. 4, *Utopia*, ed. E. Surtz and J. H. Hexter (New Haven: Yale University Press, 1965), 3–15.

20. More, letter to Dorp (1515), in *Collected Works*, vol. 15, ed. Daniel Kinney (Toronto: University of Toronto Press, 1976), 9.

21. Chambers, *Thomas More* (London: Jonathan Cape, 1935), 207.

22. Vives, *Introduction to Wisdom*, trans. M. Tobriner (New York: Teacher's College Press, 1968), 11.

23. Erasmus, *Correspondence*, vol. 11, ed. R. Mynors and J. Estes (Toronto: University of Toronto Press, 1989), 185.

24. Erasmus, *Antibarbarus*, trans. M. Phillips, in *Collected Works*, vol. 23, ed., 42.

25. Erasmus, letter to Thomas Grey (1497), in *Erasmus and His Age*, ed. H. Hillerbrand (New York: Harper & Row, 1970), 23.

26. Erasmus, letter to Paul Volz (1528), in *Erasmus and His Age*, 128.

27. Ibid., 48.

28. Marjorie O'Rourke Boyle, *Erasmus on Language and Method in Theology* (Toronto: University of Toronto Press, 1977), 37.

29. Erasmus, in *Renaissance Reader*, 83.

30. Erasmus, "Paraclesis," in Frederic Seebohm, *The Oxford Reformers* (London: Longmans, Green & Co., 1896), 326.

31. Erasmus, letter to Dorp (1515), in *Erasmus and His Age*, 84.

32. Erasmus, letter to Antony of Bergin (1513–14), in *Erasmus and His Age*, 66. See Robert P. Adams, *The Better Part of Valor: More, Erasmus, Colet, and Vives on Humanism, War, and Peace 1496–1535* (Seattle: University of Washington Press, 1962).

33. Erasmus, letter to Melanchthon (1524), in *Erasmus and His Age*, 174.

34. Ibid., 183.

35. Erasmus, letter to Melanchthon (1530), in ibid., 239.

36. Amerigo Vespucci, *Letter to Piero Soderini*, trans. George Tyler Northup (Princeton: Princeton University Press, 1916), 2.

37. Edmundo O'Gorman, *The Invention of America* (Bloomington: University of Indiana Press, 1961), 47.

38. Cited by J. H. Elliott, *The Old World and the New, 1492–1650* (Cambridge: Cambridge University Press, 1972), 10.

39. See Anthony Pagden, *The Fall of Natural Man: The American Indian and the Origins of Comparative Ethnology* (Cambridge: Cambridge University Press, 1982).

## 5. THE STRUCTURE OF HUMANISM

1. Arthur Henkel and Albrecht Schöne, eds., *Emblemata: Handbuch zur Sinnbildkunst des XVI. und XVII. Jahrhunderts* (Stuttgart: J. B. Metzlersche Verlag, 1967), col. 1537–38.

2. On "Humanism and the Disciplines," see Rabil, *Renaissance Humanism*, vol. 3.

3. Vergil, *De rerum inventoribus* (Basel: Bebel, 1536), 1.6. See W. Keith Percival in Rabil, *Renaissance Humanism*, 3:67–84.

4. Hegius, in Rabil, *Renaissance Humanism*, 3:131.

5. Guarino, "De Ordine docendi et studendi," in William Harrison Woodward, *Vittorino and Other Humanist Educators* (Cambridge: Cambridge University Press, 1987), 163.

6. W. Keith Percival, "Grammar and Rhetoric in the Renaissance," in James J. Murphy, ed., *Renaissance Eloquence* (Berkeley: University of California Press, 1983), 304.

7. Vives, cited by Richard Waswo, *Language and Meaning in the Renaissance* (Princeton: Princeton University Press, 1987), 121.

8. Dullardus, cited in G. A. Padley, *Grammatical Theory in Western Europe 1500–1700, Trends in Vernacular Grammar* (Cambridge: Cambridge University Press, 1975), 25.

9. Valla, *Antidoti in Poggium*, in *Opera*, 1:385, and *Elegantiae*, in *Opera*, 1:13.

10. Bruni, "On the Correct Way to Translate," *The Humanism of Leonardo Bruni*, 220. See Glyn P. Norton, *The Ideology and Language of Translation in Renaissance France and Their Humanist Antecedents* (Geneva: Droz, 1984).

11. *Scaligerana* (Amsterdam: Corens & Mortier, 1740), 2:285.

12. Aeneas Sylvius, "De Liberorum educatione," in Woodward, *Vittorino*, 144.

13. On this see Aldo Scaglione, "The Humanist as Scholar and Politian's Conception of the *Grammaticus*," *Studies in the Renaissance* 8 (1961):49–70.

14. Vico, *Diritto universale*, in *Opere giuridiche*, ed. P. Cristofolini (Florence: Sansoni, 1974), 2.2.1.

15. R. H. Robins, *A Short History of Linguistics* (Bloomington: Indiana University Press, 1967), 95ff., and W. Keith Percival, "Renaissance Linguistics: The Old and the New," in *Studies in the History of Western Linguistics in Honor of R. H. Robins*, ed. T. Bynon and F. Palmer (Cambridge: Cambridge University Press, 1986), 58ff.

16. Vergil, *De rerum inventoribus*, 1.13. See John Monfasani in Rabil, *Renaissance Humanism*, 3:171–235; Lisa Jardine and Brian Vickers in *Cambridge History of Renaissance Philosophy*, 173–98 and 715–45; and especially Vickers, *In Defense of Rhetoric* (Oxford: Clarendon, 1988), and Terence Cave, *The Cornucopian Text* (Oxford: Clarendon Press, 1979).

17. Salutati, cited by Vickers, *In Defense of Rhetoric*, 272.

18. Vittorino, "De Ingenuis moribus," in Woodward, *Vittorino*, 107.

19. Erasmus, *On the Method of Study*, in *Collected Works*, vol. 24, ed.

Craig R. Thompson (Toronto: University of Toronto Press, 1978), 670.

20. Agricola, cited in Noel L. Brann, "Humanism in Germany," in Rabil, *Renaissance Humanism*, 2:133.

21. Erasmus, "The Right Way to Speak," in *Collected Works*, vol. 4, ed. J. K. Sowards (Toronto: University of Toronto Press, 1985), 369.

22. Ernst Cassirer, *The Philosophy of Symbolic Forms*, trans. Ralph Manheim (New Haven: Yale University Press, 1953), 1:127.

23. Valla, *Disputationes dialecticae*, cited by Jerrold E. Seigel, *Rhetoric and Philosophy in Renaissance Humanism* (Princeton: Princeton University Press, 1968), 162.

24. Valla, *On Pleasure*, 75.

25. Pico, letter to Ermolao Barbaro, in *Renaissance Philosophy*, 1:107.

26. Melanchthon, cited in Vickers, *In Defense of Rhetoric*, 195.

27. Bruni, "On the Study of Literature," in *The Humanism of Leonardo Bruni*, 246.

28. Vives, *On Education*, trans. Foster Watson (Cambridge: Cambridge University Press, 1913), 181.

29. Guazzo, cited in Vickers, *In Defense of Rhetoric*, 273.

30. Ibid., 194.

31. John Rainold, *Oxford Lectures on Aristotle's Rhetoric*, ed. Lawrence D. Green (Newark: University of Delaware Press, 1986), 99.

32. Seigel, *Rhetoric and Philosophy*, 211.

33. Valla, *On the True Good*, 77.

34. Marjorie O'Rourke Boyle, *Erasmus on Language and Method in Theology* (Toronto: University of Toronto Press, 1977), 46.

35. Walter J. Ong, *Ramus, Method, and the Decay of Oratory* (Cambridge, Mass.: Harvard University Press, 1958).

36. Montaigne, *Essays*, 1.51 ("On the Vanity of Words").

37. Fumaroli in Murphy, *Renaissance Eloquence*, 255.

38. Bacon, *Advancement of Learning*, in *Philosophical Works*, ed. Ellis and Spedding (London: Routledge and Sons, 1905), 127.

39. Valla's "History of King Ferdinand of Spain," in *Opera*, 2:6.

40. Vergil, *De rerum inventoribus*, 1.10. See D. R. Kelley in Rabil, *Renaissance Humanism*, 3:236–70, and in *Cambridge History of Renaissance Philosophy*, 746–61.

41. Guarino, *De Ordine*, 169.

42. Bruni, *History of Florence*, in *Humanism and Liberty*, ed. Renée Neu Watkins (Columbia: University of South Carolina Press, 1978), 28.

43. Cicero, *De Oratore*, 2.9.36.

44. Valla, *De rebus a Ferdinando Hispaniarum rege*, in *Opera*, 2:6.

45. Budé, *De l'Institution du prince*, fol. 16.

46. Vergerio, *De ingenuis moribus*, 106.

47. Dionysius of Halicarnassus, *De arte rhetorica*, 11.2.

48. Bruni, "On the Study of Literature," 245.

49. Machiavelli, *Discourses*, in *The Chief Works*, 1:278.

50. See especially Peter Fraenkel, *Testimonia Patrum* (Geneva: Droz, 1961).

51. Sleidan, *The General History of the Reformation* (1556; London: Edward Jones, 1689).

52. Melanchthon, *Opera quae supersunt omnia* (Halle: C. A. Schwetschke, 1834–60), vol. 11, col. 306, and 12:705.

53. Agrippa, *Of the Vanitie and Uncertaintie of Artes and Sciences*, trans. James Sanford (London: Henry Wykes, 1569), ch. 5.

54. Bodin, *Method*, 11.

55. Gaillard, *Methode qu'on doit tenir en la lecture de l'histoire* (Paris: Pierre Cavellat, 1579), 151.

56. Arnaldo Momigliano, *The Classical Foundations of Modern Historiography* (Berkeley: University of California Press, 1990), 48–53.

57. Erasmus, *De copia*, in *Collected Works*, vol. 24, 674.

58. Heinsius, *The Value of History*, trans. G. Robinson (Cambridge, Mass.: privately printed, 1943), 10.

59. Vergil, *De rerum inventoribus*, 1.8. See Danilo Aguzzi-Barbagli in Rabil, *Renaissance Humanism*, 3:85–170; Concetta Carestia Greenfield, *Humanist and Scholastic Poetics 1250–1500* (Lewisburg, Pa.: Associated University Presses, 1981); Bernard Weinberg, *A History of Literary Criticism in the Italian Renaissance* (Chicago: University of Chicago Press, 1961); Baxter Hathaway, *The Age of Criticism: The Late Renaissance in Italy* (Ithaca, N.Y.: Cornell University Press, 1962); Thomas Green, *The Light in Troy: Imitation and Discovery in Renaissance Poetry* (New Haven: Yale University Press, 1982); David Quint, *Origin and Originality in Renaissance Poetry* (New Haven: Yale University Press, 1983); and G. W. Pigman III, "Versions of Imitation in the Renaissance," *Renaissance Quarterly* 33 (1980):1–32.

60. Greenfield, *Humanist and Scholastic Poetics*, 201.

61. *Boccaccio on Poetry*, trans. Charles G. Osgood (Princeton: Princeton University Press, 1930), xxxvi.

62. See Erwin Panofsky, *Studies in Iconology* (New York: Harper & Row, 1962), 33.

63. Greenfield, *Humanist and Scholastic Poetics*, 219.

64. Guarino, *De Ordine*, 170.

65. Greenfield, *Humanist and Scholastic Poetics*, 135.

66. Salutati, "Letters in Defense of Liberal Studies," in *Humanism*

*and Tyranny,* ed. E. Emerton (Cambridge, Mass.: Harvard University Press, 1925), 316.

67. *Boccaccio on Poetry,* 117.

68. Tasso, "On the Art of Poetry," in *Renaissance Philosophy,* 1:821. See Hathaway, *Age of Criticism,* 140.

69. *Castelvetro on the Art of Poetry,* trans. A. Bongiorno (Binghamton, N.Y.: Medieval and Renaissance Texts and Studies, 1984), 4.

70. Hathaway, *Age of Criticism,* 45.

71. Weinberg, *History,* 2:715.

72. Hathaway, *Age of Criticism,* 330.

73. Weinberg, *History,* 2:767.

74. Sidney, "A Defence of Poetry," in *Miscellaneous Prose of Sir Philip Sidney,* ed. K. Duncan-Jones and J. van Dorsten (Oxford: Clarendon Press, 1973), 78.

75. See Antonio Perez-Ramos, *Francis Bacon's Idea of Science and the Maker's Knowledge Tradition* (Oxford: Clarendon Press, 1988).

76. Weinberg, *History,* 2:791.

77. Bacon, *De augmentis scientiarum,* in *The Philosophical Works,* 439. See Donald Lemen Clark, *Rhetoric and Poetry in the Renaissance* (New York: Columbia University Press, 1922), 93, and George A. Kennedy, *Classical Rhetoric and its Christian and Secular Tradition from Ancient to Modern Times* (Chapel Hill: University of North Carolina Press, 1980).

78. Vico, *On the Most Ancient Wisdom of the Italians,* trans. L. M. Palmer (Ithaca, N.Y.: Cornell University Press, 1988), 96.

79. Weinberg, *History,* 2:767.

80. Vico, *On the Study Methods of our Time,* trans. E. Gianturco (New York: Liberal Arts Press, 1965).

81. Vico, *The New Science,* trans. T. Bergin and M. Fisch (Ithaca, N.Y.: Cornell University Press, 1961), 69ff.

## 6. BEYOND HUMANISM

1. Vergil, *De rerum inventoribus,* 1:16. See Jill Kraye in *Cambridge History of Renaissance Philosophy,* 303–86, and Charles Trinkaus, *In Our Image and Likeness: Humanity and Divinity in Italian Humanist Thought* (Chicago: University of Chicago Press, 1970).

2. Petrarch, *The Life of Solitude,* trans. J. Zeitlin (Urbana: University of Illinois Press, 1924), 100 and 311, and his letter to Rienzi (1347) in *Petrarch,* ed. David Thompson (New York: Harper & Row, 1971), 81.

3. *Renaissance Philosophy of Man,* 36–46.

4. Cited in Trinkaus, *In Our Image,* 2:14.

5. Garin, *Italian Humanism*, trans. Peter Munz (New York: Harper & Row, 1965), 29.

6. Bruni, "An Isagogue to Moral Philosophy," *The Humanism of Leonardo Bruni*, 268.

7. E. F. Rice, *The Renaissance Idea of Wisdom* (Cambridge, Mass.: Harvard University Press, 1958).

8. See Katherine Park and Eckhard Kessler in *Cambridge History of Renaissance Philosophy*, 453–534.

9. Especially in Erasmus, *The Handbook of the Militant Christian* (1503).

10. Montaigne, *Essays*, 2:16.

11. Ibid., 3:9.

12. Ibid., 1:29.

13. Ibid., 1:23.

14. D. R. Kelley, "Second Nature: The Idea of Custom in European Law, Society, and Culture," in *The Transmission of Culture in Early Modern Europe*, ed. Anthony Grafton (Philadelphia: University of Pennsylvania Press, 1990), 131–72.

15. Vergil, *De rerum inventoribus*, 1:16. See David Cast in Rabil, *Renaissance Humanism*, 3:412–49, and P. O. Kristeller, "The Modern System of the Arts," *Journal of the History of Ideas* 12 (1951):496–527, and 13 (1952):17–46.

16. Vergil, *De rerum inventoribus*, 2.16.

17. Valla, *Elegantiae*.

18. *Renaissance Reader*, 79, 91ff.

19. Alberti, "On Painting," in *A Documentary History of Art*, ed. Elizabeth G. Holt (Princeton: Princeton University Press, 1957), 1:205, and Vasari, *Lives of the Artists*, ed. B. Burroughs (New York: Simon & Schuster, 1946), 185.

20. *Castelvetro on the Art of Poetry*, 9, and Baxandall, *Giotto and the Orators* (Oxford: Oxford University Press, 1971).

21. Alberti, "On Architecture," in *A Documentary History*, 218, and Vasari, *Lives*, 43.

22. Vergil, *De rerum inventoribus*, 1.14. See Claude V. Palisca in Rabil, *Renaissance Humanism*, 3:450–85, and his *Humanism in Italian Renaissance Musical Thought* (New Haven: Yale University Press, 1986).

23. Jean Jehasse, *La Renaissance de la critique* (Saint-Etienne: Publications de la Université de Saint-Etienne, 1976).

24. See Cesare Vasoli and Anthony Grafton in *Cambridge History of Renaissance Philosophy*, 57–74 and 767–91.

25. Walter Ullmann, *Medieval Foundations of Renaissance Humanism* (Ithaca, N.Y.: Cornell University Press, 1977).

26. D. R. Kelley, *Foundations of Modern Historical Scholarship*, 39, 66, 87.

27. Nancy Siraisi, *Medieval and Early Renaissance Medicine* (Chicago: University of Chicago Press, 1990).

28. See Pamela O. Long in Rabil, *Renaissance Humanism*, 3:486–512, and William A. Wallace and Alfonso Ingegno in *Cambridge History of Renaissance Philosophy*, 201–63.

29. See Brian Copenhaver in *Cambridge History of Renaissance Philosophy*, 264–300.

30. John S. Mebane, *Renaissance Magic and the Return of the Golden Age* (Lincoln: University of Nebraska Press, 1989), 20–21.

31. A classic work is E. Harris Harbison, *The Christian Scholar in the Age of the Reformation* (New York: Scribners, 1956).

32. Vives, *On Education (De tradendis disciplinis)*, 14, 90.

33. Ibid., 158.

34. Vico, *Study Methods*, 47.

35. Vico, *The New Science*, bk. 2.

36. Condorcet, *Sketch for a Historical Picture of the Progress of the Human Mind*, trans. J. Barraclough (New York: Noonday Press, 1955), ch. 8.

37. Le Roy, in *Renaissance Reader*, 98.

38. D'Alembert, *Preliminary Discourse to the Encyclopedia of Diderot*, trans. R. Schwab and W. Rex (Indianapolis: Bobbs-Merrill, 1963), 5.

39. Stewart, *Collected Works*, ed. William Hamilton (Edinburgh: T. Constable & Co., 1854), 1:49.

40. Perelman and Obrechts-Tyteca, *The New Rhetoric* (Notre Dame: University of Notre Dame Press, 1969), 1.

41. Gadamer, *Truth and Method*, trans. G. Barden and J. Cumming (New York: Seabury Press, 1975), 5, 389.

42. Ibid., 241.

43. Sartre, *Existentialism* (New York: Philosophical Library, 1947), 11–61.

44. Heidegger, *Basic Writings*, trans. D. Krell (London: Routledge & Kegan Paul, 1977), 193–242.

45. Montaigne, *Essays*, 3.2; cf. 1.26.

46. Grassi, *Heidegger and the Question of Renaissance Humanism* (Binghamton, N.Y.: Medieval and Renaissance Texts and Studies, 1983), 13, and *Renaissance Humanism* (Binghamton, N.Y.: Medieval and Renaissance Texts and Studies, 1988)

47. Burckhardt, *The Civilization of the Renaissance*, 341.

# Bibliographic Essay

---

$T$wo recent publications, both with full, critical, and up-to-date references, make an extensive bibliography unnecessary: Albert Rabil, Jr., ed. *Renaissance Humanism: Foundations, Forms, and Legacy,* 3 vols. (Philadelphia: University of Pennsylvania Press, 1988), and Charles B. Schmitt and Quentin Skinner, eds., *The Cambridge History of Renaissance Philosophy* (Cambridge: Cambridge University Press, 1988). See also Anthony Goodman and Angus MacKay, eds., *The Impact of Humanism on Western Europe* (London: Longman, 1990), and J. H. Burns, ed., *The Cambridge History of Political Thought c. 1450–c.1700* (Cambridge: Cambridge University Press, 1991).

The interpretation of Renaissance humanism has emerged from a great tradition beginning with the classic Jacob Burckhardt, Georg Voigt, and John Addington Symonds, and including more recently Ernst Cassirer, Alfred von Martin, Paul Oskar Kristeller, Hans Baron, Eugenio Garin, Augustin Renaudet, and Wallace K. Ferguson, who surveys the whole canon in his *The Renaissance in Historical Thought: Five Centuries of Interpretation* (Boston: Houghton Mifflin, 1948); also now William Kerrigan and Gordon Braden, *The Idea of the Renaissance* (Baltimore: Johns Hopkins University Press).

Selections of primary texts appear in Ernst Cassirer, Paul Oskar Kristeller, and John Herman Randall, Jr., eds., *The Renaissance Philosophy of Man* (Chicago: University of Chicago Press, 1948), and Arthur Fallico and Herman Shapiro, eds., *Renaissance Philosophy,* 2 vols. (New York: Modern Library, 1967). Some of the major authors of Renaissance humanism are well served by translations, especially Petrarch, Bruni, Erasmus,

---

More, Machiavelli, and Montaigne, and to some extent Ficino, Pico, Vives, and Vico. This is less true of others, including Boccaccio (Latin works), Salutati, Budé, Melanchthon, the Scaligers, and in general the tradition of philology. Notable recent additions are Petrarch, *Letters on Familiar Matters*, 3 vols., translated by Aldo S. Bernardo (Albany: State University of New York Press, 1975–85); *The Humanism of Leonardo Bruni*, translated by Gordon Griffiths, James Hankins, and David Thompson (Binghamton, N.Y.: Medieval and Renaissance Texts, 1987); Marsilio Ficino, *The Letters*, 3 vols., translated by the Language Department of the London School of Economics (London: Shepheard-Walwyn, 1975–); the Yale edition of the works of Thomas More; and the Toronto edition of Erasmus' works and correspondence (still in progress).

"Civic humanism" is an aspect pursued especially by Baron, *The Crisis of the Early Italian Renaissance*, 2d ed. (Princeton: Princeton University Press, 1966), and *In Search of Florentine Humanism*, 2 vols. (Princeton: Princeton University Press, 1988); Garin, *Italian Humanism: Philosophy and Civic Life in the Renaissance*, translated by Peter Munz (New York: Harper & Row, 1965); Walter Ullmann, *Medieval Foundations of Renaissance Humanism* (Ithaca, N.Y.: Cornell University Press, 1977); Marvin Becker, *Florence in Transition*, 2 vols. (Baltimore: Johns Hopkins University Press, 1967–68), and *Civility and Society in Western Europe 1300–1600* (Bloomington: University of Indiana Press, 1988); Gene Brucker, *The Civic World of Early Renaissance Florence* (Princeton: Princeton University Press, 1977); Donald Weinstein, *Savonarola and Florence* (Princeton: Princeton University Press, 1970); Lauro Martines, *The Social World of the Florentine Humanists, 1390–1460* (Princeton: Princeton University Press, 1963); J.G.A. Pocock, *The Machiavellian Moment: Florentine Political Thought and the Atlantic Republican Tradition* (Princeton: Princeton University Press, 1975); William Bouwsma, *Venice and the Defense of Republican Liberty* (Berkeley: University of California Press, 1968); Margaret L. King, *Venetian Humanism in an Age of Patrician Dominance* (Princeton: Princeton University Press, 1986); Charles L. Stinger, *The Renaissance in Rome* (Bloomington: University of Indiana Press, 1985); Jerry H. Bentley, *Politics and Culture on Renaissance Naples* (Princeton: Princeton University Press, 1987); and extensive commentaries (surveyed by Rabil, *Renaissance Humanism*, 1:141–74).

On Renaissance humanism in general, the essential books in English (besides Rabil's *Renaissance Humanism*) begin with the work of Paul Kristeller, most comprehensively represented in *Studies in Renaissance Thought and Letters*, 2 vols. (Rome: Edizione di Storia e Letteratura, 1956–85). Three of his more useful festschriften, with articles pursuing his lines of investigation, are Edward P. Mahoney, ed., *Philosophy and Humanism: Festschrift for Paul Oskar Kristeller* (New York: Columbia University Press, 1976); Heiko Oberman and T. A. Brady, Jr., eds., *Itinerarium Italicum: The Profile of the Italian Renaissance in the Mirror of Its European Transformations* (Leiden: E. J. Brill, 1975); and James Hankins, John Monfasani, and Frederick Purnell, Jr., eds., *Supplementum Festivum: Studies in Honor of Paul Oskar Kristeller* (Binghamton, N.Y.: Medieval and Renaissance Texts and Studies, 1987). Also useful are the surveys of R. R. Bolgar, *The Classical Heritage and Its Beneficiaries* (Cambridge: Cambridge University Press, 1954); *Classical Influences on European Culture, A.D. 500–1500* (Cambridge: Cambridge University Press, 1971); *Classical Influences on European Culture, A.D. 1500–1700* (Cambridge: Cambridge University Press, 1976); and above all E. R. Curtius, *European Literature and the Latin Middle Ages,* translated by Willard R. Trask (New York: Pantheon Books, 1963).

On the origins, background, and particular themes, see especially George Holmes, *Florence, Rome and the Origins of the Renaissance* (Oxford: Clarendon Press, 1986) and *The Florentine Enlightenment, 1400–1450* (New York: Pegasus, 1969); Charles Trinkaus, *The Scope of Renaissance Humanism* (Ann Arbor: University of Michigan Press, 1983); Elizabeth Eisenstein, *The Printing Press as an Agent of Change: Communications and Cultural Transformations in Early Modern Europe,* 2 vols. (Cambridge: Cambridge University Press, 1979); Deno Geanakopolos, *Interaction of the "Sibling" Byzantine and Western Cultures in the Middle Ages and the Italian Renaissance (330–1600)* (New Haven: Yale University Press, 1976); and Eugene F. Rice, Jr., *The Renaissance Idea of Wisdom* (Cambridge, Mass.: Harvard University Press, 1958).

Among the best studies of individual authors are Thomas Caldecot Chubb, *Dante and His World* (Boston: Little, Brown & Co., 1966); Charles Till Davis, *Dante and the Idea of Rome* (Oxford: Clarendon Press, 1957); Ernest Hatch Wilkins, *Life of Petrarch* (Chicago: University of Chicago Press, 1961); A. S. Bernardo, *Petrarch, Scipio and the "Africa": The Birth of Humanism's Dream* (Baltimore: Johns Hopkins University Press, 1962); Vittorio Branca, *Boccaccio: The Man and His Works,* translated by R. Monges (New York: New York University Press, 1976); Ronald G. Witt, *Hercules at the Crossroads: The Life, Works, and Thought of Coluccio Salutati* (Durham, N.C.: Duke University Press, 1983); Joan Gadol, *Leon Battista Alberti: Universal Man of the Early Renaissance* (Chicago: University of Chicago Press, 1969); P. O. Kristeller, *The Philosophy of Marsilio Ficino,* translated by Virginia Conant (New York: Columbia University Press, 1943); W. G. Craven, *Giovanni Pico della Mirandola, Symbol of His Age: Modern Interpretations of a Renaissance Philosopher* (Geneva: Droz, 1981); Denys Hay, *Polydor Vergil* (Oxford: Oxford University Press, 1952); Roland H. Bainton *Erasmus of Christendom* (New York: Scribners, 1969);

Richard Marius, *Thomas More* (New York: Random House, 1984); David O. McNeil, *Guillaume Budé and Humanism in the Reign of Francis I* (Geneva: Droz, 1975); Carlos G. Noreña, *Juan Luis Vives and the Emotions* (Carbondale: Southern Illinois University Press, 1989); Charles G. Nauert, Jr., *Agrippa and the Crisis of Renaissance Thought* (Urbana: Illinois University Press, 1965); Sebastian de Grazia, *Machiavelli in Hell* (Princeton: Princeton University Press, 1989); Walter J. Ong, *Ramus, Method, and the Decay of Dialogue* (Cambridge, Mass.: Harvard University Press, 1958); Donald Frame, *Montaigne: A Biography* (New York: Harcourt, Brace & World, 1965); and Lisa Jardine, *Francis Bacon: Discovery and the Art of Discourse* (Cambridge: Cambridge University Press, 1974).

For the scholarly aspect of the humanist movement, see especially Rudolph Pfeiffer, *History of Classical Scholarship from 1300 to 1850* (Oxford: Oxford University Press, 1976); L. D. Reynolds and N. G. Wilson. *Scribes and Scholars*, 2d ed. (Oxford: Oxford University Press, 1974); Roberto Weiss, *The Renaissance Discovery of Classical Antiquity* (Oxford: Oxford University Press, 1969); Deno Geanakopolos, *Greek Scholars in Venice: Studies in the Dissemination of Greek Learning from Byzantium to the West* (Cambridge, Mass.: Harvard University Press, 1962); John Monfasani, *George of Trebizond: A Biography and a Study of His Rhetoric and Logic* (Leiden: E. J. Brill, 1976); Beryl Smalley, *The Study of the Bible in the Middle Ages*, 2d ed. (Oxford: Oxford University Press, 1952), and *English Friars and Antiquity in the Early Fourteenth Century* (Oxford: Oxford University Press, 1960); Eugene F. Rice, Jr., *Saint Jerome in the Renaissance* (Baltimore: Johns Hopkins University Press, 1985); Jerry H. Bentley, *Humanists and Holy Writ: New Testament Scholarship in the Renaissance* (Princeton: Princeton University Press, 1983); Donald R. Kelley, *Foundations of Modern Historical Scholarship: Language, Law and History in the French Renaissance* (New York: Columbia University Press, 1970); John D'Amico, *Theory and Practice in Renaissance Textual Criticism: Beatus Rhenanus between Conjecture and History* (Berkeley: University of California Press, 1988); Anthony Grafton, *Joseph Scaliger: A Study in the History of Classical Scholarship* (Oxford: Clarendon Press, 1983); and William McCuaig, *Carlo Sigonio: The Changing World of the Late Renaissance* (Princeton: Princeton University Press, 1989).

A brief selection from the vast literature on the five *studia humanitatis* (besides Rabil, *Renaissance Humanism*, vol. 3): For grammar, see G. A. Padley, *Grammatical Theory in Western Europe, 1500–1700* (Cambridge: Cambridge University Press, 1976). For rhetoric, see James J. Murphy, ed., *Studies in the Theories and Practice of Renaissance Eloquence* (Berkeley: University of California Press, 1983); Brian Vickers, *In Defense of Rhetoric* (Oxford: Clarendon Press, 1988); Jerrold E.

Seigel, *Rhetoric and Philosophy in Renaissance Humanism* (Princeton: Princeton University Press, 1968); John W. O'Malley, *Praise and Blame in Renaissance Rome* (Durham, N.C.: Duke University Press, 1979); and Victoria Kahn, *Rhetoric, Prudence, and Skepticism in the Renaissance* (Ithaca, N.Y.: Cornell University Press, 1985). On poetry and literary topics more generally, C. C. Greenfield, *Humanist and Scholastic Poetry, 1250–1500* (Lewisburg, Pa.: Bucknell University Press, 1981); Bernard Weinberg, *A History of Literary Criticism in the Italian Renaissance*, 2 vols. (Chicago: University of Chicago Press, 1961); B. Hathaway, *The Age of Criticism: The Late Renaissance in Italy* (Ithaca, N.Y.: Cornell University Press, 1962); Arthur F. Kinney, *Continental Humanist Poetics* (Amherst: University of Massachusetts Press, 1989); Thomas M. Green, *The Light in Troy: Imitation and Discovery of Renaissance Poetry* (New Haven: Yale University Press, 1982); David Quint, *Origin and Originality in Renaissance Literature: Versions of the Source* (New Haven: Yale University Press, 1983); Richard Waswo, *Language and Meaning in the Renaissance* (Princeton: Princeton University Press, 1987); Michael Murrin, *The Allegorical Epic* (Chicago: University of Chicago Press, 1980); and Ernesto Grassi, *Renaissance Humanism: Studies in Philosophy and Poetics* (Binghamton, N.Y.: Medieval and Renaissance Texts and Studies, 1988). On history, see Wallace K. Ferguson, *The Renaissance in Historical Thought;* Myron P. Gilmore, *Humanists and Jurists: Six Studies in the Renaissance* (Cambridge, Mass.: Harvard University Press, 1963); Donald J. Wilcox, *The Development of Florentine Humanist Historiography in the Fifteenth Century* (Cambridge, Mass.: Harvard University Press, 1969); Erich Cochrane, *Historians and Historiography in the Italian Renaissance* (Chicago: University of Chicago Press, 1981); Nancy S. Struever, *The Language of History in the Renaissance: Rhetoric and Historical Consciousness in Florentine Humanism* (Princeton: Princeton University Press, 1970); A. G. Dickens and J. M. Tonkin, *The Reformation in Historical Thought* (Cambridge, Mass.: Harvard University Press, 1984); Donald R. Kelley, *Foundations of Modern Historical Scholarship;* and Arthur Ferguson, *Clio Unbound* (Durham: Duke University Press, 1979). On moral philosophy, see Charles Trinkaus, *In Our Image and Likeness: Humanity and Divinity in Italian Humanist Thought*, 2 vols. (Chicago: University of Chicago Press, 1970), and George W. McClure, *Sorrow and Consolation in Italian Humanism* (Princeton: Princeton University Press, 1991).

For political and social thought, see Quentin Skinner, *The Foundations of Modern Political Thought*, 2 vols. (Cambridge: Cambridge University Press, 1978); Anthony Pagden, ed., *The Languages of Political Theory in Early Modern Europe* (Cambridge: Cambridge University Press, 1987); Donald R. Kelley, *The Human Measure: Social Thought in the Western Legal*

*Tradition* (Cambridge, Mass.: Harvard University Press, 1990); Felix Gilbert, *Machiavelli and Guicciardini: Politics and History in Sixteenth Century Florence* (Princeton: Princeton University Press, 1965); J. H. Hexter, *The Vision of Politics on the Eve of the Reformation* (New York: Basic Books, 1973); Robert P. Adams, *The Better Part of Valor: More, Erasmus, Colet and Vives on Humanism, War and Peace, 1496–1535* (Seattle: University of Washington Press, 1962); and Walter Kaiser, *Praisers of Folly: Erasmus, Rabelais, Shakespeare* (Cambridge, Mass.: Harvard University Press, 1963).

On philosophy (besides *The Cambridge History of Renaissance Philosophy*), see Ernst Cassirer, *The Individual and the Cosmos in Renaissance Philosophy,* translated by M. Domandi (New York: Harper & Row, 1963); P. O. Kristeller, *Eight Philosophers of the Italian Renaissance* (Stanford: Stanford University Press, 1964); Eugenio Garin, *Italian Humanism: Philosophy and Civic Life in the Renaissance;* Arthur Field, *The Origins of the Platonic Academy in Florence* (Princeton: Princeton University Press, 1988); Charles B. Schmitt, *Aristotle and the Renaissance* (Cambridge, Mass.: Harvard University Press, 1983); James Hankins, *Plato in the Italian Renaissance* (Leiden: E. J. Brill, 1990); and Richard H. Popkin, *The History of Skepticism from Erasmus to Spinoza,* rev. ed. (Berkeley: University of California Press, 1979).

On science, again from a huge literature, see Eugenio Garin, *Science and Civic Life in the Italian Renaissance,* translated by P. Munz (Garden City, N.Y.: Anchor Books, 1969); Alexandre Koyré, *From the Closed World to the Infinite Universe* (Baltimore: Johns Hopkins University Press, 1957); Timothy J. Reiss, *The Discourse of Modernism* (Ithaca, N.Y.: Cornell University Press, 1982); Nicholas Jardine, *The Birth of History and Philosophy of Science* (Cambridge: Cambridge University Press, 1984); Paul L. Rose, *The Italian Renaissance of Mathematics: Studies on Humanists and Mathematicians from Petrarch to Galileo* (Geneva: Droz, 1975); and Paolo Rossi, *Philosophy, Technology and the Arts,* translated by S. Attanasio (New York: Harper & Row, 1970).

On humanist education, Paul F. Grendler, *Schooling in Renaissance Italy: Literacy and Learning, 1300–1600* (Baltimore: Johns Hopkins University Press, 1989); Anthony Grafton and L. Jardine, *From Humanism to the Humanities* (Cambridge, Mass.: Harvard University Press, 1986); and William Harrison Woodward, *Studies in Education during the Age of the Renaissance, 1400–1600* (Cambridge: Cambridge University Press, 1906; rpt., 1967).

For the fine arts the classic works, see Erwin Panofsky, *Renaissance and Renaissances in Western Art* (Stockholm: Almqvist & Wiksells, 1960) and *Studies in Iconology: Humanistic Themes in the Art of the Renaissance*

(Oxford: Oxford University Press, 1939); and Jean Seznec, *The Survival of the Pagan Gods: The Mythological Tradition and Its Place in Renaissance Humanism and Art* (New York: Pantheon Books, 1953). See also Michael Baxandall, *Giotto and the Orators: Humanist Observers of Painting in Italy and the Discovery of Pictoral Composition, 1350–1450* (Oxford: Oxford University Press, 1971) and *Painting and Experience in Fifteenth Century Italy* (Oxford: Oxford University Press, 1972); Samuel Y. Edgerton, Jr., *The Renaissance Recovery of Linear Perspective* (New York: Basic Books, 1975); Rudolf Wittkower, *Architectural Principles in the Age of Humanism* (London: Warburg Institute, 1949); and Claude V. Palisca, *Humanism in Italian Renaissance Musical Thought* (New Haven: Yale University Press, 1986).

On religion, see John F. D'Amico, *Renaissance Humanism in Papal Rome: Humanists and Churchmen on the Eve of the Reformation* (Baltimore: Johns Hopkins Press, 1983); E. Harris Harbison, *The Christian Scholar in the Age of the Reformation* (New York: Scribners, 1956); Heiko Oberman, *The Harvest of Medieval Theology: Gabriel Biel and Late Medieval Nominalism* (Cambridge, Mass.: Harvard University Press, 1963) and *Masters of the Reformation: The Emergence of a New Intellectual Climate in Europe* (Cambridge, Mass.: Harvard University Press, 1981); and Lucien Febvre, *The Problem of Unbelief in the Sixteenth Century: The Religion of Rabelais*, translated by B. Gottlieb (Cambridge, Mass.: Harvard University Press, 1982).

On humanism beyond the Alps (besides Rabil, *Renaissance Humanism*), see James H. Overfield, *Humanism and Scholasticism in Late Medieval Germany* (Princeton: Princeton University Press, 1984); Lewis W. Spitz, *The Religious Renaissance of the German Humanists* (Cambridge, Mass.: Harvard University Press, 1963); Franco Simone, *The French Renaissance: Medieval Tradition and Italian Influence in Shaping the Renaissance in France*, translated by H. Gaston Hall (London: Macmillan, 1969); Werner L. Gundersheimer, ed., *French Humanism, 1470–1600* (New York: Harper & Row, 1969); Roberto Weiss, *Humanism in England during the Fifteenth Century*, 2d ed. (Oxford: Oxford University Press, 1957); James C. McConica, *English Humanists and Reformation Politics under Henry VIII and Edward VI* (Oxford: Clarendon Press, 1965); Fritz Caspari, *Humanism and the Social Order in Tudor England* (Chicago: University of Chicago Press, 1954); and Maria Dowling, *Humanism in the Age of Henry VIII* (London: Croon Helm, 1986).

On the occult tradition, see Frances A. Yates, *The Occult Philosophy in the Elizabethan Age* (London: Routledge & Kegan Paul, 1979); D. P. Walker, *This Ancient Theology: Studies in Christian Platonism from the Fifteenth to the Eighteenth Century* (Ithaca, N.Y.: Cornell University Press,

1972); J. S. Mebane, *Renaissance Magic and the Return of the Golden Age: The Occult Tradition and Marlowe, Jonson, and Shakespeare* (Lincoln: University of Nebraska Press, 1989); and Ingrid Merkel and Allen G. Debus, *Hermeticism and the Renaissance* (Wash., D.C.: Folger Shakespeare Library, 1988).

On the place of women, see Patricia A. Labalme, ed., *Beyond Their Sex: Learned Women of the European Past* (New York: New York University Press, 1980); Margaret Ferguson, M. Quilligan, and N. J. Vickers, eds., *Rewriting the Renaissance: The Discourses of Sexual Difference in Early Modern Europe* (Chicago: University of Chicago Press, 1986); Katharina M. Wilson, ed., *Women Writers of the Renaissance and Reformation* (Athens: University of Georgia Press, 1987); and Margaret L. King and Albert Rabil, *Her Immaculate Hand: Selected Works by and about the Women Humanists of Quattrocento Italy* (Binghamton, N.Y.: Medieval and Renaissance Texts, 1983)

# Index

Aeneas Sylvius (Pope Pius II), 80
Agrippa of Nettesheim, Henry Cornel-
    ius, 48, 99
Agricola, Rudolf, 24, 56, 57, 88
Alberti, Leonbattista, 16, 25, 50, 52,
    120–21
Alciato, Andrea, 123–24, 127
Alembert, Jean le Rond d', 129
Alexander of Roes, 5
Alfonso V, King of Aragon, 35
Ancients and Moderns, 6, 53, 61, 72,
    82, 98, 141
anthropology, 45–49, 78, 103, 119,
    126, 130, 132, 134
*antiquitas*, 30, 32, 35, 36, 81, 98
Archimedes, 125
Aristotle (Aristotelianism), 3, 4, 8, 21,
    22, 34, 35, 36, 37, 40, 42, 44, 45, 47,
    49, 50, 51, 57, 62, 72, 96, 103–7,
    110, 115–16, 119, 123–25, 127, 129
*ars arengandi*, 88
*ars dictaminis*, 3, 88
*ars grammatica*, 76–82, 95, 99, 100, 105,
    122
*ars historica*, 94–102, 105, 122, 132
*ars poetica*, 95, 99, 102–10, 122
*ars praedicandi*, 88

*ars rhetorica*, 36, 76, 82, 88–94, 96, 99,
    105, 120, 122, 131
Athens, 93
Augustine, St., 10, 46, 65, 113–14,
    116, 125, 136
*auctores*, 6, 26
Aulus Gellius, 2, 3
Averroës, 9, 125
Avignon, 11, 18, 113

Bacon, Francis, viii, 27, 32, 94, 101,
    108–9, 119, 125, 129, 131
Baldus de Ubaldis, 16
barbarians (barbarism), viii, 7, 14, 36,
    43, 56, 66, 58, 71–73, 139, 141
Barbaro, Francesco, 29, 30
Barbaro, Ermolao, 33, 43, 55, 91, 127
Baron, Hans, 14, 20, 39, 111, 134
Bartolus of Sassoferrato, 16, 35, 49
Baxandall, Michael, 120
Beatrice, 7
Beatus Rhenanus, 58, 98
Beccadelli, Antonio, 111
Bentley, Richard, 79
Bessarion, Cardinal, 41
Biondo, Flavio, 31, 62, 98

Boccaccio, Giovanni, 13, 26, 29, 63, 66, 102–4, 117, 135
Bodin, Jean, 50, 52, 100
Boethius, 35, 36, 38
Bologna, 19
Bologna, University of, 8, 15
Bourges, 124
Brothers of the Common Life, 66
Browning, Robert, 79–80
Bruni, Leonardo, 1, 13, 14, 19–25, 29, 36, 40, 42, 49, 53, 60, 62, 78, 91, 95, 97, 98, 115–16, 120, 123, 127, 135, 141
Budé, Guillaume, 24, 32, 39, 46, 50, 57, 60–62, 64, 65, 81, 88, 97, 124, 126–27
Burckhardt, Jacob, 2, 59, 135

Cabalism, 31, 41, 57, 126
Caesar, Julius, 13, 22
Calvin, Jean, 24, 46, 61, 126
Cambridge, 63
Campanella, Tommaso, 106–9
Cario, Johann, 98
Casaubon, Isaac, 79
Cassirer, Ernst, 41, 42, 48, 89, 134
Castelvetro, Ludovico, 105, 107
Caxton, William, 63
Celtis, Conrad, 58
Chambers, R. S., 65
Charlemagne, 5
Charles IV, Emperor, 12, 13
Charron, Pierre, 119
Christine de Pisan, 26
Chrysoloras, Manuel, 24, 40, 62
Cicero (Ciceronianism), 2, 9, 10, 19–26, 28, 29, 34, 35, 36, 48, 50, 61, 65, 74–75, 90, 85, 95–98, 98, 102, 104, 112, 113, 115–16, 118, 130, 139
Cimabue, 120
civic humanism, viii, 14–23, 27, 49–54, 72, 93, 120–21, 123
civil science, 15–16, 52–53, 73, 92, 123–24, 136
*civilitas*, 28, 35
Clement VI Pope, 12
Colet, John, 63–64, 67–69

Columbus, Christopher, 71–72
Condorcet, M. J. A., 33, 129
Constantine, Emperor, 38
Constantinople, 40
Cooper, Thomas, 77
Copernicus, Nicolaus, 125
Crinito, Pietri, 55
Croce, Benedetto, 134
Cujas, Jacques, 79, 124

Dante, 2, 4–7, 10, 18, 20, 21, 22, 30, 34, 45, 47, 49, 71, 78, 92, 103, 120, 125
Decembrio, Pier Candido, 17
Demosthenes, 61, 62
Derrida, Jacques, 82, 89, 134
Descartes, René, 27, 101, 128–29, 131–32
Diderot, Denis, 129–30
dignity of man, viii, 45–49, 112–19, 130, 134
Dilthey, Wilhelm, 134
Diogenes Laertius, 123
Dionysius of Halicarnassus, 97
*docta ignorantia*, 41, 42
Donation of Constantine, 37–39, 101
Dorp, Martin, 65
DuBellay, Joachim, 107
Dullardus, Johannes, 78
Du Perron, Davy, 93
Du Vair, Guillaume, 117

Eisenstein, Elizabeth, 31
Eliot, George, 79
encyclopedia, 3, 27, 32, 44, 46–47, 60, 63, 67, 74, 76, 81, 95, 100, 102, 103, 104, 108, 109, 112, 117, 120–31
Epicureanism, 3, 37, 112, 116
Erasmus, Desiderius, 6, 18, 24, 25, 27, 33, 39, 46, 50–53, 55–57, 60–61, 63–70, 79, 81, 88–90, 93, 101, 117, 120, 126–27
Euclid, 125
Euripides, 91
Existentialism, 134

Ferguson, Wallace, 32
Ferrara, 24, 31, 40

Fichet, Guillaume, 59
Ficino, Marsilio, 9, 13, 42–48, 53, 55, 64, 104, 114, 120, 123, 126
Filelfo, Francesco, 17
Florence, 2, 13, 14, 17–24, 31, 35, 40, 49, 71, 95, 97, 98, 115, 120, 141
Fontius, Bartolommeus, 104
fortune, 16, 50, 52, 71, 114
Foucault, Michel, 134
Francis I, King, 61
Franciscan order, 12, 19
Frederick II, Emperor, 4, 12
Friedell, Egon, 31

Gadamer, Hans-Georg, 132–34
Gaffurio, Franchino, 121
Gaguin, Robert, 60
Gaillard, Pierre Droit de, 100
Galen, 89, 124, 125
Galileo Galilei, 27, 101, 125, 131
Garin, Eugenio, 39, 134
Geneva, 61
Gesner, Konrad, 82
Ghibellines, 4, 15, 17, 22, 49
Gibbon, Edward, 30, 31
Giotto, 120, 141
golden age, 60, 67
Goggio, Bartolommeo, 26
*grammatica speculativa*, 77
Grassi, Ernesto, 39, 135
Grocyn, William, 63, 64
Guarino Veronese, 24, 29, 46, 62, 77, 92, 95, 104
Guazzo, Stefano, 92
Guelfs, 15, 17–20, 22, 40, 49, 120
Gicciardini, Francesco, 101

Habsburg Donation, 13, 102
Haskins, C. H., 8
Hauser, Henri, 33
Hegius, Alexander, 24, 56, 77, 80
Heidegger, Martin, 134–35
Heinsius, Daniel, 102
Henry VII, Emperor, 4, 11, 12
hermeneutics, 80, 132–35
Hermeticism, 31, 41–43, 45, 111, 126
Herodotus, 62, 99, 100

Hesiod, 101
Heynlin, Jean, 60
Hippocrates, 125
historicism, 39, 133
Holmes, George, 24
Homer, 28, 29, 95, 102, 104, 128
Horace, 99, 103, 105, 106
Housman, A. E., 79
*humanitas*, vii, 3, 4, 23, 33, 35, 129–30
Hume, David, 119
Humphrey, Duke of Gloucester, 63
Hus, Jan, 24
Husserl, Edmund, 134
Hutton, Ulrich von, 59

*institutio*, 23–25, 28, 29, 42, 50–51, 127, 131
Isidore of Seville, 81, 124

Jerome, St., 9, 65, 67, 92, 113
John of Salisbury, 4, 77
Julius II, Pope, 68–69
Justinian, 23, 37, 60, 119

Kant, Immanuel, 133
Kelly-Gadol, Joan, 26
Kepler, Johann, 125
Kristeller, P. O., 3, 5, 6, 39, 111, 122, 134

La Boétie, Etienne de, 54
La Croix du Maine, François de, 62
Landino, Cristoforo, 42, 104
La Popelinière, Henri de, 100
Latini, Brunetto, 92
Laura, 7
Lefèvre d'Etaples, 60, 125
legal humanism, 37, 60
Leo X, Pope, 68
Leonardo de Vinci, 121
Le Roy, Louis, vii, viii, 61–62, 72, 100, 120, 129
Lessing, Gotthold, 33
*Lex Regia*, 11
liberty, 17, 18, 20, 22, 23, 40, 50, 59, 99
Linacre, Thomas, 63, 64
Lionardi, Alessandro, 106

Lipsius, Justus, 112
Livy, 28, 29, 35, 37, 41, 49, 51, 97
Locke, John, 129
Lombards, 14, 22
López de Gómara, Francesco de, 72
Louvain, 67
Lucretius, 125
Luther, Martin, 39, 46, 57–59, 61, 68–70, 93, 98, 126

Machiavelli, Niccolò, 10, 13, 15, 18, 23, 25, 50–56, 71, 97, 98, 101, 101, 113
Manetti, Giacomo, 46, 114
Mantua, 24
Maritain, Jacques, 132
Mark, St., 71
Marxism, 134
Medici (family), 40
Medici, Cosimo de', 23, 41, 42, 71
Medici, Lorenzo de', 55
Medici, Piero de, 55
Melanchthon, Philip, 24, 57, 70, 91, 92, 98, 99, 127
mercantile humanism, 19
method, 27, 77, 94, 121, 125
Milan, 17, 18, 19, 20
Milieu, Christophe, 100
misery of man, viii, 45–46, 114, 130
Momigliano, Arnaldo, 100
Montaigne, Michel de, 48, 53–54, 62–63, 72, 93, 118–19, 130–35
Monte Cassino, 29
Montefeltro, 25
Montpellier, University of, 8
More, Thomas, 51, 63–65, 68, 69
Moses, 97, 102
Mount Ventoux, 10, 113, 125
Murphy, James, 88

Naples, 19, 24, 35
Neoplatonism, 41–44, 47, 64, 126
Nero, Emperor, 30
Newton, Isaac, 129
Nicholas V, Pope, 19
Nicolas of Cusa (Cusanus), 41–42, 47, 131
Nietzsche, Friedrich, 59

Obrechts-Tyteca, L., 132
Orbellis, Nicolas, 74
O'Gorman, Edmundo, 71
Ottoman Empire, 31
Ovid, 7
Oxford, 63, 125

Padua, 24, 26, 124, 125
*paideia*, 2, 67, 132
Palmieri, Matteo, 25
Panofsky, Erwin, 103
Paolo Emilio, 60, 98
Paris, 125
Pasquier, Etienne, 100
Patrizi, Francesco, 107, 109
Paul, St., 59, 64
Pelagianism, 46
Perelman, Chaim, 132
*Perfect Merchant*, 19
Peter, St., 12, 69
Petrarch, Francesco, 1, 7–13, 16, 17, 18, 20–24, 28, 29, 30, 32, 62, 34–41, 48, 52, 53, 55, 56, 62, 63, 66, 67, 71, 74, 75, 88–90, 95, 96, 102, 104, 112–15, 118–20, 123, 124, 126, 135, 136, 141
philology, 13, 32, 33, 35–39, 60–61, 80–82, 85, 110, 126–28, 131, 135, 136
Pico della Mirandola, Giovanni, 9, 13, 42–46, 55, 56, 64, 65, 91, 114, 125–27, 134
Piero della Francesca, 120
Pindar, 119
Pisa, 15
Plato (Platonism), 3, 4, 9, 28, 34, 40–45, 47, 50, 50, 61–62, 90, 101, 104, 107, 123, 125
Pletho, George Gemistos, 40
Pliny, 28, 125
Poggio Bracciolini, 13, 29, 30, 31, 35, 62, 63
Poliziano, Angelo, 55, 60, 79, 85, 99, 124, 125, 127
Polybius, 51
Pomponazzi, Pietro, 47
Pope, Alexander, 119

posterity, viii, 9, 12, 23
posterity, viii, 7
printing, viii, 26, 27, 30–33, 39, 56, 59, 72, 89, 128–29
pseudo-Dionysius, 41, 64
Ptolemy, 125
Pyrrhonism, 48, 63, 118, 119, 131

*quadrivium*, 3, 74, 103, 121, 131
Quintilian, 24, 25, 26, 29, 34, 75, 77, 78

Rabelias, François, 62
Ramus, Petrus, 57, 93
Republic of letters, 30, 33, 56, 66, 89, 96
*restitutio*, 32, 60, 62, 80
Reuchlin, Johann, 57
Rho, Antonio da, 116
Rienzi (Cola di Rienzo), 11–13, 30
Robert of Anjou, 4
Robortello, Francesco, 106
Rome, 11–15, 18, 19, 24, 30, 31, 35, 51, 53, 75, 93, 98, 113, 136–40
Ronsard, Pierre de, 62
Rousseau, J. J., 48

Sacco, Catone, 116
Salutati, Coluccio, 9, 13, 15, 20, 29, 49, 63, 82, 104, 114–15, 123–25
Sartre, Jean-Paul, 134
Savonarola, 55
Scaliger, J. C., 106
Scaliger, J. J., 79, 81
Schiller, F. S. C., 132
Scholasticism, 4, 6, 8, 35, 36, 38, 42, 43, 44, 57, 63, 65–68, 74, 77, 78, 89, 96, 103, 111, 125, 141
Scipio Africanus, 25
Selden, John, 79
Seneca, 61
Sextus Empiricus, 48, 117, 123
Seyssel, Claude de, 62
Sewell, Elizabeth, 107
Seznec, Jean, 32
Sidney, Philip, 107, 108
Siena, 19

Sigismund, Emperor, 25
Sigonio, Carlo, 75
Silvester I, Pope, 38
Siraisi, Nancy, 124
skepticism, 48–49, 70, 99, 101, 112, 117–19
Sleidan, Johann, 99
Socrates, 4, 25, 44, 90, 112, 121, 125
Sophists, 90
Stewart, Dugald, 33, 129
Stoicism, 3, 35, 37, 112, 116–17, 119
*studia humanitatis*, 3, 8, 18, 22, 23, 24, 25, 28, 33, 34–35, 39, 43, 47, 55, 57, 66, 72–119, 122, 123, 130, 136, 138
*studium*, 5, 6, 28, 40, 121, 122, 128
Sulla, 22

Tacitus, 29, 49, 57–59, 72
Tasso, Torquato, 105
Theophrastus, 121
Thomas Aquinas, 5, 42
Thucydides, 49, 61, 62, 101, 121
translation of empire, 5, 58, 139
translation of studies, 5, 56, 58, 60, 122, 139
Trapezuntius, George, 40
Traversari, Ambrogio, 123
*trivium*, 3, 24, 40, 74, 95, 104
Turin, 67

Ullmann, Walter, 123
*uomo universale*, 25, 53

Valla, Lorenzo, 29, 33, 35–39, 43, 47, 49, 57, 58, 60–62, 66–68, 78–79, 82, 90, 91, 94, 96, 99–101, 115–17, 120, 124, 126–27, 129, 131, 132, 136–41
Vasari, Giorgio, 120
Vaucluse, 7
Vegio, Maffeo, 85, 116
Venice, 16, 19, 26, 49
Vergerio, Pier Paolo, 16, 24, 46, 82, 97
Vergil, Polydore, 63, 72, 76, 82, 94, 98, 100, 102, 121
Verona, 9
Vespasiano da Bicci, 26, 29
Vespucci, Amerigo, 71

Vicenza, 26
Vickers, Brian, 32, 88
Vico, Gianbattista, 27, 28, 32, 48, 73, 80, 81, 101–3, 109–10, 128, 132–33, 135
Vincent of Beauvais, 45
Virgil, 7, 10, 21, 67, 104, 105, 112, 119
virtue, 16, 21, 23, 25, 50–52, 58–59, 113–16
Visconti, Giangaleazzo, 17, 18, 20
*vita activa*, 22, 115
*vita contemplativa*, 22, 47, 113, 115
Vitruvius, 103, 120, 125

Vittorino da Feltre, 24, 25, 26, 46, 62
Vives, Juan Luis, 26, 46, 65, 69, 78, 88, 90, 91, 99–101, 126–28
Voltaire, F. M. A., 33

Weiss, Roberto, 15, 30, 49, 63
wisdom, 10, 41–44, 65, 90, 91, 100, 108–10, 116, 127–28, 135–36
Wolf, F. A., 79
Wycliffe, John, 24

Zoroaster, 44
Zwingli, Ulrich, 66, 126

# The Author

Donald R. Kelley, James Westfall Thompson Professor of History at Rutgers University, has taught at the University of Rochester, Harvard University, the State University of New York at Binghamton, and other universities. He studied at Harvard and Columbia universities and the University of Paris. A member of the American Academy of Arts and Sciences and executive editor of the *Journal of the History of Ideas*, Kelley has held fellowships from the Guggenheim Foundation (twice), the Institute for Advanced Study in Princeton, The National Humanities Center, the American Council of Learned Societies, the National Endowment for the Humanities, the Shelby Cullom Davis Center (Princeton), the Newberry and Folger Shakespeare Libraries, and other institutions. His publications include *Foundations of Modern Historical Scholarship* (1970), *The Beginning of Ideology* (1981), *History, Law, and the Human Sciences* (1984), *The Human Measure* (1990), *The History of Ideas: Canon and Variations* (edited, 1990), *Views of History: Antiquity to the Enlightenment* (edited, 1991), *The Shapes of Knowledge* (edited with Richard Popkin, 1991), and chapters concerning the Renaissance for the *Cambridge History of Renaissance Philosophy* (1988), *Renaissance Humanism* (ed. A. Rabil, 1988), and the *Cambridge History of Political Thought 1450–1700* (1991).

# The Editor

Michael S. Roth is the Hartley Burr Alexander Professor of Humanities at Scripps College and professor of history at the Claremont Graduate School. He is the author of *Psycho-Analysis as History: Negation and Freedom in Freud* (1987) and *Knowing and History: Appropriations of Hegel in 20th-Century France* (1988), both published by Cornell University Press. He is currently writing about contemporary strategies for representing the past in the humanities and about conceptualizations of memory disorders in the nineteenth century.